W9-BSF-406

# Exploring
# **Black and White**
# Photography Second Edition

# Exploring
# **Black and White**
# Photography

### Second Edition

**Arnold Gassan**
*Retired, Ohio University*

**A. J. Meek**
*Louisiana State University*

**WCB Brown & Benchmark**
P U B L I S H E R S

Madison, Wisconsin · Indianapolis, Indiana
Melbourne, Australia · Oxford, England

**Book Team**

Editor  *Kathleen Nietzke*
Developmental Editors  *Susan J. McCormick/Deb Reinbold*
Production Editor  *Jane E. Matthews*
Designer  *David C. Lansdon*
Art Editor  *Carla Goldhammer*
Permissions Editor  *Mavis M. Oeth*
Art Processor  *Brenda A. Ernzen*
Visuals/Design Developmental Consultant  *Donna Slade*

A Division of Wm. C. Brown Communications, Inc.

Vice President and General Manager  *Thomas E. Doran*
Executive Managing Editor  *Ed Bartell*
Executive Editor  *Edgar J. Laube*
Director of Marketing  *Kathy Law Laube*
National Sales Manager  *Eric Ziegler*
Marketing Manager  *Carla Aspelmeier*
Advertising Manager  *Jodi Rymer*
Managing Editor, Production  *Vickie Putnam Caughron*
Manager of Visuals and Design  *Faye M. Schilling*

Design Manager  *Jac Tilton*
Art Manager  *Janice Roerig*
Photo Manager  *Shirley Charley*
Publishing Services Manager  *Karen J. Slaght*
Permissions/Records Manager  *Connie Allendorf*

**Wm. C. Brown Communications, Inc.**

Chairman Emeritus  *Wm. C. Brown*
Chairman and Chief Executive Officer  *Mark C. Falb*
President and Chief Operating Officer  *G. Franklin Lewis*
Corporate Vice President, Operations  *Beverly Kolz*
Corporate Vice President, President of WCB Manufacturing  *Roger Meyer*

Cover photograph © John Running: Photographer, Inc.

Computer graphics generated by Arnold Gassan and McCullough Graphics, Dubuque, IA. Computer graphic editing by Diane Schoenbaum.

Copyright © 1989, 1993 by Wm. C. Brown Communications, Inc. All rights reserved

Library of Congress Catalog Card Number: 91-76863

ISBN 0-697-12523-8

No part of this publication may be reproduced, stored in a retrieval system, or transmitted, in any form or by any means, electronic, mechanical, photocopying, recording, or otherwise, without the prior written permission of the publisher.

Printed in the United States of America by Wm. C. Brown Communications, Inc., 2460 Kerper Boulevard, Dubuque, IA 52001

10  9  8  7  6  5  4  3  2  1

# Contents

# Preface

This text deals only with black-and-white photography. Silver process black-and-white photography offers more creative freedoms (and demands more control) by the photographer than does color. Black-and-white pictures excite us in ways that differ from color pictures—perhaps because black-and-white photography at its best separates us from the sensual world of color and lets our eye explore abstraction of form and discover visual analogies all too easily hidden by color.

Photographic processes and equipment are constantly changing. Electronic imaging may well overcome traditional film-based photography. As this edition goes to press, Kodak announced **Photo CD,** which is digitized compact disk storage and reproduction of filmed pictures using a TV set. This transitional print-replacement product intended for the nonprofessional combines traditional cameras and silver-based films with electronic technology to replace silver-based prints.

Manipulations of the picture through digitized reconstruction has become commonplace in advertising and editorial illustration. Yet despite these developments, the traditional *silver process* photographic black-and-white print has continuing beauty and attractiveness. Not that making good

pictures is ever really easy. Annie Leibowitz, a photographer noted for her portraits in *Rolling Stone* and other magazines, said in a National Public Radio interview that "Today, if I take five photographs a year that are good—that's wonderful."

For most photographers, there is something magical about developing film in orange light, watching a special negative be enlarged until it is the size and proportion of the print you want; exposing a piece of blank, white paper to the (always mysterious) negative; immersing that blank paper gently into a clear chemical solution in a shallow tray, and watching it while a dim, ghostly image appears and becomes clear; holding the picture *you* wanted when it is fully realized.

Developing your own negatives and making your own prints means you decide how dark or light the image should be, what contrast should appear between the shadows in trees and the highlights in clouds. You decide whether the print would be better small—something to be held in the hand—or large and displayed on the wall, and exactly how it is finally proportioned.

It is gratifying to develop film and print negatives in your own darkroom, but making your own black-and-white photographs requires much more in-

volvement with photographic materials and processes than does color slides or purchasing prints from a photofinisher. Excellence of control is gained only by personal work and time spent experimenting with materials. Besides a camera and film, you need special photographic solutions, a darkroom in which to process the film and to print the negatives, and space in which to finish the prints.

My personal belief is that the best way to learn is to take a camera and make pictures, then develop the film and make prints. When working with new photographic materials, follow the suggestions made by the manufacturer but look critically at what you have made and think hard about how you wish to change the way of seeing or the craft. Finally, start again at the beginning. When your imagination runs dry, outline a photographic project. Each step of this cycle utilizes intuition, craft, and analytical thinking.

The text has been reorganized to fit a variety of teaching methods. The first chapters deal with looking at and talking about photographs. As photography moves from silver to electromagnetic recording, it is more important than ever that photographic meaning be understood. These chapters draw upon several years of work with Minor White, graduate study of art history and painting, twenty years experience teaching photographic art history and observing changes in that area, doctoral research in measuring how perceptions of photographs are changed by life experiences, and clinical experience.

Technical controls are important because camera and darkroom skills are used to modify content and achieve creative goals. Technical controls are a major problem faced by all beginning and intermediate photographers. Chapter 3 presents camera controls. The darkroom is discussed next and chapters 5 through 7 outline step-by-step exposing and developing film and prints. Lighting and advanced techniques follow. Possible health hazards are clearly noted in the text.

Finally, professional concerns about making a living, and some legal and ethical photographic problems, are outlined in chapter 12. Appendixes list sources of equipment, information, and chemicals. For photographers who have access to a densitometer, *parametric controls* are presented in appendix 9.

The general illustrations for the text have been chosen to provide a commentary on the text. The pictures are obtained from young photographers, from historical collections, and from the author's own files. Although most of the contemporary pictures used here are 35mm, other formats are also included.

Once, in a summer workshop, Ansel Adams said you don't make a photograph just with a camera, you bring to the act of photography all the pictures you have seen, the books you have read, the music you have heard, the people you have loved. Minor White put it a bit differently another summer, in another workshop, when he said that if you let yourself really see what is in front of your camera, and are true to yourself, something magical often results when you expose the film.

## Acknowledgements

With this edition, A. J. Meek, Louisiana State University School of Art, becomes coproducer. New illustrations have been provided by graduate students from the Louisiana State University photographic arts program.

New photographs in this edition have also been provided by students from Agfa-Beseler competitions. Other illustrations for this text have been made available with the generous assistance of the Ansel Adams Publishing Trust; the Library of Congress, and the American Folk Life Center of the Library; the National Archives; the New Orleans Collection; and the University of Louisville Photographic Archives. Nikon Corporation lent me the cutaway single-lens reflex camera and zoom lens, and Wilson's Camera Shops in Athens, Ohio, lent many other pieces of equipment used to provide text illustrations.

Restructuring of the text was suggested by several advisors, and I wish to thank them for the hard work they did. Also thanks to the faculty, graduate, and undergraduate students at Ohio University who allowed me to use their pictures. The School of Visual Communication and the School of Art at Ohio University initially provided equipment, facilities, and a supportive environment.

The reviewers are Raymond J. Brooks, Winona State University; Kathleen Campbell, State University of New York; Emmette Jackson, Sam Houston State University; Michael D. Sherer, University of Nebraska; Darilyn R. Rowan, El Camino College; and Wendall A. White, Stockton State College.

Arnold Gassan

# 1 Looking at Photographs

Figure 1.1
**Top of Stuart Haby's Dresser. Texas, 1945. Esther Bubley.** The photograph captures in an instant a cross section of a Texas rancher's life, providing a record of significant details.

Esther Bubley, University of Louisville Photographic Archives.

## Begin Photography by Looking at Photographs

Photographs permit us to communicate to the world what we see that no one else might otherwise see. Figure 1.1 shows a record of details that reflect a man's entire life: three bottles of hair tonic, two very clean combs, two hair brushes, hard-worn western spurs, a religious statue, a box of small-bore cartridges and three high-velocity rifle cartridges, an alarm clock, a horse figurine, a handkerchief, a cardboard fan, a hand mirror, a lace-edged runner covering the dresser, and a battered plaster dog. Taken as they are found together, these commonplace things strongly evoke the personality of the man. The photographer has added point-of-view, selection and composition, camera controls, and light.

The things we discover and make visible in our pictures symbolize what we feel by using the elements of value, form, light, space, color, and texture. We make pictures both to describe what is there before the camera, and to make associations between what is obviously there and what might be there. The photographer is helpless to communicate if the viewer does not look carefully at the picture.

---

The earliest photographs widely known by the public were made by Daguerre, a painter. When his small metal plate images were first presented, another painter examined them and proclaimed that from that day, painting was dead! He meant that the painter's struggle to describe the visible world with such sufficient detail and exactitude to fool the eye was no longer the first goal for the artist.

The goal of creating a consensual optical reality was codified by Leon Battista Alberti in 1435 when he described how to create a drawing of a small bit of the world that had "correct" perspective. An Alberti drawing is a kind of "magic window" on the world that exactly resembles a photograph. What the perspective drawing (and the camera itself) ignores is what happens *outside the frame,* and that was a problem of aesthetics largely left unaddressed until late nineteenth century French painters began to look at photographs.

---

## Photography, Science, Art, and Reality

The original purpose of photography was to describe perspective as the eye saw it. To this end, lenses were designed to produce "normal" images where straight lines in nature appeared straight on the print. The assumptions of nineteenth century art were nurtured by photographers and remained dominant in photography well into the twentieth century until other artists redefined the purpose of art.

Definitions of purpose in contemporary photography like contemporary art are torn without hope of repair. One definition of photography derives from the belief that the scientifically accurate description of the scene before the camera is adequate and appropriate. Another definition is that the purpose of the photographer is to discover "significant form," use the camera to isolate it and the controls of the process to enhance it. A third definition argues that photographs are messages without a code whose meaning is always new, for meaning is the result of interpretation based on current social, political, and aesthetic fashions. One generation interprets a photograph as viewed by Marxism, the next as viewed by feminists. What is important is that *no photographic record is unbiased and transparent.* Finally, photographic methods are used by many artists to create "new" realities—assemblage, collage, montage, overlays—that have little to do with Alberti's one-eyed vision that photography inherited.

You will inevitably bring your own concerns to any photograph. The purpose of this chapter and the next is to provide you with an introduction to tools that can be used to assess what it is you are examining when you look at a photograph. To that end, *documentary photography* is the term used in this text, with the understanding that it is the descriptive quality of the photograph that is of concern.

---

Popular photography dates from George Eastman's production of the Kodak system in 1889, but the true "invention" of photography dates to 1839. It was fifty years after Daguerre presented his unique copper-plate images to the public in France before George Eastman created what seemed to be an ideal way to make pictures. Figure 1.2 shows how his camera easily recorded moments of personal discovery. With the Eastman camera, you bought a photographic system: the camera was already loaded with film; you pointed it at your personal world, pressed the shutter, advanced the film, pulled a string to cock the shutter again, and when all the film was exposed, you mailed the camera back to Kodak. The film was then removed from the camera and developed, prints were made and mounted on cardboard, and the camera was reloaded and returned to you, along with the prints. This system freed photographers from photographic chemistry and darkroom tedium. The price of this freedom was that the photographer lost control of the middle steps—everything that happened between the *click* of the shutter and the excitement of the finished print. The photographer lost the magic that came with seeing his/her own pictures develop.

---

## Photographic Composition and Art Traditions

Compositional traditions for two-dimensional representations created by painters were adapted by most early photographers. This was due in part because most early photographers were painters who had been economically displaced by the daguerreotype, which quickly became a cheap replacement for painted portraits. Yet the compositional traditions of painting have always been slightly at odds with the documentary nature of the photograph. The painter always has the capacity to select what to keep in and what to leave out as the painting is created. The photographer does this with difficulty.

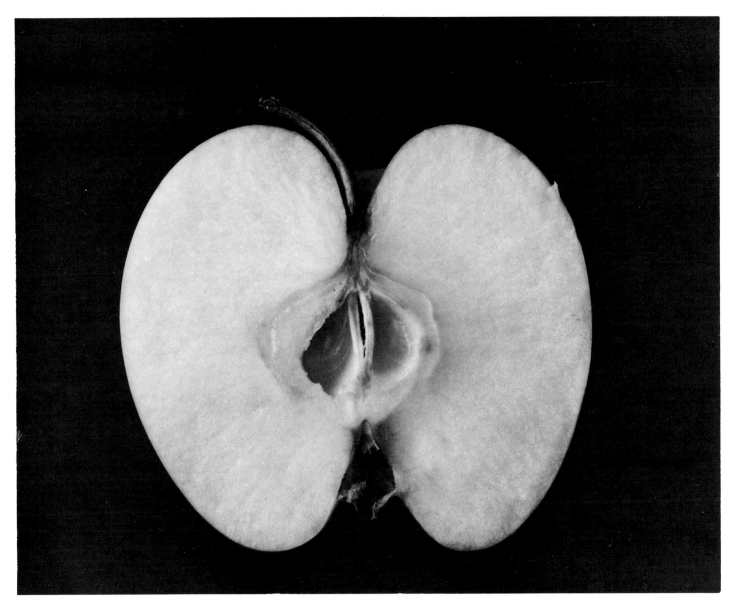

Figure 1.2
**Great Mother of Big Apples. Steve
Ballance.** The "obvious" form of the apple
is both descriptive and suggestive, and the
interior figure/ground forms evoke the
message of the photograph's title.
Courtesy of the photographer.

## Figure and Ground

The principal subject in the picture is often referred to as the **figure**, and the surrounding frame as the **ground**, with the relationship between them being the **figure/ground** dialogue. This notation is useful when describing the obvious arrangement of shapes in the photograph.

Figure/ground relationships also define some of the content. The relationship between the figure and the ground is actually quite limited; there are really only three compositional patterns that appear repeatedly:

1. Closed, or simple figure/ground

2. Multiple figure/ground relationships

3. Open figure/ground

When the subject is centered, attention is automatic. Figure 1.2 is an example of a closed, superficially simple figure/ground relationship. The light shape of the apple floats in the solid black of the frame. And yet there is another figure/ground within the apple, as you discover the shadowy shape of the seed pocket within the apple itself. Rarely does one only find a single figure/ground relationship, though often one shape is dominant, as in this illustration.

Multiple figure/ground compositions often happen by default and they often weaken a picture, but creating complex figure/ground relationships can be an effective photographer's tool when used with care. Figure 1.3*A* is a photograph of an American Indian church in which a complex set of

a.

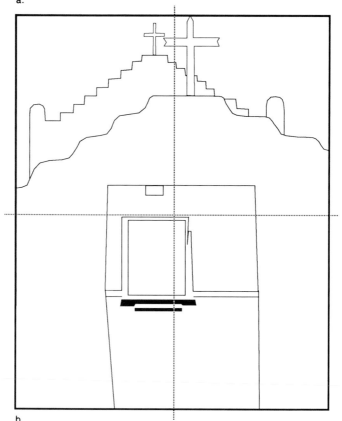

Figure 1.3
**a. Indian Pueblo Church, New Mexico. Ansel Adams.** Nominally a documentary photograph made for the U.S. Department of the Interior, the picture became a complex photographic art statement. Framing, point of view, length of lens, and depth-of-field controls were used to reveal complex form seen by the photographer.
**b.** Figure/ground analysis of Adams' photograph of the Indian pueblo church.

**a.** Print by National Archives; reproduction courtesy of the Trustees of the Ansel Adams Publishing Rights Trust. All rights reserved.

b.

figure/ground relationships can be discovered. Part of the strength of this picture is in the complexity of the form relationships. One discovers rectangles within rectangles in the lower half of the picture detailed in figure 1.3B. All of the shapes in the lower half are also in a dialogue with the stairwell walls and the crosses in the upper half of the picture.

While a closed figure/ground composition directs our attention to the photograph itself, the broken, or open, figure/ground composition often has a more subtle impact; it suggests we look past the photograph to the real objects that were before the photographer's camera. Figure 1.4A is the same church photographed twenty years later from an oblique angle, and figure 1.4B is an analysis of that picture, which demonstrates how the open framing created by the strong diagonals interacts with the frame-within-a-frame of the doorway to produce two different photographs in one, creating a different visual complexity and energy.

a.

Figure 1.4
**a. Indian Pueblo Church, New Mexico. Arnold Gassan.** An oblique view using the adobe patio wall to frame a portion of the pueblo residence changes the meaning of the array of crosses. The "empty" center and the angled view encourages the eye to move back and forth across the picture.
**b.** Figure/ground analysis of the author's photograph of the Indian pueblo church.
**a.** Photo by the author.

b.

Figure 1.5A is an example of open forms created with curves. It is an historically early large-format, wet-plate documentary photograph of a great western valley and river. The dominant form in the picture is the loop of the river, which (as seen in fig. 1.5B) creates an open shape closed only by the edge of the frame.

## The Centered Image

The centered image (or an image firmly tied to a corner of the frame) is considered to be stable (compared to an eccentric placement in the frame), and something special happens when the figure is centered. It seems that the subject is influenced by the boundary of the frame more than the boundary is affected by the subject, as shown in figure 1.6A, which is diagramed in figure 1.6B.

When the subject is dead center, it is not "dead" because there are tensions in all directions; to a sensitive eye, a subject in balance in the middle may sustain great tension. When the subject is dispersed, or moved away from the center, as shown in figure 1.7A and the diagram in figure 1.7B, the entire frame becomes a pattern and that, in turn, becomes the apparent subject of the photograph.

Photographs are made to describe objects and events, to reveal significant form, and to disclose personal insights. Some photographs are more powerful as documents, others are effective as visual poems, and some can hardly be described in verbal terms because they are so singularly visual and formal in content.

The camera does not seek out significant form. A camera thoughtlessly describes whatever is in front of the lens, and it is up to the photographer to select what the lens will record, by selecting a point of view and controlling the photographic process to produce significant form from chaotic events. The inclusiveness of the lens places great demands on the photographer; while a painter can make a scene tidy, the camera describes what is before it, and the photographer must edit what the camera might record.

a.

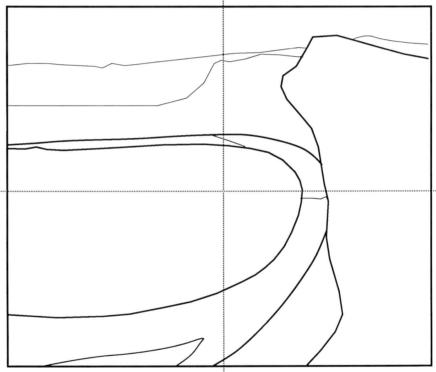

b.

Figure 1.5
**a. Green River. William Henry Jackson.** An early wet-plate documentary photograph. The photographer sought out significant form and combined it with accurate description of the vast spaces as well as specific geologic information. **b.** Figure/ ground analysis of Jackson's landscape photograph.

**a.** National Archives.

a.

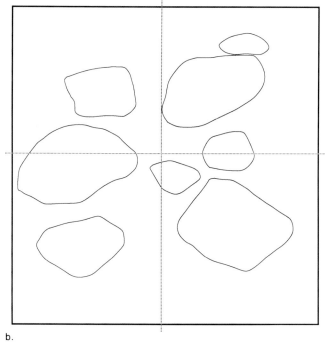

b.

Figure 1.6
**a.** Photograph of rocks seen as a stable central cluster form in the frame. **b.** The simplified drawing of forms (as suggested in assignment #2) shows the figure/ground relationships of **a.**

a.

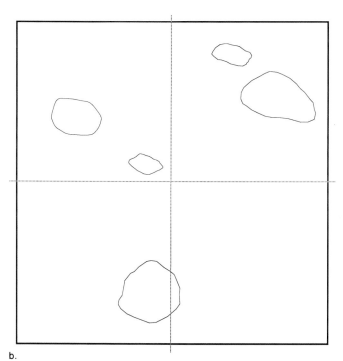

b.

Figure 1.7
**a.** Photograph of rocks seen as a dispersed pattern within the frame. **b.** The simplified drawing of forms (as suggested in assignment #2) shows the figure/ground relationships of **a.**

The photograph as art has many possible meanings. While some critics believe art should be concerned only with formal structure, others note that art has multiple definitions, including even creating objects that have commonplace utility.

## Composing Photographs

Traditions are useful even as they inhibit. Rules of composition have reflected the spirit of each period in Western art. One can look at classic art from Greece and feel the intense quiet produced by balance and symmetry about the centerline, or jump forward to the sixteenth century and admire the writhing, spiraling energy created by baroque painters who compose across the frame with strong diagonals.

The different traditions in photographic art strongly reflect the country and time in which each began. Early nineteenth century artists presented their subjects in relatively simple, *centered* relationships. In French art, there was an obvious move from centeredness (as in the heroic paintings by David) to the asymetrical paintings with significant fragmentary details at the edge created by the painter Edgar Degas.

Suggestions used in painting and drawing still frequently appear as ''rules'' for composing shapes within the frame to guarantee a pleasing photograph. These rules are effective but they also inhibit. A picture made by rules will be pleasant but lack the unexpected. As John Szarkowski said in *Photography Until Now,* ''Good photographs are often more richly unfinished than other pictures, are *wilder,* in the sense that they have in them more elements that are not fully understood and domesticated.''[1]

Three examples of useful compositional rules are

1. Place the horizon about one-third from the top or bottom of the frame, and automatically create a pleasant balance of forms
2. Pose the portrait so that the subject's eyes are about one-third from the top of the frame
3. Place the major figures within the frame to create a triangle with a wide base near the bottom of the picture, the apex centered near the top

The mechanical traditions are found everywhere in art, even in surreal photographs like that by Clarence John Laughlin (fig. 1.8). Here, the sinister and pathetic figure evoked by the eroded small concrete statue was placed in the frame by the photographer in the same way it would have been placed by an eighteenth century portrait painter.

What is important is not so much *how* the picture is composed as *how the composition affects the viewer's interaction.* Too much concern with the geometry of the photograph may distract from the viewer's understanding of deeper relationships between the photographer and the photograph.[2] Look again at figure 1.1 and you will see that the battered leering plaster dog figurine is at the center of the picture and yet the ''subject'' is the whole array of objects and their clear description of a neat, vain, hunting, hardworking Texas rancher.

## The Many Kinds of Photographs

The **straight** photograph is an unmanipulated print made from a single negative by a conventional camera. It is a picture that draws details from an instant in the world and describes relationships between objects with accuracy and surfaces with fidelity. The ''purely'' descriptive photograph was often referred to as a *documentary photograph.* This description is correct but not exclusive: what happens when the objects seen by the camera have been *assembled to be photographed?*

---

Photography is a technological medium, totally dependent on machine-made equipment and machine-made images. As the technology of photography has changed, the kind of image it was possible to make also changed. As technology changed, photographic aesthetics changed.

- Camera obscura described in 1558; originally just a darkened room with what amounted to a pinhole lens. Light entering a small hole in one wall created an inverted image of the scene outside on the opposite wall. The hole was replaced with a convex glass lens, and within a generation, the room shrank into a transportable tent that was used to assist artists drawing landscape or cityscape.
- Photosensitivity of silver salts described in 1725 by Johann Schulze. This ability of silver salts to darken in light was explored by Josiah Wedgewood and Humphry Davy in 1802. They made simple silhouette prints on paper coated with silver salts, but could not stop the paper from continuing to darken.
- Other photosensitive materials tried by Joseph-Nicéphore Niépce, in France, who made a successful photoetching in 1823.
- Daguerre in 1835 accidentally discovered the fact that a little light unalterably but invisibly changed the silver salts and this latent (i.e., hidden) image could be made visible by use of another chemical process, and so he discovered what we call *development.*

Figure 1.8
**Figure from the Underworld, Out of the Earth. Clarence John Laughlin, 1951.** This documentary photograph of an eroded concrete funerary sculpture creates an air of surreal fantasy because the photographer's title directs the viewer's imagination.

© Historic New Orleans Collection; print courtesy of the author.

Daguerre used mercury metal fumes to develop the picture, which consisted of a thin layer of exposed silver salts on a copper mirror. Each **daguerreotype** exposure was unique, and copies were impractical. As important as development was his use of sodium thiosulfate, nicknamed *hypo,* to *stop* the darkening or development of the image.

Before the end of 1839, Daguerre manufactured and sold a camera exposing a "full plate" about 6 1/2 inches by 8 1/2 inches, with a lens aperture of about f–15.

An ideal documentary photograph might be said to describe what was before the lens in as unbiased and transparent a way as possible. The choice of lens, contrast, and point of view enhances our sense of the print's transparency and encourages us to look through the surface of the picture as though it were a magic window, as though the camera were casting a spell over time itself. But other responses always intrude. For example, the nominally documentary photographs made by the FSA photographers reveal consistent personal traits interacting with their broadly defined documentary assignments. It is clear on examining the Library of Congress FSA collection that while most of those photographs obviously provide historically interesting cultural and social data, some are more clearly aimed at the emotions, some at our aesthetic sensibilities, and some hold all three aims in balance.

The descriptive power of the camera is often deceptive, yet the term *documentary photograph* implies something more than merely accurate description; it suggests a discovery of significant aesthetic, conceptual, or intuitive relationships between things as they were—discovered and then documented by the photographer using the camera in an honest, simple dialogue.

The photographer may function as an artist or as a technician. Paul Klee wrote that the artist made the invisible visible. The technician describes; the artist perceives underlying form and discloses hidden meaning. Photographs may do both—describe what is there and suggest what the photographer saw only in his mind's eye.

Photographic aesthetics have undergone many changes in recent years; during the past generation there has been and is now significant critical interest in photographs that seem more like paintings than descriptive photographs. Paralleling this is a review of what unmanipulated camera realities might mean when coupled with political concerns. Two examples are feminist reevaluations of advertising and Afro-American views of what inner city scenes mean.

## Classification of Photographs

Classification is necessary in order to know what is being described. Without classification, one can't be sure when others are talking about the same object. In art as in nature, objects fall into categories, and just as a naturalist speaks of **taxonomy,** which is classifying according to the natural relationships between animals, or objects, the arts also need to be classified. Without knowing the class of picture being examined, a naive response is all that can be expected—a simple utterance of "pretty" or "nice."

A number of writers on photography have suggested ways of classifying and looking at the photograph, which you may wish to investigate. Suggested readings include:

- Jonathan Green, *A Concise History of American Photography*
- Naomi Rosenblum, *World History of Photography*
- John Szarkowski, *The Photographer's Eye, Mirrors and Windows: American Photography since 1960,* and *Photography Until Now.*

Regardless of the system being used, the response to the photograph will always depend to some degree on its descriptive power. Also, any knowledge of the subject or of the photographic processes used will affect your definition, as you examine any photograph. Many photographs exist in more than one category (e.g., documentary photographs often also reflect a photographer's search for significant form).

Photographs can be outlined broadly as follows:

- Art
- Social documentary
- Scientific documentary
- Journalistic interpretation
- Product and fashion figure
- Snapshots, personal inventories
- Self-therapy

Not only the initial purpose but also the way a photograph is used affects categories and evaluations. Because each viewer rediscovers the photograph in light of what is often an unstated personal agenda, there need to be neutral ways to describe the photograph, because no matter what the photographer's intention may have been, a picture is responded to in terms of the viewer's needs of the moment.

Here are three categories that permit you to describe the photographic subject, the photographer's craft, and the photographer's relation to the medium itself. These are ways of classifying photographs:

- Functions of the subject being photographed
- Photographer's attitude toward the subject
- Traditions within the medium itself

First, when describing pictures by subject, realize that a person can only photograph people (portraits, social landscape, fashion, nudes), places (architecture, cities, landscapes), things (abstracted details, scientific subjects), and the form relationships between shapes.

Second, when attempting to classify photographs by the photographer's attitude toward the subject, attempt to discover whether the object before the camera is most important or whether the photograph itself is the object of attention.

The photographer sometimes attempts to become unobtrusive or transparent, so that the viewer remains most aware of the subject before the camera, rather than the photographic technique. The alternative is when the photographers call attention to themselves through lighting, composition, lens and camera choices, and printing technique, and the photograph itself becomes more important than the objects before the camera.

Third, because printing craftsmanship affects the response to photographs, even when seen in reproduction in a book or magazine (although some criteria apply only to the original silver print itself), it is necessary to examine the effect of the camera and film, which includes focus and sharpness, shadow detail, exposure of the negative, development of the print, highlight detail and texture, development of the negative, and the exposure of the print; and the print presentation, which includes the full tonal range, print color, matting, mounting, framing, and sequence and set relations.

Describing a photograph carefully in terms of these criteria can help you understand what you have seen. Of course, how you choose to evaluate the photograph after you understand it is, or should be, an intensely personal process.

## Manipulated Visions

Photography differs from the other arts in that the time spent creating the photographic negative is usually literally a fraction of a second. In the classic definition of *straight photography,* the photographer often makes the finished negative statement in 1/125th of a second or less. The photographer spends months and years in training to be able to respond to an instant of time, and in that instant chooses what to see and exposes the film. The choices recorded by the lens and shutter reveal both the photographer's aesthetic, social, and political training, and almost always discloses unconscious influences as well. The finished print (whether straight, composite, or manipulated) may take many hours to produce. Producing a photographic print can be as complicated as making a print by any other process.

Within the purist tradition of photography, selection, cropping, printing, toning, organizing, reprinting, and sequencing unmanipulated photographs come close to the process of sketching, underpainting, painting, and reworking of an image by a painter. The acts of selection, sequencing, and arrangement are responsive decisions that always change the meaning of individual prints in a body of work, but they do not nullify the creative, if fleeting, glance of the photographic vision.

---

Documentary photography has repeatedly been spurred on by the discovery of "new" things that the public has not before seen. The opening of the American West and the discovery of the landscapes of Colorado, Arizona, and California found photographers as varied as Timothy O'Sullivan, William Henry Jackson, Albert Bierstadt, and Edweard Muybridge creating amazing, large-format documentary photographs. Their work flourished during the last third of the nineteenth century. Observe how the documentary movements in photographic history alternated with periods of popular photo manipulations:

- 1839—Documentary photography, centered compositions
- 1840—Documentary landscapes
- 1851—*Société Héliographique,* the first amateur photo club sponsoring photographic art
- 1855—Composite photography used to make allegorical pictures
- 1856—Documentary photographs of war scenes
- 1857—Illustrations of myths and stories, "ideal" composite landscapes
- 1880—Hand cameras and flexible, dry film encouraged amateur snapshots and renewed interest in straight photography

- 1882—Jacob Riis publishes documentary slum photos illustrated with flash powder
- 1885—P. H. Emerson's writings promote soft-focus art photos
- 1892—*Linked Ring* photo group exhibits photos as art
- 1893—Photo-Club of France exhibits "First Exhibit of Photographic Art"
- 1900—Single-lens reflex cameras begin to replace view cameras
- 1903—*Photo-Secession* supports photos resembling paintings
- 1905—Lewis Hine documents sweat shops with Graflex (4″ × 5″ single-lens reflex)
- 1924—35mm snapshots enlarge realm of photographic documentation
- 1930—Flashbulbs let pictures be made anywhere
- 1931—Harold Edgerton demonstrates electronic flash
- 1935—FSA documentary propaganda project begins
- 1936—*Life* magazine begins weekly publication
- 1945—Robert Capa, David Seymour, William Vandivert, and Henri Cartier-Bresson found Magnum Photos to market documentary 35mm photography
- 1967—Present wave of photographic manipulations surfaces.

---

When the photograph itself is painted upon, or collaged into a mixed-media presentation, it becomes a painting by default and a different critical language is required than when a straight photograph is being discussed. In the second case, a new language is needed, but only when the photograph is meant to be equivalent to a painting is it appropriate to borrow the art history critical language of painting.

Assembled and manipulated photographs are now part of the art mainstream, but they recall similar, earlier periods in photographic art history. There have been a series of cycles of acceptance and rejection of documentary photography since photography began. The first critical reactions to photography were positive because the new medium so accurately described the world's surface details.

Events can be created and objects assembled by the artist to be photographed, just as historical recreations and still-life paintings are traditional artist's work. Art photographs—from Edward Weston's peppers to the very large Polaroid photographs by Starr Ockenga or Sandi Fellman, or the complex verbal/visual puns created by Robert Cumming—often consist of objects assembled and lighted only for the purpose of being photographed. These pictures are accurately descriptive but differ in spirit from photographic discoveries created in the documentary tradition.

What happened in the last fifty years can be described as alternative popularity of sharp, descriptive photographs and photo-arts, where photographic methods and technology are applied to the production of other forms of print and image making.

---

In the 1850s, *combination printing* became popular. Combination printing simply meant making a new picture by printing two or more negatives on the same sheet of paper. At the beginning of this century, there was the photography movement called **pictorialism,** which encouraged photographers to make pictures that more resembled Impressionist oil paintings or etchings than photographs as we know them.

The reaction to pictorialism and its manipulations came in the 1920s when Paul Strand, Alfred Steiglitz, Ansel Adams, and Edward Weston fostered a new commitment to straight photography.

About each generation the cycle is echoed, and twenty-five years ago a renewed interest in photography as printmaking and photographic assemblage began again to dominate photographic arts. This, in turn, has recently competed with a renewed interest in descriptive photography, revitalized by new political concepts. Documentary photographers like Robert Frank, William Klein, Diane Arbus, and Robert Adams are best understood in the light of political interpretation of the implied meanings of their photographs.

## The Purpose of the Photograph

When a large number of photographs is examined, a pattern of **intention** may be discovered within most mature work. Even when a specific intent is unknown, the work itself often reveals the intention, and that usually becomes clear when the photographs are examined in the context of their time. For example, the social and emotional suggestions of the subjects of photographs by Russell Lee in figure 1.9 and figure 1.10 are vastly different, yet his formal response to both the poverty of plantation housing and to the aesthetic excitement of dramatic sunlight on fuel storage tanks is almost identical.

An examination of photographs that have survived years of critical attention reveal that they:

- Describe a specific moment clearly
- Have a strong sense of form

Either the descriptive or the formal aspect of the photograph may dominate, but both usually exist.

The apparent content of a photograph is often a result of its context, as well as the words that appear in a title or caption that accompanies it. Words that accompany the photograph also change or direct the viewer's attention and affect the meaning. One always needs to also examine the original context for which a photograph was made. Captions and words in the photo itself must be scrutinized carefully, especially if they are out of our own time. Identifying how the photograph was used by the photographer and others in its own time will help in recognizing its original purposes. This effort needs to be made in order to isolate the photograph from editorial decisions made by others.

Figure 1.9
**Negro Cabins. Russell Lee.** Mississippi plantation workers' housing, taken in 1936 for the Farm Security Administration. The picture can be interpreted in many ways.

However, regardless of the politics of the picture, there is a strong formal structure that is repeated often by the photographer. Library of Congress, FSA Collection.

Figure 1.10
**Baytown Refinery, Texas, 1949. Russell Lee.** Refinery storage tanks photographed by "axis" lighting (see chapter 9), which exaggerates the cylindrical forms of the tanks. The photograph was made while

working for Standard Oil, which continued the documentary project of American life begun by the Farm Security Administration. University of Louisville Photographic Archives.

## The Response to the Photograph

We are surrounded by picture sources, which offer us a constant supply of new images. The problem is that we often look without truly registering what it is we are seeing. Like other skills, it takes work and practice to learn to see what we are looking at. Research on how the mind interprets visual information indicates that we look for differences in patterns, and largely ignore everything else.[3]

We expect to see what we are trained to see. This training is a result of our daily experiences and our sense of pleasure about what we willingly watch and what we turn away from. Some of our training is societal and culturally determined, and some reflects our reactions to deeply felt personal events.

The photograph in itself tells us nothing. Ultimately, the photographic print is only a record of the light available to the lens during the fraction of a second when the shutter was opened. In black-and-white photography, that information is further abstracted because color is eliminated and only value remains. All other information we ascribe to the photograph is either intellectual reconstruction of meaning, or emotional **projection,** which is a psychological term describing many otherwise inexplicable responses to photographs. Projection is a defense against self-disclosure. A viewer projects himself onto the picture and, when confronted by an ambiguous image, his own personality traits, needs, goals, desires, fears, etc., are perceived in the image.

The information presented in the photo may have little to do with your responses, feelings, and emotions. When the print is finished, one may wish to ask what it is for and what it means? Most photographers hope that their photographs communicate clearly, but few realize that what others see is not what the photographer saw. Looking at pictures means to respond, and to understand the response, but it also means to discover the information contained in the picture.

## Photographic Information

The lens of the eye makes a retinal image that is interpreted by the brain; it is in that translation that "reality" is conceived. Because of the congruence between our own visual experience and the photographic experience, most of us view the photograph as a magical window opening onto reality. The photograph is merely a two-dimensional construction of gray values, created by a lens system that approximates what our eyes see.

The information available from a photograph is very complex. A photograph's content is the sum of our knowledge of the original scene illustrated in the picture; our insight into art and photographic history; and personal needs, desires, and fears that we bring to the photograph and project onto it. This variability of content is true of all photographs. It has been said that a documentary photograph is only as good as its documentation. For example, a photograph from the mid-1860s may tell us about the clothes worn and the styles of hair. But a response to that photograph should also reflect the difficult and tedious daguerreotype or collodion wet-plate photographic procedures, where exposures lasted for minutes, and one could not ask for fleeting, or more charming, poses.

---

The photographs that have been selected to illustrate this text are drawn in part from large public collections. Sizable photographic art collections are stored at the Museum of Modern Art, New York, New York, and the George Eastman House, Rochester, New York. Unfortunately, only a small fragment of these (and many of the other collections cited here) are available for view at any one time. But for dedicated research purposes, contact staff at these sources for information and viewing schedules: The Gernsheim Collection, The University of Texas, Austin, Texas; Kuhn Memorial Library, Baltimore, Maryland; Chicago Art Institute, Chicago, Illinois; University of Nebraska, Lincoln, Nebraska; University of New Mexico, Albuquerque, New Mexico; Center for Creative Photography, Tucson, Arizona; Friends of Photography, The San Francisco Museum of Modern Art, San Francisco, California; The Library of Congress, and the National Archives in Washington, D.C.

Many specialized collections lie dormant in surprising places. Most states have accessible historical society collections. The Standard Oil collection, which is essentially a continuation of the FSA project, is at the University of Louisville, Kentucky, along with the Griswold collection. Clarence John Laughlin's negatives and prints are in The Historic New Orleans Collection.

The Library of Congress has catalogued more than 80,000 original Farm Security Administration negatives. Working prints that can be handled by you are in open files and may be studied without special access. Beginning in 1935, the photographers of the FSA made documentary photographs for seven years. The project, which was started by the U.S. government, was headed by Roy Stryker, who had a clear sense of what the photographers ought to photograph. They, in turn, took pictures of almost anything they wanted to photograph, to help in fighting the Depression, with the belief that the camera was an effective tool for education (and propaganda). When the FSA project was disbanded, at the beginning of World War II, the project was continued, for a time, by Standard Oil. In the early 1970s, there was the short-lived Documerica project, a further photographic documentation of American life. Ongoing documentary photography of life-styles continues under the aegis of the Library of Congress, American Folklife Center.

Copy prints can be purchased at moderate prices from either the Library or the Archives. An even larger accumulation of photographs (including many of the same photographers) is available in the National Archives, but a researcher's card is needed, though not difficult to obtain. Library of Congress files are alphabetical by photographer; National Archives files photographs by U.S. government agency. Dorothea Lange, for example, not only worked for the FSA, but for the War Relocation Administration and the Agricultural Economic Administration, and you will need to do preliminary research to know which agency list to request.

Photographs are commonly accepted as being truthful and they are frequently allowed in court as legal evidence, but only after they have been validated as not distorting reality, and the court receives testimony regarding the conditions under which the pictures were taken. But the photograph *is not* a transcription of reality.

The photographic experience is also largely a learned experience, in which simplification of forms, acceptance of wide-angle perspective, absence of color, juxtapositions of people and objects in the frame, and intrusions of points of view are accepted as replacements for the actual event.

Some people see in a photograph only the event that was in front of the camera; others see the photograph as pattern and light and dark shapes in the print; still others may see fantasies stimulated by the picture. Response to a picture is frequently an emotional reaction to the illusion of looking through the photo onto a separate reality; that illusion is at the heart of the photograph's power. Each viewer experiences a different photo because we each bring different life experiences to the picture.

Our unique life experiences color our responses, but there generally are commonplace responses as well. We frequently feel the same emotions many others did when we look at a picture; if we did not, there would be no consensual meaning for any photograph. Nevertheless, each person's response to the photograph is dependent on cultural training and personal experiences.

Cultural traditions are deeply embedded in what is photographed, how it is photographed, which photographs are published, how the photographs are used, and how a "good" photograph becomes a model by which you judge other photographs. To an anthropologist or sociologist, for example, the cultural event happening before the lens may be of primary importance, and the formal, aesthetic elements have little value. To an artist, the aesthetic qualities of the print may well come first, and the objects before the camera have little value.

Figure 1.11
**Women Shelling Pecans. Lewis Hine.** A flashpowder-lighted photograph. Hine documented immigrant labor and child labor in American slums and factories in an effort to promote better working conditions and fair labor laws.
Print courtesy of the author.

## Examples of Interpretation

The photograph by Lewis Hine in figure 1.11 is an early example of a carefully posed and arranged flashpowder-lit photograph made by a sociologist in his struggle to reveal the way the poor in New York were forced to live and work early in the century. It is also an emotionally complex picture. Two adults are shown at work hulling pecans by hand, drawn from an enormous cloth sack. The tablecloth is soiled with their work. A child eats broken nutmeats. Two infants are being cared for as the women work. A neighborhood boy attempts to peek in through the glass panels in the door opening onto a tenement hall. A piece of lace is strung across the narrow doorway. Diapers and clothes dry on a line strung across a storage area where a folding bed has been put away to make space for the worktable. The photograph is lighted by flashpowder at the camera (as revealed by

the reflection in the door). Things are jammed together. These women worked ten to fourteen hours a day, fitting their children's lives around their work. One imagines living and caring for a baby in this unventilated space, trying to get enough air, light, and clean water to remain healthy.

Photographs that exist in more than one category are found in figure 1.12 and figure 1.13. The woman in the dark doorway, the strong pattern made by the roof shakes, and the composition in the photographed advertisement are of almost equal importance. Notice the overall similarity of shapes in these two photographs; this is an example of the eye perceiving shape relationships that create linkages between photographs that otherwise obviously have little in common, another way of describing when aesthetic and documentary intentions have equal weight.

Descriptive photography becomes art when the photographer's aesthetic

Figure 1.12
**Advertising, Woodbine, Iowa, 1940. John Vachon.** The photographer frequently turned his camera toward details like this as a personal interpretation of his assignment to photograph daily American life while working from the Farm Security Administration.
Library of Congress, FSA Collection.

Figure 1.13
**Boone County, Arkansas, Rehabilitation Clients, August 1935. Ben Shahn.** Shahn is one of the few FSA photographers who used 35mm. A shy man, he often used a lens prism on his Leica, which permitted him to appear to photograph at right angles to the subject.
Library of Congress, FSA Collection.

sense dominates. John Vachon worked for the FSA and then as a *Life* and a *Look* staff photographer. His photographic abstraction of a billboard is documentary in the most literal sense, a fragment of a small American town. Superficially, the photo does little to describe Depression America. The in-camera selection and editing create a surreal arrangement of facial parts. This documentary photograph is a tiny sample from a large body of photographic expression. It reveals a photographer concerned with the discovery of significant form and social documentation.

Ben Shahn was a painter and designer who worked three years as a photographer for the FSA in order to make a living during the depths of the Depression. Figure 1.13 shows a woman standing in front of a log house. There is little information within the picture itself that unequivocally tells us where and when the picture was taken. These are the facts of the photograph. The proportions of the image are those of the 35mm camera, so the picture could have been made any time in the past sixty years. The woman is white, thin, and careworn. The log cabin and the woman's appearance might lead one to suspect an Appalachian scene, but the picture could also have been made in Alaska or Canada. It is not clear from the picture itself just why these people were photographed. It is only in examining the caption that one discovers the woman and girl were recipients of a Depression-era U.S. government aid program. This fact justified the documentary act of the photographer; the caption completes the photo.

Figure 1.14
Untitled, 1936. Arthur Rothstein.
Library of Congress, FSA Collection.

## Hidden Meanings

The meaning of the documentary photograph usually becomes clear when the viewer knows the implied social references. But sometimes the meaning may still be elusive, even though the picture seems dramatically self-evident.

Figure 1.14 shows a man peering under the hood of an old Ford truck. A puddle of liquid on the pavement implies the car has overheated. The model of the truck, the narrowness of the road, the bareness of the road shoulder, and the absence of guard rails or fences date the scene. The tires are bald, and the sidewall of one tire is peeling away. The truck is piled high with household goods. At a glance, one might think this was a

typical, migrating "Okie" during the Depression years. But the man is wearing a solid leather coat and a good hat; he has a thick, hand-rolled cigarette in his mouth. The license plate is from Tennessee. He may just be moving from one place to another, and what we have is a dramatic photograph that entertains us, but we do not really know what is happening.

The two families shown in figures 1.15 and 1.16 show how misleading the apparent information in a photograph often is, and how difficult it is to define photographic intention when the picture is viewed uncritically, without relevant social and historical information. Both these pictures are "straight" and "unmanipulated," and they both affect our emotions. When you first

look at them they are documentary photographs without documentation.

Both groups were photographed indoors, and the photographer used flash bulbs. Figure 1.15 shows a smiling, well-fed black family. The quality of the highlights and the sharpness of the shadows reveal the flash light as source. Artificial light would have been required for both indoor family portraits. Figure 1.16 shows what seems to be a very poor white family. In this scene, flashbulbs are the obvious choice, given there is not enough light, the slow films available (about ISO 32), the depth of field, the obvious fact that there is no electricity in the house, and the historical fact that electronic flash was not yet available when the picture was made.

Figure 1.15
**Feggen Jones and Family, 1936. Arthur Rothstein.** An example of propaganda to encourage a country in the midst of the Depression.
Library of Congress, FSA Collection.

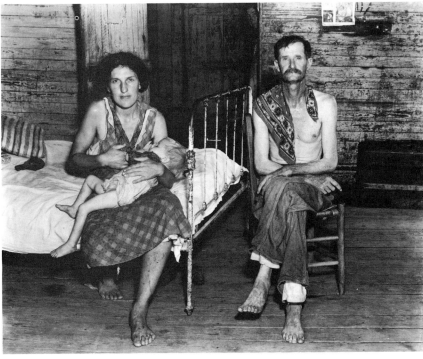

Figure 1.16
**Bud Fields and His Daughter-in-Law. Walker Evans.** A dialogue between the photographer and the subject is captured by the camera.
Library of Congress, FSA Collection.

The history of these people is vividly described in *Let Us Now Praise Famous Men*.[4] In this book, the Fields' are solemn, badly clothed, dirty, and poorly fed. The poverty of the white family is clearly revealed in the bed frame with peeling paint, the pillow without a case, the rough wooden walls without paint, the failed attempts at personal cleanliness, and the clothes they wear.

Walker Evans' picture (fig. 1.16) seems to be a complete description of the people before his camera, posed in the solemn, passive way they might have been photographed almost a century earlier. A flashbulb used indoors flattens the family into a frieze against the poverty and intimacy of their house. Arthur Rothstein (fig. 1.15) also used a flashbulb to freeze a fleeting gesture of the familiar, happy grin we all know how to make for the camera into an unlikely propaganda. The Feggens' are cheerful, well-clothed, and well-fed. The black man and his wife are neatly dressed—he in clean overalls, she in a very good dress—for their class and the year. They are posed against a plain, white wall that reveals nothing about where they live, or their daily lives. Seen in the historical context of the Depression, and against the history of the status of black people in America, in the South, and in the 1930s, this picture is at best an untypical idealization.

A final comparison illustrates how similar subjects offering similar information can arouse profoundly different responses. The well-nourished young woman in figure 1.17 is striding toward the camera. She is comfortably dressed in boots, soft blue jeans, and a work shirt. Her face and body are relaxed. Compare her to the tenant farmer's wife in figure 1.18 (the negative was cropped by the photographer).[5] Her thin body is covered by a stiff, badly made dress that is coarse, torn, and dirty. She stands among debris, barefoot on bare earth. Her frozen, awkward stance symbolizes the poignancy of the uneducated American poor during the Depression of the 1930s. The 1980s photograph records the health and comparative wealth and freedom common even in Appalachia a half-century later. These pictures also reflect different styles of documentation, as well as different cultural generations. One is rigid and bound, the product of the 4″ × 5″ view camera; the other free and casual, a "typical" 35mm snapshot.

## Information and Emotion

Look carefully at any picture and you will respond at some level. As you respond, feelings give rise to some thoughts. To understand how these thoughts relate to the photograph, it is necessary to catalogue the information presented in the photograph and to acknowledge your own emotions.

All photographs offer information and have an independent aesthetic content. The "art" photograph may be more clearly conceived as an aesthetic statement, but it too has descriptive information (unless its photographic underpinnings have been completely concealed or destroyed through manipulation). On the other hand, the documentary photograph made for journalism, fashion, technical, or even medical and scientific purposes often reveals formal concerns that intrude on the viewer and cause differential responses that may or may not be congruent.

The person or event in front of the camera is the obvious subject, but as has been shown in these examples, not the only subject. No photograph is only about the subject. There is no way to predict what emotions any given photograph will produce in a particular viewer. The photographer's training and the aesthetic traditions and conventions of the viewer (asking why the picture was made at all; responding differently when and where the picture is viewed) inevitably affect the selection of subject matter, point of view, type of lens and film, print contrast, lighting, and composition.

Photographic content is a sum of the descriptive information, the cultural associations, and the personal projections triggered by the print. In a broad sense, a pattern of emotional response can be predicted, but ultimately content is individual to the viewer. Individual responses are dependent on the context in which the picture is seen, its position on the printed page and what is adjacent to it, the words associated with it, and its sequence in a group of photographs.

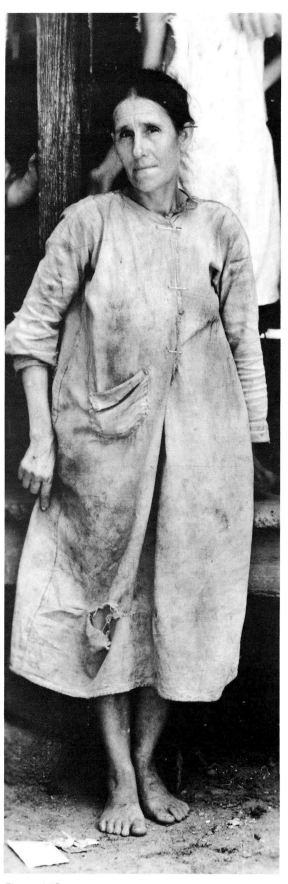

Figure 1.17
Young Appalachian Woman, 1986. Mike
DuBose.

Courtesy of the photographer.

Figure 1.18
Wife of Tenant Farmer, Georgia, 1936.
Walker Evans.

Library of Congress, FSA Collection.

## Summary

Look carefully at every detail in the photograph. Examine the cultural, technical, and aesthetic assumptions you bring to the picture. The photograph offers emotional and aesthetic stimuli, patterns, and abstracted form, in addition to the detailed description of events. Response is affected by contemporary photographic fashions. This response may or may not be appropriate. The response you have to the photograph is a mixture of what is obvious in the picture, what you know or understand about the events described, and what you project onto the picture. Projection is unconscious and involuntary, and usually difficult to assess.

In a broad sense, we always make photographs of people, places, or things. Yet each photographer responds to the most commonplace subject in an individual way. The more you reveal your own inner response to any subject, the more interesting your photograph will be—you are the only person who can reveal your vision.

Rules of composition permit us to safely make pleasant pictures but also inhibit us from reaching out and making pictures that become more vital by breaking the rules. Dull pictures are often the result of trying to make pictures that look like "good" pictures (i.e., conforming to a standard way of seeing, or photographing only acceptable subjects, like sunsets or kittens or pretty girls). The photographs and the photographers that interest us most are those that look at common subjects and offer new insights, whether into the spirit of the subject, the aesthetic form it might evoke, or a new way of presenting the subject in the print.

## Discussion and Assignments

What is fashionable in the arts of a society always reflects current social as well as aesthetic priorities. The pictures made in any era that are honored and preserved (in galleries, personal collections, archives) reflect both the aesthetic and the political modes of the time. Technical improvements change photographic aesthetics. As cameras, lenses, and film change, so do the pictures that are made.

Consensual content can be discovered by discussion; it is what you and the others around you agree on what a picture means. Implied content is usually not consensual because it depends on what you bring to the image. Content is always affected by photographic techniques (lens, contrast, lighting, etc.), by the context in which the picture is seen, the sequence in which pictures are seen, and by the words that may be associated with the picture. The words may be as brief as captions or as extensive as the volumes written on photographic history.

### Assignment 1

Have a friend provide several mounted photographs (without titles) of people, places, or events you probably do not know well. Without talking about these, examine one of these for exactly a minute, then turn it face down. Then do the following.

1. Immediately write down words that came to mind while looking at the picture.

2. On a second sheet of paper, list *everything* you saw in the photograph.

3. On a third sheet of paper, make a careful sketch of the principal shapes in the photograph as you remember them.

Turn the photograph face up and compare the contents of your three sheets of paper with your new perception of the photograph. Try to discover what you failed to see or remember, and what you have distorted or lost in your sketch. Repeat this for each of the other prints.

### Assignment 2

Take the most powerful (interpret that word as you will) photograph from the first assignment (or use another picture if you wish). Using transparent drafting paper and a black felt-tip pen, make careful tracings of the photograph, placing the tracing paper over the photograph and drawing the border of the print, in the following ways.

1. Draw complete outlines around all the important highlight areas (those places that are light gray to white) on the first tracing.

2. Draw complete outlines around all the shadowed areas (middle gray to black) on the second sheet.

Color the enclosed areas solid black on each drawing. Place these tracings on clean cardboard so they can be seen as objects for themselves. Put the original photograph away and compare the tracings to each other. Study patterns made by the highlights and by the shadows and see what these patterns suggest to you.

## Notes

1. John Szarkowski, *Photography Until Now* (New York: The Museum of Modern Art, 1989). 2. "Compositional structure also has been treated as though it consisted of rigid geometrical patterns that were to coincide with salient points of the pictorial design—an activity in which the intellect can rejoice as long as it pays no attention to the fact that the eye fails to discover any such mechanical relation between the compositions of the masters and the superimposed geometry." Rudolf Arnheim, *Toward a Psychology of Art* (Berkeley, California: University of California Press, 1966), 20. 3. B. Julesz and J. R. Bergen, "Textons, the fundamental elements in preattentive vision and perception of textures," *The Bell System Technical Journal,* vol. 62, no. 6 (July–August 1983), 1619–45. 4. James Agee and Walker Evans, *Let Us Now Praise Famous Men* (New York: Houghton Mifflin, 1960). 5. The Library of Congress identifies the woman as Mrs. Tengle, but she is identified as Mrs. Ricketts in Stott, *Documentary Expression and Thirties America* (New York: Oxford University Press, 1978).

# 2 Talking about Photos

Figure 2.1
**Japanese Family Waiting Shipment to Manazar, 1942. Dorothea Lange.** The viewer's identification with the girl awaiting shipment to a wartime concentration camp is enhanced by the point of view. Lange frequently used a *twin-lens reflex* camera, which encouraged a low point of view, seeing children at their own level rather than looking down on them.
**National Archives, Bureau of Agricultural Economics.**

## Basics

First, catalogue the contents of the photograph, then decide what you think this catalogue means. In chapter 1, you were given methods to classify the kind of picture you were looking at, what the nominal subject of the picture was, whether it directed you toward the subject or directed your attention toward the photographer, how camera and film used affected the picture, and how print technique affected your response. With this primary information you can begin to ask the final questions that will lead to understanding of the picture:

1. What is the initial, obvious meaning?

2. What hidden meanings surfaced during the examination?

3. How does the information in the picture compare to the feelings it evoked in you?

This work may be hard at first, if only because it calls for you to make a public statement that may not agree with what your friends think and feel.

It helps to write down, or to say out loud, what you think of a photograph. If you do not have a classmate or a friend to talk with, write down your responses. Putting ideas and emotions into careful words is always hard work, but worth the effort: you clarify what you feel and discover what you think.

The first task is to discover what exists in the picture. The second is to learn how much of your response to the picture comes from within you and is involuntary and projective in nature. The photograph and the photographer are always at the mercy of the viewer. It is the author's opinion that often neither the viewer nor the photographer realizes what is communicated by the photograph and what is brought to it by the individual viewer.

---

Illusionary detail was at the heart of photography for the first half-century and continues to be the principal pleasure photography offers. It is not surprising that buildings, newly discovered Egyptian ruins, churches, cathedrals, monuments, and landscapes were the first subjects. David Octavius Hill and Robert Adamson in Scotland, and Maxime du Camp, Louis-Désiré Blanquart-Evrard and William Powell Frith in Egypt became famous for their documentary photographs. Documentary pictures of cities sold very well and a few professional photographers offered fantastically detailed records of places few could ever expect to see any other way.

Professional photographers in the nineteenth century often made the same pictures in several different formats, not the least important was the square print for the stereopticon viewer. The illusion of deep three-dimensional space required by the stereo pair viewer subtly controlled photographic composition between about 1860 and 1900; photographs were planned to "read" well both as two- and three-dimensional performances. Stereo viewers were found in most houses well into this century and they disappeared only when supplanted by inexpensive movies and TV after 1945. A market for stereo travelogue views still exists in the form of plastic toy viewers.

---

Talking about photos separates the information available in the photograph from the associations and emotions you bring to the picture. Talking leads to a critical judgment, which means to apply specific criteria to the photograph.

## Criteria for Judgment

The least useful response to any photo is "I like it." There are many reasons we do not speak out easily when asked for our real thoughts, not the least being we are afraid to be different. The "I like it" response may be true or it may be just a safe reponse, but it limits discussion and keeps you from discovering what else the photograph offers.

Stating that a picture is good or bad begs the reply, "good for what?" Many pictures that are instantly successful and well-received are *sentimental,* which means they offer no new insights but only confirm what we already know and believe.[1] If the criteria for *good* is to provide insight into aesthetic, political, or social realities, then popular pictures are rarely *good* pictures.

A critical judgment is always a reflection of what *you think* is the purpose of the photograph, because evaluating a photograph means to determine what criteria apply. A *good* photograph is one that serves its intended purpose; a *bad* picture does not.

Photographs are made for many different reasons, but they are often used for purposes other than their original use. Chapter 1 noted that the context in which the photograph is seen will change its apparent content and value.

Critical confusion arises when criteria and purpose are not correlated. This happens when the documentary photograph is expected to look like a painting, or a journalistic demand for a centered image is imposed on a formalist image.

---

Compare Cartier-Bresson, a photographer trained as a painter, and Garry Winogrand. Cartier-Bresson spoke of photographing the "decisive moment." His was a *planned* moment (he was filmed for TV demonstrating how he waited and watched to finalize an anticipated composition). Winogrand photographed *within the moment.* Cartier-Bresson produced complex photographed designs; Winogrand revealed actions in the process of creating form.

Other photographers who seem to respond to the instant (rather than primarily to formal concerns) are Geoff Winningham and Mark Cohen. Compare their photographs to the carefully composed and fabricated pictures by Guy Bourdin, Helmut Newton, Robert Heinecken, Deborah Turbeville, or Bea Nettles, to name a few. There are other possibilities (e.g., where composition is subservient to content as in the work of Ralph Eugene Meatyard or Robert Cummings, who have an intellectual, narrative purpose).[2]

---

Before you make a decision about good-and-bad, decide on criteria, examine the informational and the aesthetic qualities of the photograph, and relate these to the purpose to which the photograph is being put. Only then can an insightful critical judgment follow easily. Without criteria, good-or-bad and acceptance or rejection are hard to justify except as personal whims.

## Composition and Meaning

Regardless of its context, whether it is found in a newspaper or in a painter's collage, the photograph creates a momentary illusion of reality. The psychological reality that is created on viewing the photograph is so powerful that Edward Weston was widely quoted as saying that composition "is the strongest way of seeing," rather than composition depending on tradition and rules. Photographic composition is a complex response to individual insight and art training.

Every shape and value within the frame affects meaning. In figures 2.2 and 2.3, the psychological event determines the composition. Placement of the principal figure within the frame controls feelings. Look at figure 2.2A, a self-portrait. The subject is conventionally centered; at first look, it is balanced, quiet, stable. Look at the picture again: the centered figure of the woman on the porch is not simple. The four vertical posts and the horizontal barrier of the rope, which the woman herself holds, create a box or an arena that limit her. The formal suggestion of these is a frame within the frame. The subtle underlying feeling is of an entrapment (self-imposed or not).

Figure 2.2B is a nontraditional figure-ground, one that violates "rules" of composition by placing the "subject" at the edge to evoke emotion. Now examine the forms in the picture: the light shape of the barn at right balances the form of the face to the left. But aside from figure-ground, there are other elements. First, there is motion to the left (suggested by the woman's hair, the angle of her head, and her face being placed near the frame). Second, there is a claustrophobic feeling with her face so close to the lower left corner. Third, there is a strong hint of a stern face in the facade of the barn.

Figure 2.2
**a.** The first of two psychological portraits: the subject is centered, seemingly open and confrontive, yet hemmed in by a rope.

**b.** By moving the woman close to the camera and at the edge of the frame, both movement and emotion are created.
Photos by Amy Boyer and Tom Jares.

Figure 2.3
**Field Hockey. Sid Hastings.** Sports action photography almost always centers the subject in the frame. The purpose is to reveal peak action and there is no intention to create a more "interesting" composition that might draw the viewer's eye away from the action and focus on the picture itself. Here, a 300mm lens used at a large aperture creates a narrow depth of field (see chapter 3) to isolate the players from an intrusive background.
Courtesy of the photographer.

figure 2.4. The two children at the right momentarily draw the eye away from the woman, who is the nominal subject. Looking back and forth between them reinforces the illusion of participation.

Sport and event photographers are trained to make simple and effective peak action pictures by using use skills that are partly learned and partly intuitive. Sport pictures are most often *centered compositions,* because the picture does not call attention to itself but to the event being documented.

The content of photographs is often influenced by other arts known to the photographer or to the viewer, who always brings personal perceptions to the photograph. The medium itself imposes content; for example, professional photographers in the nineteenth century often made selected compositions based on the dramatic space that could be evoked in the stereographic picture, and then simply made supplementary exposures on larger film from which to make other prints. Later, with the rise of pictorialism, popular compositional standards were derived from painting. In our time, there are few photographers who do not plan their photos as two-dimensional compositions, following either painting or journalistic traditions; the photographers who seek to discover what is essentially "photographic" are very rare.

## Context and Content

Photographic content is constantly redefined because all photographs are made and seen within a technical, cultural, and art context:

- Technical aids define what kind of picture can be made at a given point in history (i.e., camera type, lens and film speed, etc.)
- Social conventions permit certain pictures; prevent or inhibit others
- Aesthetic traditions in the arts interact, rewarding some images, discarding others

Today's meaning of a photograph is changed by its context. Contextual influences must be identified and named

The classical rules of composition are most often correct for photographs intended to describe only what is obvious, with little suggestion of alternative meanings. The photojournalist's record of peak action in a hockey game (fig. 2.3) is an example where the photographer wished to describe *only what happened* and responded according to form, without conscious planning.

The camera often is aimed like a gun, and the most popular composition has a centered subject. Also note that visual space is usually shallow in event-oriented photographs (the photographer is object-centered), but there are other ways to create a *window of illusion,* where we invite the viewer to mimetically participate. This window of illusion can be reinforced by using an off-centered composition and a secondary subject, as shown in

Figure 2.4
**Woman with a Camera. Arnold Gassan.**
The subject is balanced in the frame by the two children on the sidewalk and the filigree of the tree against the sky. The subject of the picture is in the discrepancies between the woman's dress and posture and the Appalachian details.
Photo by the author.

before a picture can be fully understood (and eventually evaluated). When any photograph is viewed out of its own time, both the subject before the camera and the photographic techniques used inevitably are reinterpreted.

We automatically tend to judge a picture by what is technically possible photographically to do now, the history of art and photography, and what is fashionable in today's art.

Examine figure 2.5*A* and compare it with figure 2.5*B*. They were made almost half a century apart, and both use supplemental flash lighting to provide adequate exposure. Although superficially similar in terms of the documentary intent, the older picture reflects the tradition of the photographer confronting the subject, which dates from the beginning of photography, while in figure 2.5*B,* the photographer and the subjects pretend the photographer is not present. This was possible because of improvements in lens design, high-speed films, and portable electronic flash. In other words, the implicit content in these photographs changed because the technology of film and lighting changed.

a.                                           b.

Figure 2.5
**a. Smith Feed Store, Powell, Wyoming, June 1944. Edwin Rosskam.** The confrontive pose and use of direct flash are typical of the documentary style of the Standard Oil documentary project.
**b. Clinton and Mae Iroller, Patrick County,** Virginia, 1978. Carl Fleischauer. Although superficially similar to Rosskam's photograph (**a**), the subjects act as though the camera did not exist in this *flash-filled* picture (see chapter 9). This scene was photographed for the American Folklife Center Blue Ridge documentary project, one of a series of ongoing documentary projects, which emulate work done by the FSA.

**a.** University of Louisville Photographic Archives.
**b.** American Folklife Center, Library of Congress.

Photographs have three kinds of content when we:

- Catalogue or name things in the picture
- Decide by consensus
- Individually interpret the picture

The consensual content of a photograph is the sum of information. Content is affected by contemporary references.

While there is no "objective" photograph, some photographic decisions are more obviously "aesthetic" and call attention to themselves and the decisions the artist/photographer made about style. Each photographer makes a choice as to how to frame a photograph; no matter how hard one tries, all photographs record subjective editorial decisions. For example, few documentary photographers have been as self-effacing as Dorothea Lange; most impose a more obvious compositional frame about the subject, which makes you more aware of the photographer behind the camera.

Figure 2.6 is a classic documentary picture, composed and photographed to allow the subject before the camera to be seen for itself. It is a picture by Lange from work done for a government bureau. It shows a 1930s version of a truck stop—a place to buy gasoline, liquor, and food. The information available from the photograph includes details of commercial architecture, automobile styles, advertising, and economic data (the price for gas). Examine only the last: the gas seems cheap, until one realizes the picture was made in 1940 and, allowing for inflation, gasoline at 21 cents in 1940 would cost about $3.00 today.

Figure 2.7 is a **cliche-verre** by Lazlo Moholy-Nagy.[3] Significance of form and manipulation of process and materials are at the heart of meaning in this photo-print. Contemporary art history references (to Cubism, to De Stijl painting) are brought to the picture, and one also inevitably responds to questions on how the photographic process was used to make the print. In preparing this book, the Moholy-Nagy photo-print was deliberately placed close to figure 2.8, a "documentary"

Figure 2.6
**Cotton Town, Arizona, 1940. Dorothea Lange.** Lange is best known for her sympathetic and emotional photographs of people in distress, but when one examines a complete file in the National Archives, it is apparent that with each assignment subject she set about photographing as much about the environment in which the downtrodden lived as she could. These supplementary pictures provide the factual documentation that supports the empathic, emotional images.

National Archives, Bureau of Agricultural Economics.

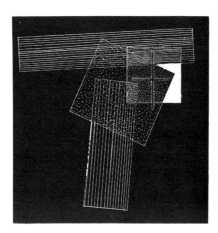

Figure 2.7
**Abstraction. L. Moholy-Nagy, ca. 1930.** This *cliche-verre* is typical of the artist's work, both in that photographic materials are a means to the image and in the parallels between this construction and what was currently important in the other arts.

Library of Congress.

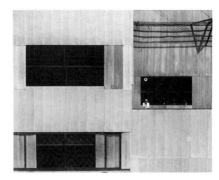

Figure 2.8
**J & L Mill Building, 1940. Ivan Massar.** Note how a careful alignment of the camera permits rigid geometric drawing in the photograph. As you look at photographs, always make note of when the picture was made: often there are important references to other art aesthetics, as between this composition and the paintings of several American abstractionists.

University of Louisville Photographic Archives.

Figure 2.9
**Union Election, Local 600, 1938. Arthur Siegel.** Every man wears a cap or a hat and the clothing is heavy and loose. Note the varying expressions of the men, some of whom question the photographer's action.
Library of Congress, FSA Collection.

photograph of the wall of a steel mill (made in 1940 by Ivan Massar, working for Standard Oil). Although Massar's picture is a straight photograph, even to the tiny figure of the man used as a highlight to enliven the third dark rectangle, it is as much an abstraction of form—a linear composition—as Moholy–Nagy's photographic print. The steel mill documentary also differs from the cliche-verre in having smooth intermediate gray tones, which make the photograph different from all other kinds of prints. In both illustrations, the photographer interposed himself between the viewer and the print: formal aesthetic concerns dominate these pictures.

## Social Climate

Each photograph reflects the social as well as the political and cultural climate of the time in which it was made. Responses to the photograph include unconscious as well as conscious reactions based on cultural programming. Programming is sometimes obvious and sometimes quite subtle. Look carefully at the photograph to discover:

- What events and subjects are photographed
- What is *not* being photographed
- The photographer's attitudes toward the subject

Photographs used to describe and photographs used as art are separated by the photographer's intentions and aesthetics. Any camera and film can be used to make the picture, but this text has shown that what is presented is always just a transcription, not the actual event before the camera. Even the very definition of what is documentary is variable.

The photographer offers us the camera's reality, not our reality. Figure 2.9 is an historical photograph by Arthur Siegel of a union election in the 1930s. Without a caption, one sees a line of men. The caption tells us they are waiting to vote in a union election. This was an event of great political significance and these elections were always emotional and often dangerous. When the photo was made, in 1938, union recognition voting was bitter and often violent. The photographer interpreted an otherwise banal business election by transforming the line of waiting men into a monumental frieze. He made them larger than life by choosing a low camera angle and eliminating the background.

Figure 2.10
**Cheyenne Woman, 1910. Edward S. Curtis.**
Portrait lighting remains unchanged and
the photographer used a single strong
source (see chapter 9) high and to the left,
an example of what is still called
"Rembrandt" lighting to describe this
woman's features.

Figure 2.11
**San Ildefonso Pueblo. Ansel Adams.** The
"snapshot" is the camera recording the
event in the instant, revealing the energy
and confusion of the world.

Print by National Archives, Department of the Interior;
courtesy of the Ansel Adams Publishing Rights Trust.
All rights reserved.

Compare figure 2.10, the Edward
S. Curtis studio portrait of a Cheyenne
woman, with Ansel Adams' snapshot,
figure 2.11, of Indian festival dancers.
Instead of a carefully planned, "artistic" reality, figure 2.11 has men in
traditional costumes being watched by
people in everyday clothes. The background is a building that has both traditional adobe walls and modern
windows. The dancers' awkward ges-
tures, the bland lighting, and the accidental overlapping shapes of dancers
and watchers typify a **snapshot.**[4]
Curtis' picture has a dark drama created by careful lighting, somber tones,
and shallow depth of field, and the
"reality" is all made up. Adams' picture is a casual, yet historically accurate, record of a mid-afternoon
performance of an ancient ritual. It is
also the flip side of Siegel's picture of
union men in that it accepts the event
at its own level and refuses to direct
the emotional response of the viewer.

## Point of View and Caption

Meaning is changed by changing point
of view. Figure 2.12A is a photograph
through an open doorway; compare it
with figure 2.12B, the same entry hall
and staircase. The photographer has
moved just within the doorway. The
first photo is a record of the entry to a
place, a glance from the corner of the
eye, a casual encounter. The second is
an emotionally evocative abstraction of
form, a dialogue between patterns of
light and shade, transparency and solidity. Both photographs describe the
same physical space, but the difference in the point of view transforms
them.

Point of view influences the
meaning of a photograph as shown by
the images of women seen in figure
2.13 and figure 2.14. Certainly, there
are other effective photographic elements at work here: lighting, camera,
costume, distance, and the captions all
modify meaning. But the point of view
is dominant. In Walker Evans' photo-

graph, the camera was centered on
the woman's face, producing an eye-
to-eye confrontation: you look at her
and she looks back. In Marion Post
Wolcott's photo, the camera was held
at waist level, looking up. (The angle of
view and the square format strongly
suggest a twin-lens reflex was used.)
The upward angle makes the figure of
the woman slightly ennobled, larger
than life. The upward angle from the
low point of view also permits Wolcott
to include details like the clothesline
and palm tree, details that enrich the
visual texture and also add information
and help define meaning.

Wolcott's caption supposedly
offers us the very words the subject
was saying while the picture was being
made, and it also has a profound effect
on the meaning of the picture. There is
no way to avoid a reaction to words
accompanying a picture when we look
at the image. Captions of photographs
are much like words to a song; once
we know them we can hardly hear the
music without remembering the words
as well.

a.

Figure 2.12
**a. Untitled.** The light, space, a feeling of possibilities, *something* catches the photographer's eye: the 35mm camera

b.

permits her to make an instantaneous response.
**b. Untitled.** Stepping closer to the same subject, allowing the space and the light to

define themselves, a second picture is exposed and the implicit subject is discovered.

Photos by Sheila Flemming.

Figure 2.13
**Allie May Burroughs, 1935. Walker Evans.**
The photographer and the woman confront one another. Evans used a 4″ × 5″ view camera on a tripod; a flashbulb controls contrast. Compare the openness and lack of mystery here with the romantic manipulation of light in figure 2.10.
Library of Congress, FSA Collection.

Figure 2.14
**Canal Point, Florida: "We never lived like hogs before." Marion Post Wollcott.** Low point of view, the woman's averted gaze, and the caption each modify meaning. The intention is to affect your emotions.
Library of Congress, FSA Collection.

## Matters of Style

Identifying photographic style, and how it modifies content, is necessary when talking about pictures. The technological sequence of camera styles ranges from the tripod-mounted, inflexible view-camera to the waist-level twin-lens reflex camera, to the immense freedom of the eye-level 35mm miniature camera. This progression may seem inevitable in retrospect. The constriction or freedom of each camera imposes significant difference of style.

---

Edward Curtis' portraits (see fig. 2.10) are *reconstructions,* made about 1910. They are made-for-photography realities modeled on portrait painting conventions standardized centuries earlier. It is important to know that the "reality" he photographed no longer existed; it was only a romantic dream.

Originally published in a Carnegie-endowed multivolume photogravure portfolio, Curtis' commissioned photographs of vanished Indian ways of life are examples of romantic art photography masquerading as documentation; they are productions of lustrous, beautiful printmaking. Curtis frequently had to make or supply costumes and ornaments appropriate to the rank or station of his impoverished subjects. On looking at the photo, our response is to the style of lighting and to the aesthetics of photo-printmaking at least as much as it is to the woman, and our response to the woman is determined in large part by the changing fashions of how we "should" respond to Native Americans.

---

There are stylistic differences in printing. In the nineteenth century, a warm brown print color was desired, and this is still found in black-and-white portraiture. For forty years, "art" photography was identified by soft-focus prints on paper with a "canvas" texture. Even the early work of Edward Weston and Ansel Adams was printed this way. For the past sixty years, the ideal print has been a sharp, glossy, blue-black, contrasty print with brilliant highlights. Yet, within the last twenty-five years, there has been a growing movement to replace the glossy print with print manipulations—overpainting, toning, hand-coloring, collage, and montage.

Style always affects perceived meaning. Style refers to changing modes of fashion in ways of making photographs. Style also refers to things seen in the picture: autos, architecture, and costumes, such as those worn by the women in figure 2.13 and figure 2.14. These strongly affect meaning. Both women wear dresses of traditional cut and material, but Evans' view-camera lends itself to passive confrontation, while Wolcott's picture was made possible by the twin-lens reflex, a camera that permitted her to choose an unusual point-of-view, and to focus and photograph quickly. The candid camera style suggests a mobile, restless, if not self-determining subject. The traditional view-camera required the subject to stand quietly in place while the photographer disappeared under a dark cloth and focused and prepared the camera. One had to be passive until the film was exposed—a willing partner to the photographic dialogue.

The photographer's personal style of interacting with the subject, as well as photographic equipment, documentary style, printing, and pictorial composition, all affect meaning. Figure 2.15A shows a neatly dressed woman wearing good clothes and a necklace while she is feeding chickens. She is fully conscious of the photographer's presence. Although the picture may look candid, these details reveal an interaction between the subject and the photographer. Dorothea Lange obviously had an open dialogue between her camera and subject.

Photographic composition is also important, and figure 2.15B is a schematic analysis of the picture, which shows how the spatial relationships are affected by the great depth of field produced by a moderate wide-angle lens, and the careful placement of the figure against the tree behind the subject. A slow shutter speed was used (evidenced by the blurred chickens). The subject of the photograph is the woman in her environment, and the photograph is a record of the photographer's understanding of the pattern of that life. Lange is in the yard, the interaction is intimate, and the photographer allows her subject to dress up to feed her chickens.

Made a generation later, figure 2.16A is a contemporary 35mm documentary of a black man leading a cow. The nominal subject is the man and the cow and the chain. These are seen as a pattern within the frame; all else is reduced to blur. The photographer stood isolated at a distance and used a long lens, which produced a narrow depth of field and transformed the subject into a cardboard cutout. The schematic analysis in figure 2.16B discloses clearly how the small camera with a long lens *selects* a thin slice of time and space, while the photographer remains at a psychological and cultural—as well as physical—distance from the subject.

a.

b.

Figure 2.15
a. Woman Feeding Chickens, Putnam
County, Georgia, 1941. Dorothea Lange.
The picture illustrates the primary tradition
in photography: the woman feeding
chickens is fully aware of the photographer,
and the process becomes interactive.
b. Schematic analysis of a, showing deep
compositional space.

a. National Archives, Bureau of Agricultural Economics.

a.

b.

Figure 2.16
a. McKinley Brim Leading Betsy, 1978.
Terry Eiler. The alternative tradition in
photographic documentation is to isolate
the photographer from the subject,
sometimes by catching the subject
unaware or (in this case) by photographing
from a distance and using a telephoto lens.
b. Schematic analysis of a, showing shallow
compositional space.

a. American Folklife Center, Library of Congress.

## Symbolic Content

A photograph may be both descriptive and symbolic. Figure 2.17 and figure 2.18 are documentary photographs of kitchens, made within a year of one another and in the same part of the United States. Paul Carter's picture describes a proposed "ideal" farm kitchen for rural America in the 1930s: one sees a coal-fired oven; stove; sink with running water; icebox for food storage; smooth, clean walls; storage cabinets; shelves; and tight wooden flooring. All these were rare or non-existent.

Walker Evans' picture reveals the bitter reality of a 1930s tenant farmer's kitchen in Georgia: one sees a crude wood-fired stove, a ragged pile of kindling, old pots and pans hung from the wall, wood walls with only traces of paint and cracks open to the weather, a rough floor with large cracks, and a chair without a seat. This picture could be remade even today on some farms in Appalachian and rural America.

Both pictures are documentary, and each also reveals clear aesthetic intent, in the way they are composed. The Carter photograph was intentional propaganda, made to show what life could be like; in its time, it was symbolic of an ideal way to live. The Evans photograph has become symbolic to us of the life of the rural poor during the Depression.

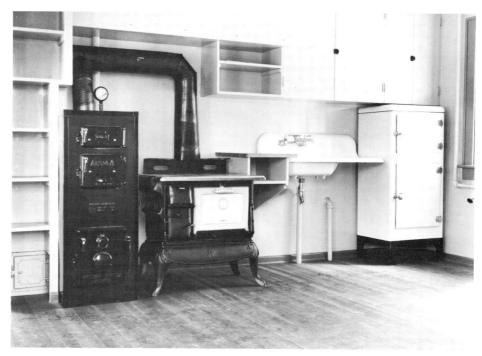

Figure 2.17
Resettlement Administration Housing, 1936–1937. Paul Carter.
Library of Congress, FSA Collection.

Figure 2.18
Corner of Bud Field's House, 1935. Walker Evans.
Library of Congress, FSA Collection.

What is seen as symbolic content in photographs may not withstand scrutiny. Figure 2.19*A* is a dramatic picture of a man working in a cotton field in Arizona, photographed by Dorothea Lange. This picture has often been reproduced with captions describing the worker's exhaustion or distress. Hand held in front of his staring face, the gesture holds you, the viewer, at bay. The photo hints of fear, exhaustion, and anger. It is vivid, clearly a symbolic gesture—one that easily lends itself to emotional interpretation. But this obviously symbolic gesture may be nothing more than the action of a hot man wiping his mouth with the back of his hand.

Figure 2.19*B* is another Lange picture taken a moment before or after. The same man is seen merely resting, leaning against a rough timber, his cotton sack slung over his shoulder. Unlike the first, the second picture is not melodramatic or threatening. Both pictures are suggestive, but their mood is different; the low point of view enhances the power of the figure in both, and the clear sky provides a neutral ground for the worker. The apparent symbolism of the first picture is a result of the photographer's skill in capturing a gesture that for a fleeting moment portrayed a feeling common to the times. This was enhanced by her editing and by her printing that selection; the gesture caught by her camera has come to symbolize the time, but it is a result of editing and captioning.

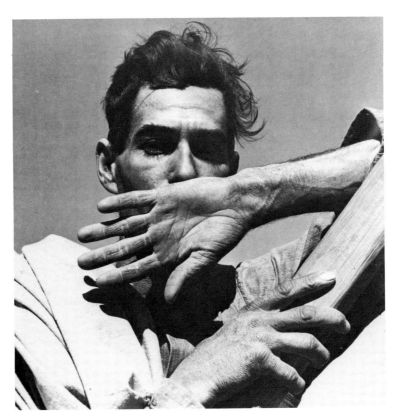

a.

b.

Figure 2.19
a. Cotton Worker, Arizona, 1942 (hand raised). Dorothea Lange.

b. Cotton Worker, Arizona, 1942 (hand down). Dorothea Lange.

National Archives, Bureau of Agricultural Economics.

## Deciding for Yourself

The portraits in figure 2.20 and figure 2.21 are presented to help you discover how apparent content is influenced by composition, point of view, contrast, lighting, symbols, placement of the subject, and costume. In figure 2.20, the man is posed against a winter-dead landscape. The picture is made from below a normal horizon, looking through the dark frame of a water-streaked screen. Details are hidden behind the streaks of water. The picture is two layers: the screen and the man in the landscape. The screen rigidly and literally "cuts the man off at the knees," and at the right is a heavy shadow cross. The man has a symmetrical, heavy, stolid pose and he is glued to the ground.

Figure 2.21 shows the same man standing in the middle of an arena, in open light, clearly defined against the fence and the background trees. The horizon line has moved up to face level. Though the same hat is worn, the irregular line of the brim is almost jaunty. His arms are akimbo and the slight downward foreshortening makes the body float upward.

What you see as the content of each picture is actually an amalgam of the descriptive information found here; the cultural, aesthetic, and life-experience associations you may bring from experiencing similar scenes; and the involuntary projective emotional response each picture triggers in you.

## Critical Judgment

Look for the information available in the photograph. Be willing to work at talking about what you see and what you feel. The emotions aroused by feelings need to be dug out before you evaluate a photograph. Make a catalogue of emotions and consensual information, to be sure you understand the difference between what is physically present and what actually may be the subject of the picture. The apparent content of the photograph is the sum of:

- Consensual information
- Personal associations
- Involuntary projections

a.

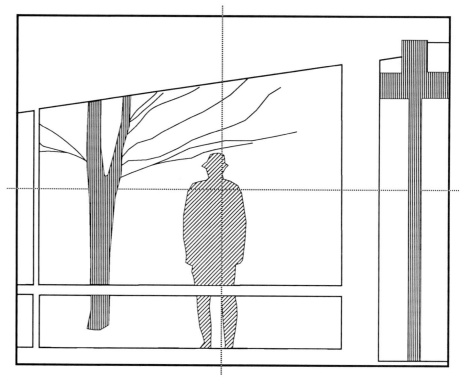

b.

Figure 2.20
**a. Untitled. Frederick M. Schreiber.** A psychologically suggestive portrait. The light, the rain, the pose, the composition all affect the meaning.
**b.** Schematic analysis of **a,** showing how the dominant shapes interact.
a. Courtesy of the photographer.

Only descriptive information recorded by the lens is available to all viewers. Associations generated by a photograph may be similar for you and other viewers raised in the same culture (i.e., from the same socioeconomic class, from the same schools; people who have read the same books, seen the same films, know the same jokes, watch the same TV shows), but even that is not guaranteed. Projections are inevitably individual, variable, and cannot be compared; frequently, the projective content is not even directly available to the viewer, but must be inferred by comparing your response to others—and being surprised at what others see.

Content assessment is necessary to understanding the photograph. Critical judgment of a photograph means to determine its contemporary and historical value. Making a critical judgment means to evaluate the following elements:

- The craftsmanship of the picture
- The appropriateness of its use
- The quality of insight into the event

Evaluating these requires suitable criteria, and knowledge of the medium and the historical context. Photographs can be good and not be likable; they can be bad and be quite pleasant to see. As you experience more and more photographs, work at becoming aware of how you make judgments and how these evaluations change as your awareness of the visual world enlarges.

a.

b.

Figure 2.21
**a. Untitled. David Myers.** The same portrait subject as in figure 2.20 is seen in a different visual space, with open light. Note how framing the subject with the fence rail and open space change the feeling.
**b.** Schematic analysis of **a.**

a. Courtesy of the photographer.

## Summary

Catalogue the contents of the photograph as a means to understanding the content. Place the picture in an historical context so as to understand the limitations under which the photographer worked. A number of research collections of photographic prints are listed, but many small, local collections are available and often overlooked. Judgement requires establishing criteria, and criteria may be drawn from art history, politics, and photographic technical history. Content is affected by context: if the picture is seen in a museum, it has different meaning than if seen in a newspaper, and if it is captioned, the words will change the meaning. Historically, judgements change because pictures are not seen in the context in which they were made. Pictures made as documentation are reexamined in the light of changing politics and aesthetics. The content of the picture is determined, in part, by what the viewer brings to it, and this is controlled both by the social climate and by the viewer's personal experiences.

## Discussion and Assignments

Discovering the limits of consensual knowledge about a photograph is not difficult, and often proves to be exciting.

### Assignment 1

Work with four or five other photographers and have each person bring a photograph he or she is willing to investigate (these can be new or historical pictures). Do not talk about the pictures or offer any response before beginning the assignment. Keep the pictures separated (i.e., place them on a print rail or a table and then study them one at a time). Use a separate sheet of paper for each picture. Write answers to the following questions:

1. What is the mood of the picture?

2. What was the photographer trying to convey?

3. What do you think is the story of the picture?

4. What technical or craft manipulations are present that affect the meaning (lighting, contrast, tone, etc.)?

5. If the picture is not contemporary, can you tell from the picture when it was made?

6. What other question do you think is important to ask?

When you have each finished, tape all the answer sheets for a given picture to the wall above the print and compare the answers. Find out how much information was held in common within the group and how much divergence there was. If you feel comfortable about it, discuss the differing answers to discover where they came from.

### Assignment 2

Choose three photographs of your own that you think are clear visual statements. Use prints that are not matted and that you are willing to have damaged by frequent handling. Over a week or ten days, offer these three prints to at least twenty people; some of them may be people you know, but the majority should be comparative strangers, and at least half should not be artists or photographers or communications majors (i.e., people with special skill or training in visual communication). As you hand them the prints, ask them to answer these questions:

1. What is the picture about?

2. Is there anything you would change in it?

3. Does it remind you of any other photograph?

Write down the answers as they are given to you. When the entire project is completed, see what kind of consensus your pictures achieve, and how you feel about the results.

## Notes

1. "Sentimental art, for instance, attempts to force preexistent emotions upon us." Annie Dillard, *Living by Fiction* (Perennial Library New York: Harper & Row, 1982), 26. 2. See *American Photography,* by Jonathan Green for examples of these photographers. Green also provides a useful historical and critical framework for their work. 3. *Cliche-verre* is literally "drawing on glass," and describes any hand-made negative. The first cliche-verre was apparently made in the 1840s by the French painter Jean-Baptiste-Camille Corot, who scratched drawings into the emulsion of fogged plates provided by friends. They then made prints of his drawings. The cliche-verre is close to the photogram in that both are photographic printmaking without a camera. Contemporary variations on the cliche-verre have been created by Man Ray, in the 1920s; Francis Bruggiere, who painted on glass; Henry Holmes Smith, who poured thin films of syrup on glass sheets and used these to make negative shadows of the liquid forms on film, and then made dye-transfer color prints of the abstract shapes he had created; and by Frederick Sommer, who caught swirls of oily smoke on glass, then printed these to create surrealistic figures. 4. *Snapshot* was adapted to photography by Sir John Herschel, who used the bird-hunting term to describe an instantaneous photograph, made without careful consideration because the target was moving. The snapshot is often the most sincere, if the least pretty, version of the documentary photograph simply because it is a genuine response to the subject and the moment of the event, rather than an artistically planned reconstruction. Herschel also suggested, in 1839, that the original camera image of reversed values be called a **negative** and the subsequent print from it be a **positive**.

# 3 Camera Controls

Figure 3.1
**Untitled. Tisa Tylor.** The photographer "panned" the camera to keep the image of child and wagon at the same place on the film during a long exposure. The result is to isolate these from their surroundings and to reveal the private world of the child at play.
Courtesy of the photographer and Agfa-Beseler.

## Basic Camera

All cameras consist of a lighttight box with a shutter and a lens, which projects an image on a photosensitive surface.

The 35mm camera permits the photographer to use the camera in hand, rather than locked onto a tripod. Modern lenses and films produce pictures with detail rivaling those made by large-format view-cameras a generation ago. Today's 35mm camera has motorized film advance, interchangeable lenses, automated aperture, an electronic shutter to control exposure, and a light-metering system with a computer that can interactively program both shutter and aperture.

---

The contemporary small camera is a very distant descendant of the **camera obscura,** or darkened room first used in the fifteenth century with an image-forming lens in one wall that projected an image onto another wall. The optical magic of seeing a complete landscape outside projected inside on a wall was soon made transportable and was used by artists for three centuries until modern photography was invented.

The camera obscura became smaller and turned into the view-camera, a big box on a stand. The view-camera is still central to professional scientific, architectural, advertising, and other photography where very fine detail, excellent tonal range, and a large negative are required. But the popular amateur camera has steadily grown smaller and smaller until—in the 1930s—the 35mm camera began to dominate.

---

## The 35mm Camera

Figure 3.2 illustrates how to load and begin making pictures with a contemporary 35mm camera. In general, the following checklist should be observed when preparing to load a camera and make pictures:

1. Check frame counter and rewind to be sure camera is empty.

2. Open camera back.

3. Insert film leader in takeup.

4. Place cassette in camera body.

Figure 3.2

**a.** Check the frame counter before opening the camera back. When the frame counter is at **S,** it indicates that there is no film in the camera. The shutter control knob on this camera allows the photographer to select specific shutter speeds, and allow through-the-lens (TTL) metering automatically to control the aperture (**A**) or choose another exposure program.

**c.** Pull out of the cassette only the film needed. The cassette is locked in by the rewind shaft. With the film in place, close the camera back and gently rewind to take up slack.

**b.** Insert the narrow tab of fresh film from the cassette into the camera take-up reel slot. After it is fully engaged, lay the film across the back of the camera. Film perforations must engage teeth on the take-up sprocket. Avoid pushing in on the shutter (just to the left of the take-up spindle).

**d.** Advance the film and press the shutter button, then repeat. This will move fresh, unexposed film into position to make pictures. The rewind crank (at left) should turn as the film advances, but if it does not, the film is probably not loaded properly. Open the back of the camera and reconnect the film in the take-up reel slot.

5. Advance film a bit to verify loading.

6. Close back; take up rewind slack.

7. Advance film and trip shutter twice.

8. Watch rewind to be sure film is moving.

9. Set camera meter to correct film speed.

10. Set aperture and shutter.

11. Note your camera posture.

12. Look.

13. Expose film.

14. Rewind film immediately after exposing the last frame on the roll.

**e.** Confirm that the ISO (film speed) number is correct for the film being used. New cameras adjust this automatically.

**f.** Locate the aperture control (shown here at 5.6) and the shutter (shown at 1/60 of a second).

**g.** After the last frame has been exposed, release the rewind control on the camera and immediately use the rewind crank to rewind film completely into the cassette.

**h.** Hold the camera by supporting it with your entire body: poor posture will limit sharpness in your pictures. The posture shown is bad because the photographer's arms are away from the body there is little; support for the camera.

**i.** A monopod supports the camera with longer exposures, yet leaves you free to move.

**j.** Correct posture places arms under the camera, braced comfortably against the body. Camera weight is transferred to the body and the pictures will be sharper at slower shutter speeds.

Your eyes and mind do not see a black-and-white image, and the photograph does not recreate what you see. Your eyes work in partnership with your brain to assemble a three-dimensional reality for two-dimensional perceptions, but the camera selects only pattern. Just as the black-and-white

photograph is a translation from color to value, so is it also a translation from three dimensions to two. You will learn to discover what the camera sees as you become skilled. Rather than demanding the camera mimic what you see, let yourself concentrate on seeing with the camera at first.

It takes a lot of practice with the camera and in the darkroom to be able to predict what a photograph will look like. You will need to experiment a lot with your camera, film, and the printing materials and processes outlined here in order to understand what effects they have on the translation from your visual impulse to the finished photograph. After several rolls of film have been exposed, developed, and printed, you will begin to understand more fully what you want to photograph, how you wish to photograph, and why you may want to take over the camera control. Remember, the picture you make is not what your eye saw.

With early cameras and with the contemporary view-camera the photographer replaced the film in the camera with a sheet of lightly etched (or "ground") glass, then covered the back of the view camera with a large black cloth. This made a dark space in which one could study the dim inverted image projected by the lens onto the ground glass.

Large view cameras have not changed much since the 1840s. The contemporary professional photographer using an 8 × 10 inch view-camera still hides under a black cloth and looks at the image projected on a ground glass. Viewing and focusing become the same operation, since the photographer can see exactly what image the lens will make.

After focusing the view-camera, the photographer had to close the shutter and replace the ground glass with the film, which was carried to the camera in ingenious flat boxes called film-holders. In the effort to simplify photography, it was necessary to do away with the ground glass and the focusing cloth required by the view-camera, as well as the heavy box of film-holders.

A problem for many photographers is that the ground glass image in the view-camera is both upside down and reversed left-to-right. When photography was invented the portable camera obscura had already been used by artists for a century. It had a mirror behind the lens at 45° which reflected the light up onto a ground glass—and inverted the image at the same time. This structure was adapted for small photographic cameras.

Most of us have had experience with a camera at some time. Fortunately, with the operating ease of modern cameras you can let the camera take care of the actual exposures at first, rather than distracting yourself and worrying much about exposure calculations. We are far more

Figure 3.3
**Untitled. Frederick M. Schreiber.** A simple plastic lens from a "toy" camera was used by the photographer. The circular image is the natural product of the lens; it is convention to crop a rectangular form.
Courtesy of the photographer.

Figure 3.4
**Vesuvius. Photographer unknown.** The first two models of the Kodak camera revealed the circular image each lens makes. The Kodak system empowered amateur photographers.
Print courtesy of Arnold Gassan.

ready to begin making 35mm pictures than we realize. Almost all new 35mm cameras have automatic exposure controls available if we want to use them. Some cameras can only be used in an automatic mode. As you become more advanced, you may wish to more selectively use these features. If you are purchasing a camera now, it is important to choose a camera that allows you to take charge in the future, when you may want to.

Begin photographing by trusting your camera. If you can manually control the shutter on your camera, set it at 1/60th or 1/125th of a second for the first roll of film you use. These shutter speeds will be fast enough to eliminate most blur when photographing outdoors, and still permit a reasonably small aperture setting.

## The Lens

A lens consists of curved glass. As light leaves air and enters glass, it moves more slowly. A ray of light entering glass at an acute angle is bent. The curvature of the glass and the kind of glass used in the lens determine how much the light will bend.

A simple lens consists of a single piece of glass or plastic with the sides curved to bend the light so that parallel rays entering the lens are bent to intersect *(focus)* at about the same point in space. Figure 3.3 shows the circular image made by a simple plastic lens from a toy plastic camera. Compare it with the circular image of figure 3.4, made a century ago with the first Kodak camera.

Simple lenses do not bend all colors of light equally, and to make pictures where the focus is the same for all colors requires the use of several pieces of glass and the use of different types of glass.

Light coming from a great distance appears to travel in parallel lines, and a well-made lens will bend parallel rays of colored or white light so that they do meet precisely at a common point on the **focal plane.**

The **focal length** is the distance from the optical center of the lens focused on something very far away to the focal plane. This "far away" distance is called *optical infinity* (marked ∞ on the camera lens), and for a 50mm lens is anything more than about 50 yards away. For example, a lens that brings objects at 500 yards into sharp focus when the lens is 100mm from the film would have a focal length of 100mm.

## Aperture

The amount of light a lens can pass is controlled by the aperture. The size of the aperture is usually set by an aperture control ring on the lens. The contemporary small camera aperture consists of several thin metal blades that overlap to form a calibrated centered opening in the lens system. The purpose of this variable opening is to control the amount of light that can pass through the lens. Figure 3.5 illustrates how the size of the lens opening relates to the *f-number* of the aperture.

In order to predict an exposure, one must be able to compare the light-gathering power of a lens, regardless of its size. A lens that is 6 inches in diameter can obviously allow more light into the camera than can a 1 inch lens of the same focal length. The actual brightness of the image made on the film is calculated by using the f–number of the lens. The f–number is the ratio of the focal length divided by the effective diameter of the lens, and it indicates the ability of the lens to provide focused light on the picture plane.

$$f = \frac{\text{focal length}}{\text{diameter of lens}}$$

For example, a lens with a focal length of 100mm is 50mm in diameter, and the f–number would then equal 100/50 or f–2.

F–numbers are often misleading in that the whole area of the lens is rarely used. There are serious distortions and loss of image sharpness on many lenses when they are used "wide open," and correction of these errors in optical design and the manufacturing are reflected in the much higher cost of some lenses. If a very "fast" lens (one with great light-gathering power) plus maximum image sharpness and minimum distortion is needed, one expects to pay dearly.

Lens advertising is reflected in the f–numbers as well. Camera and lens manufacturers often advertise "half-stop" increases in lens size as a big gain. The whole-stop sequence is f/4, f/2.8, f/2, and f/1.4, and f–1, but popular lens sizes are f/1.1 and f/2.2 *which are only half-stop gains* over much less expensive lenses.

Simple lens in a supporting barrel, with an aperture placed behind the lens: Light from a distance is bent by the lens to converge to a point on the focal plane. The aperture limits the light from the lens. A simple camera consists of a lens, an aperture, a shutter, and film placed at the focal plane.

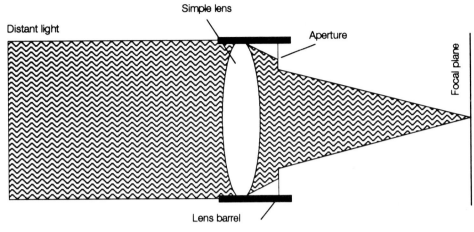

a.

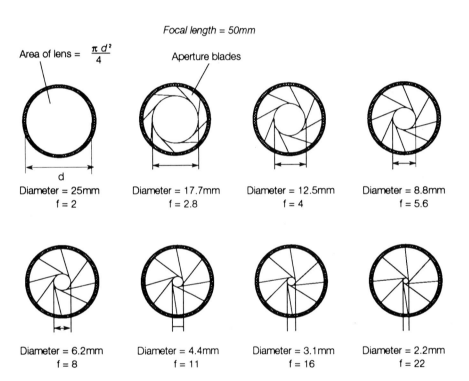

A typical 35mm camera lens has a focal length of 50mm (about 2 inches), with a lens about 25mm (1 inch) in diameter. With the iris full open, the lens is about f–2. Close the iris to about 0.7 the diameter (17.7mm), the *area* through which light can pass has been reduced by half, and the lens opening is now f–2.8. Reduced a further 0.7 to 12.5mm, the area of the opening will be halved again: the lens opening is now f–4. This pattern continues through to the smallest opening.

b.

Figure 3.5
**a.** Light from a distant source is bent to converge on a point at the focal plane.
**b.** The diameter of the lens aperture controls the f–number of the lens.

Lens numbers are standardized; each of the following common f-numbers has a 2:1 ratio of light transmittance compared to an adjacent number:

f-1  1.4  2  2.8  4  5.6  8  11  16  22  32

This ten-stop range is rarely available on any single lens. Many 35mm lenses stop down only to f-16, though lenses designed for professional use may close down to f-32.

Most contemporary lenses have *detents* in the aperture control ring, which physically indicate that one has moved from one f-number to the next, without having to look at the control ring.

Almost all 35mm cameras now also have automated apertures: these remain fully open for maximum focusing screen brightness when the camera is being focused, "stop down" for an instant to control the light during exposure, then reopen to full aperture again immediately afterward so the photographer can continue to monitor the scene. A difficulty with these apertures is that it is difficult to see what the actual depth of field is going to be, and often critical time is wasted in focusing.

## Field of View

Early in the development of photograpy, it was generally agreed that a lens with a field of view of about 38° was **normal**. This angle of view approximates the sharp area you see in focus when staring straight ahead with one eye closed. Figure 3.6 illustrates the range of focal lengths easily available to a photographer today, and how the field of view changes with focal length.

Lenses with many fields of view other than "normal" are used in today's photography. A **wide-angle** lens is one that accepts light from an angle of more than 40°. Modern wide-angle lenses have fields of view exceeding 90° (fig. 3.7). The extreme wide-angle lenses produce curved lines where the eye sees straight lines and are sometimes called **fisheye lenses**.

Figure 3.6
Photographs made without moving the camera: changing point of view by changing focal length of lens. **a.** 24mm lens field of view.

**b.** 55mm lens field of view.

**c.** 105mm lens field of view.

d. 180mm lens field of view.

e. 300mm lens field of view.
Photographs by Chris Polydoroff.

The normal focal length lens for any given film size is also approximately the same length as the diagonal of that film format. A 35mm film frame measures 24 × 36mm, with a diagonal of about 44mm, and the normal lens for a 35mm camera has been established by custom as 50mm. The normal lens for a 6 × 6cm camera is 80mm. Lenses commonly available for 35mm cameras range from 18mm to 400mm, with both shorter and longer lenses being available.

The longer the focal length, the narrower the field of view. Great magnifications of the subject can be produced by lenses with very long focal lengths. Simple lenses with long focal lengths have been replaced by telephoto lenses, which are complex lens systems that produce a magnified image but do not require a long barrel. A contemporary, lightweight, 400mm telephoto lens for a 35mm camera measures only about 9 inches, yet if it were simply a conventional lens, it would require a barrel about 16 inches long, far too long and heavy to be useful without resorting to a tripod mount.

Figure 3.7
**Cropduster. Ben Brink.** A "fish-eye" 15mm lens attached to the wing of the plane and triggered by an IR remote control reveals curvature of straight lines, which are the characteristic distortion of the extreme wide-angle lens.
Courtesy of the photographer.

## Choice of Lens

The focal length of the lens controls angle of view and to some degree also controls the apparent depth of space in the photograph. A long lens selects a smaller target area from the subject, and because the field of view is smaller, a long lens makes a picture with less vivid separation of near and far subjects. However, a photographer with a sensitive eye can produce photographs that enhance or minimize distance relationships with lenses of almost any focal length. Visual separation of objects at different distances from the camera is controlled more by composition, lighting, value relationships, and by the aperture used, than by lens focal length.

Few photographers can afford all the lenses available for any given camera system. Most professionals now use a moderate wide-angle lens (either 35mm or 28mm) as the "normal" lens. As a rule of thumb, many professionals feel a 2:1 change in focal length from one lens to the next is both effective in terms of compositional impact and economy. Using this logic, supplementary lenses would best be 18mm (half the 35mm), 80mm, 110–150mm, and 210–300mm. Much shorter (10–15mm) and much longer (500–1,000mm) lenses are available but, as they are more expensive to design and manufacture, the price rises sharply for extremely long or short focal lengths.

## Zoom Lenses

As a result of new glass technology developed in Japan after World War II, lens design changed dramatically in the 1950s. Computer-assisted design of lenses further accelerated the evolution of lens change. One result was the production of economical and optically excellent variable-focus or **zoom lenses.**

The zoom lens permits you to have a wide range of focal lengths instantly available. The effective focal length of the zoom lens is continually variable by moving a sliding collar, which rearranges the optical construction of the lens, producing the effect of having many lenses with different focal lengths. The internal complexity of a Nikon zoom lens is shown in figure 3.8.

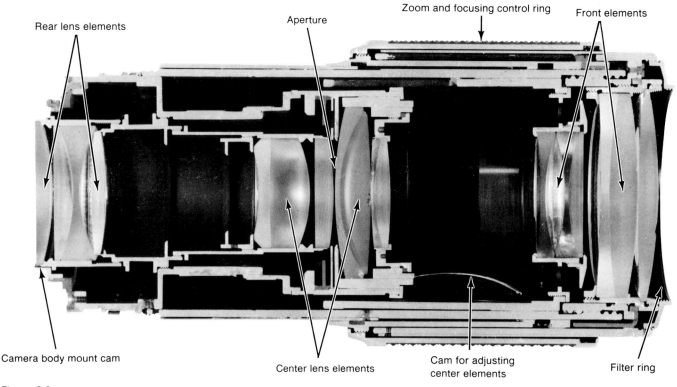

Figure 3.8
Cross section of a Nikon zoom lens.

The zoom lens is surprisingly complicated because not only is the effective focal length constantly variable, but because the position of the focal plane must remain constant while zooming. The immense optical/mechanical design problems this need presented initially produced lenses that were obviously less sharp than conventional lenses. Although there may still be a small loss of quality compared to a fixed focal length lens, that loss is difficult to identify in pictures made with newer zoom lenses.

Contemporary zoom lenses cover a wide range of focal lengths within a single unit (e.g., 28 to 85mm, or 70 to 210mm). Zoom lenses are made to cover a number of different ranges of focal lengths, but the 70–210mm lens has proven to be the most popular for professional work. This lens replaces at least two standard lenses, approximates the longest lens that is normally hand held, and reduces both capital outlay and the physical effort of carrying extra lenses.

## Viewing and Focusing

Predicting exactly what the camera would see before the film is exposed has always been a major problem for the photographer.

The *reflex* camera is a variation on ground-glass focusing. This was the method of focusing in Daguerre's first camera, which was simply an adaptation of the portable camera obscura. But the large internal mirror made the camera too bulky for films larger than 4 × 5 inches. The basic structure of Daguerre's camera was retained when the reflex camera was reintroduced. The contemporary reflex camera was born at the beginning of this century. When the shutter was tripped, the mirror flipped up to cover the ground glass and uncover the film plane.

Different viewfinders have replaced the ground glass and helped the photographer anticipate what the camera will photograph. The most simple viewfinder is none at all. The first Kodak camera was marketed in 1889 and was shaped like a shoe box, with a simple lens centered in one end. The camera was merely pointed toward the subject. The photographer aimed it with an arrowhead imprinted on the top of the camera body. Despite its crudeness, many wonderful pictures were produced.

The wire *sportsfinder,* adapted from military gunsights, was a step above the Kodak arrowhead. A stiff wire frame was mounted on the top front of the camera, and a locating post stuck up at the rear. Looking over the post and through the wire frame, one saw approximately what the camera saw. The 4 × 5 "press" camera used this (seen in old movies on TV), and some specialized sports and scientific cameras still use this simple sighting device.

Optical viewfinders that produce a *virtual-image* (one that is not projected onto a ground glass but that exists only for the photographer's eye) are used on many 35mm cameras. There is no ground glass to absorb the light; the image is very bright and clear. It is used on the Leica and many other popular small cameras and was the standard viewfinder for 35mm cameras until reflex viewing became popular in the 1950s.

Virtual-image viewfinders did not help the photographer focus the lens. Most early 35mm cameras required one to guess at camera-to-subject distances. A popular 35mm accessory in the 1940s was an expensive supplementary **range finder,** which clipped onto the accessory shoe on top the camera. These were derived from military distance-measuring devices. Only the most expensive cameras included range finders, which calculated the camera-to-subject distance. Also called **split-image** range finders, these present two overlapping images in the center of the frame. When

the images exactly overlap, the distance from the range finder to the subject is known. Split-image range finders are now built into most cameras and are mechanically coupled to the lens.

**Virtual-image** viewfinders are often coupled to other ranging devices. New 35mm cameras are focused by pulsed, solid-state infrared (IR) *autofocus* controls. Polaroid cameras use ultrasonic pulses. The reflected IR or sound pulses are timed and measured by a solid-state computer in the camera, which controls and uses small motors to mechanically focus the lens.

Ground-glass focusing and framing was also done by using two lenses of the same focal length, one mounted directly above the other. The lenses were attached to a common lensboard and moved together. The *twin-lens* reflex camera was very popular for forty years, beginning in the 1920s. In effect, there were two cameras; one just for viewing, one for taking pictures. A fully corrected lens was used for exposing film and a simpler lens for viewing.

The twin-lens system corrected image reversal but had *parallax* error. Parallax is the compositional error created by the vertical spacing between the viewing and the taking lens. This becomes significant when photographing close to the subject. Image reversal occurs because the mirror corrects the vertical but not the lateral reversal of the ground-glass image.

The 35mm single-lens reflex camera (**SLR**) began to dominate photography in the 1950s, when *pentaprism* reflex viewing and focusing, interchangeable lenses, and fast, fine-grain films were made available. The pentaprism (a five-sided glass prism) fits on top of the reflex ground glass and corrects the left-to-right image reversal. The single-lens reflex camera with pentaprism excited both professional and amateur photographers because the camera became almost an

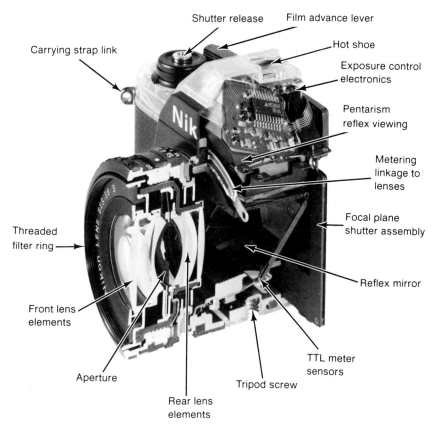

Carrying strap link

Shutter release

Film advance lever

Hot shoe

Exposure control electronics

Pentarism reflex viewing

Metering linkage to lenses

Focal plane shutter assembly

Reflex mirror

TTL meter sensors

Tripod screw

Rear lens elements

Aperture

Front lens elements

Threaded filter ring

**Figure 3.9**
Cross section of a 35mm single-lens reflex camera.

extension of the photographer's eye. A relaxed, natural posture was encouraged by the pentaprism and quick, precise focusing and accurate previewing were combined. Many SLRs also have split-image focusing as well as ground-glass optical focusing.

The 35mm single-lens reflex camera triumphed when **TTL** (through-the-lens) metering was added in the 1960s. The victory was completed when tiny integrated circuits became available, which allowed computerized electronic control of both aperture and shutter.

Figure 3.9 shows a cross section of a popular single-lens reflex camera, showing film storage, lens, metering controls, mirror, and shutter relationships. The lens-to-film distance inside the camera is optically identical to the lens-to-ground-glass distance. When the lens is focused (moved toward or

away from the film), the changing image is seen on the ground glass and the photographer chooses a correct focus.

## Depth of Field

Depth of field is defined as the range of distance from the nearest to the farthest subject from the camera that will appear *acceptably* sharp in a print. The depth of field is limited by the focal length of the lens, the aperture used, and the distance at which the lens is focused.

In a picture containing both blurred and sharp images, the eye will tend to reject an unsharp representation and select a sharp representation. A wide-open lens has little depth of field, while a lens that has been stopped down to a small aperture has a much greater depth of field.

The greatest depth of field available will always be when the smallest aperture is used on the shortest focal length lens. It should be remembered that the apparent sharpness of the image in the print is also affected by the grain of the film and the degree of enlargement. Thus, a slow, fine-grain film and a 5″ × 7″ print will produce a greater apparent depth of field than an overexposed and overdeveloped high-speed, coarse-grained negative enlarged to 11″ × 14″ because of the larger inherent grain.

While the aperture controls the amount of light that can enter the camera when the shutter is open, it also controls the depth of field (i.e., what is seen as being sharp or unsharp in the picture). The fact that the maximum aperture is used for focusing in single-lens reflex cameras is visually misleading when one is operating the camera—one does not see the actual depth of field available during the exposure. This affects both photographic content and aesthetics.

Depth of field can be controlled to produce pictures where everything is apparently in equal focus, or to isolate an object like the boat in figure 3.10, making it the only sharp focused detail in the frame.

The depth of field for any given distance and aperture can be calculated by using the depth-of-field scales on the lens, and it can actually be seen with your eye by using the *preview* control available on most reflex cameras. The preview control manually stops down the lens to any desired aperture to see (although on a darker screen) what the film can record.

The shorter the lens, the greater the depth of field. Look at the depth-of-field scales on a 28mm or 35mm focal-length lens. Set the focus on 5 feet (or 2 meters) and notice the f/16 marks embrace both ∞ and a very close distance, about 2 feet. Compare this to what you find on a 150mm lens focused on about 30 feet (or 10 meters). At f/16, the near distance is about 20 feet, and the far may just touch the ∞ sign.

Figure 3.10
A long lens and large aperture effectively
isolate the boat from the myriad details of
similar value.
Photo by Jim Zietz.

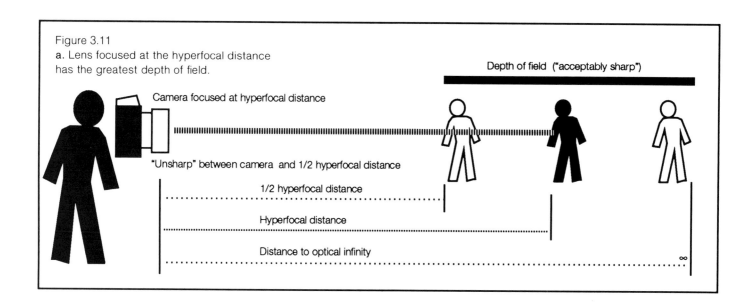

Figure 3.11

**a.** Lens focused at the hyperfocal distance has the greatest depth of field.

Depth of field ("acceptably sharp")

Camera focused at hyperfocal distance

"Unsharp" between camera and 1/2 hyperfocal distance

1/2 hyperfocal distance

Hyperfocal distance

Distance to optical infinity

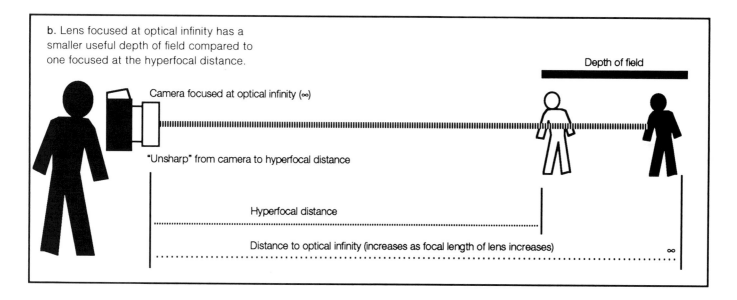

**b.** Lens focused at optical infinity has a smaller useful depth of field compared to one focused at the hyperfocal distance.

Depth of field

Camera focused at optical infinity (∞)

"Unsharp" from camera to hyperfocal distance

Hyperfocal distance

Distance to optical infinity (increases as focal length of lens increases)

## Hyperfocal Distance

Greatest depth of field is always produced by focusing on the *hyperfocal distance,* which is defined as *the nearest distance at which objects at optical infinity are also in acceptable focus.* This distance varies with the aperture. Examine the drawings of camera-to-subject distance in figure 3.11, and see how the range of distances that will produce acceptably sharp images varies.

When the lens is focused at the hyperfocal distance, everything from half the hyperfocal distance to infinity is equally unsharp. This is another way of describing what is acceptably sharp. Optical infinity is physically indicated by the ∞ sign on the focusing ring. Practically speaking, infinity (∞) is about 50 feet from the camera for wide angle and normal lenses, and 300 feet for long lenses.

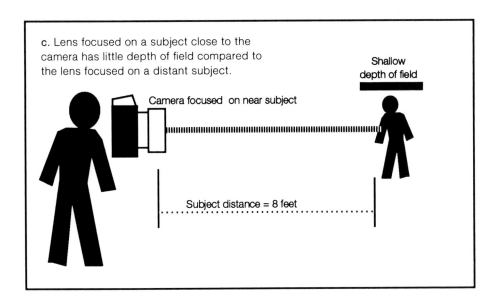

c. Lens focused on a subject close to the camera has little depth of field compared to the lens focused on a distant subject.

Shallow depth of field

Camera focused on near subject

Subject distance = 8 feet

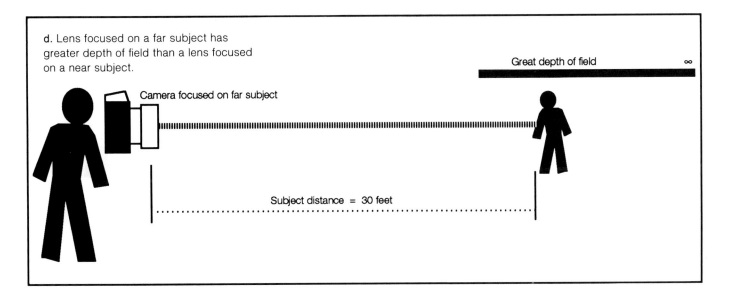

d. Lens focused on a far subject has greater depth of field than a lens focused on a near subject.

Great depth of field ∞

Camera focused on far subject

Subject distance = 30 feet

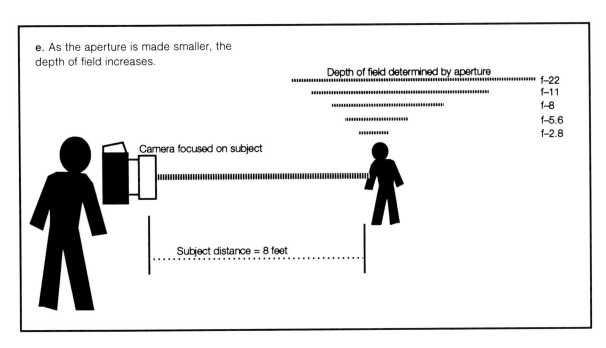

e. As the aperture is made smaller, the depth of field increases.

Depth of field determined by aperture

f–22
f–11
f–8
f–5.6
f–2.8

Camera focused on subject

Subject distance = 8 feet

## Zone Focusing

Depth-of-field marks are provided on all contemporary camera lenses, and while it is true that the objects at the plane of focus are most sharply focused, it is often convenient to use *zone focusing*. Examine figure 3.12*A* and you will see that at the indicated aperture of f–5.6, when the ∞ sign is placed next to the line for f–5.6 (on the right half of the focusing control ring) then the f–5.6 line on the left half of the focusing ring is opposite 10 feet (or 3 meters). This means that *everything between 10 feet and optical infinity is equally sharp.*

One can set the focusing control, compose, and shoot without refocusing, and there is no need to refocus when photographing subjects in that distance range. This is obviously of importance when the photographic subjects are at varying distances from the camera, or when the subject will be moving rapidly toward or away from the camera and the photographer can prefocus for a given distance zone and then be concerned only with composition and the choice of the moment of exposure.

Zone focusing lets you photograph objects distributed through deep space without refocusing, knowing they all are equally sharp. A second example is shown in figure 3.12*B*. The ∞ mark has been set opposite f–16 on the right half of the focusing control ring. Find the f–16 mark on the left half of the ring and see how it lines up with the 5 in 3.5 feet. This means that if you set the aperture at f–16 and focused as shown in figure 3.11*B,* there would be no need to refocus for any subject between 3.5 feet and infinity.

The least effective focus is shown in figure 3.12*C,* where the ∞ mark is placed opposite the ▲ focusing reference. The depth of field at f–5.6 is only from ∞ to about 20 feet. If there were subjects in the scene closer than 30 feet from the camera, they would be visibly out of focus in the picture. Refocusing and setting the 30 foot mark opposite the ▲ would increase the depth of field at f–5.6 to include from 12 feet to ∞, a much more effective use of the lens.

Figure 3.12
**a.** The lens is set at f–5.6, and the focus is set on the hyperfocal distance (determined by setting the ∞ sign opposite the line indicating the aperture being used). Focusing with the aperture marks produces the greatest depth of field for any given aperture; in this case, everything from ∞ to 10 feet will be acceptably sharp.

**b.** At the indicated aperture, the depth of field at f–5.6 is only from about 6 to 11 feet, as the focus is now set. If the aperture were reset at f–16 (the smallest opening for this lens), setting the ∞ mark opposite the 16 on the focusing ring makes possible a picture where everything from about 3.8 feet to ∞ will be equally (and acceptably) sharp.

c. Setting the focusing ring at ∞ narrows depth of field from ∞ to about 20 feet.

## Lens Focal Length Aesthetics

The focal length of the lens inevitably affects photographic aesthetics. While a lens with a long focal length has much less depth of field at any given aperture than a short (or wide-angle) lens, a long lens (with very narrow depth of field) can be used to isolate a narrow slice of space, while a wide-angle lens (with great depth of field) will tend to make everything in the scene equally sharp.

The long-lens effect resembles our focused attention when one concentrates on something and excludes everything else. A shallow depth of field is easily achieved with the long lens, as is shown in figure 3.13. This is useful for focusing attention on a single subject. The wide-angle lens can be seen to resemble a contemplative view when one simply accepts a complex view and eliminates nothing in it.

Figure 3.13
**Civil Rights March, Forsythe, Georgia. Kim Hairston.** A 300mm lens used at maximum aperture dynamically isolates the poster from the crowd.
Courtesy of the photographer.

**Figure 3.14**

**Laborer, J & L Tin Plate Department. Ivan Massar.** The isolation between figure and ground achieved by limited depth of field is part of the way the photographer subtly empowers the worker: placing the camera slightly below eye level, composing the picture along a diagonal (circular shapes roll of steel and the worker's hat/face), converging lines of overhead lights and the casual hand pointing to the steel.

University of Louisville Archives, Standard Oil Collection.

## Exposure Law

The term **exposure** describes the total amount of light that the shutter and aperture allow to reach the film. *Exposure* is also used to describe the act of making the picture and the effect light

A large aperture can limit depth of field with a lens of any focal length. In figure 3.14, a normal lens is used at a large aperture; the resulting narrow depth of field and soft-focus background interacts with the convergent pattern of the factory lights to direct your eye to the steelworker.

has on the photographic emulsion. The exposure of photographic materials is usually (but not always) the product of the exposure time and the intensity of light focused on the emulsion. This is true for *all* silver emulsions.

As the aperture is enlarged (or opened), the shutter speed must be shorter to maintain a constant exposure. Film exposure is a measure of the quantity of light. The amount of light is simply the product of lens opening and the shutter time. The aperture setting determines how intense the projected image can be, and the shutter controls how long light can

reach the film. The net exposure is the product of the intensity and the time:

$$E = I \times T$$

where **E** is exposure, **I** is light intensity, and **T** is exposure time. If **E** is to be kept constant, then an increase in **I** requires a decrease in **T**. This is called the *law of reciprocity,* because any given exposure can be made up of a wide variety of shutter-aperture combinations.

When the shutter speed is halved, then the aperture must be doubled in area to produce the same exposure. If the aperture is made smaller, then time must be lengthened proportionately to keep the exposure constant.

In practice, this simple formula is true for exposure times between about 1 second and 1/1000 of a second. Figure 3.15*A* and *B* both have the same exposure in that the product (**E**) of the aperture and shutter speed is identical for both pictures, and the negatives have similar densities. Both pictures were made of a horse moving in an indoor arena against the same background: moving the camera through an angle and tracking the horse through the long exposure obviously changed both visual space and texture.

## Shutter Speeds

Shutter speeds are standardized to exposures with a 2:1 change in time, one speed to the next. Standard contemporary shutter speeds are 1, 1/2, 1/4, 1/8, 1/15, 1/30, 1/60, 1/125, 1/250, 1/500, and 1/1000 of a second, though some new camera shutters offer longer and shorter speeds. Electronically controlled shutters actually provide exposures that are close to the indicated speeds; mechanical shutters may vary by half a stop from the indicated speed.

Shutter speeds can be chosen by the photographer to fit professional or aesthetic needs. Sports photography, for example, is usually concerned with "peak action" and that necessitates using very short shutter speeds, as shown in figure 3.16.

Figure 3.15
Two pictures made from the same point of view, with the same background for the horse, and each the same total exposure.
a. Exposed for 1/250 second at f–2.8.

b. Exposed for 1/2 second at f–32. The camera was "panned" to follow the horse during the long exposure.

Figure 3.16
**Hockey Flip. Annie Lennox.** Very short shutter speeds are often used in sports photography to freeze peak action.
Courtesy of the photographer.

A very fast shutter, which absolutely "stops" motion, is not the only way to photograph moving subjects. The photographer often can find a moment of comparative stillness, when movement nearly ceases. During these pauses, even a slow shutter may be used, as shown in figure 3.17. In this scene, despite dim gymnasium lights, the photographer captured both the motion of the dance and relatively great depth-of-field by choosing a moment when both small aperture and slow shutter speed could be used.

An alternative to freezing motion or catching a pause within a repetitive movement is to "pan," or move the camera with the moving subject; this allows some movement into the frame. Figure 3.15B is an exaggerated example combining sharp and blurred details.

## Shutter and F-stop Combinations

Contemporary cameras have aperture and shutter settings that vary by 2:1 ratios. These easily permit you to transform any metered exposure to fit a variety of conditions, depending on whether a short or a long shutter speed, or a large or a small aperture, is needed. For example, if a metered exposure is 1/60 at f–5.6, all the following exposures would produce equivalent negative densities:

Figure 3.17
**Dance Master Class. Arnold Gassan.**
Capture the essence of a movement by watching for a moment when the action pauses; it is possible to photograph with minimal blur even in very low light levels.
**Photo by the author.**

| f–1.4 | 2 | 2.8 | 4 | 5.6 | 8 | 11 | 16 |
|-------|------|------|-------|------|------|------|------|
| 1/1000 | 1/500 | 1/250 | 1/125 | 1/60 | 1/30 | 1/15 | 1/8 |

The question arises: which of these should you use? The answer depends on your aesthetics and your professional requirements. It is possible that a slightly blurred image may be more effective than a stopped action in communicating the mood of an event, as in figure 3.18.

Movement across the picture frame will be blurred unless a very short exposure (1/250th of a second or less) is used. Movement directly toward or away from the camera produces less blur. Look back at figure 2.4 and see that the two boys at the right of the picture are blurred but still recognizable in a 1-second exposure,

which was required by the small aperture needed to produce the great depth of field. A very short exposure will "freeze" the subject, but usually requires a large aperture, with little depth of field; a small aperture (f–16) will offer greater depth of field, with a risk of blurring.

## Focal-plane Shutters

The oldest basic shutter design still in general use is the focal-plane shutter (sometimes called a curtain-shutter), now standard on most 35mm reflex

cameras. The original focal-plane shutter was a long, opaque cloth strip with several metal-edged slits of different widths across it. The curtain was rolled onto a spring-loaded spindle, much like a window blind.

The curtain shutter was placed just in front of the film, near the plane of focus. When it was released, springs pulled a slit in the curtain past the film at a constant rate of speed, exposing each area of the film evenly. By choosing a slit and adjusting the spring tension, one could create exposures varying from 1/1000th of a

Figure 3.18
**Untitled. Edward Pieratt.** A slow shutter speed enhances the anxiety of being caught in the crowd by mounted police.
Courtesy of the photographer.

second to more than a second. By using a small slit and high spring tension, very short exposures for each area of the film were possible, although the curtain itself moved slowly.

The contemporary focal-plane shutter dates from the early 1920s, when E. Leitz began manufacturing the Leica camera. The Leica focal-plane shutter used two curtains to form a slit of variable width. Both curtains traveled across the film at a constant speed, but the second curtain followed the first after a delay, thus creating a virtual slit with a variable width, and therefore exposures that were also variable. The first curtain in the original Leica shutter traversed the 36mm long opening in 1/60th of a second, regardless of the shutter speed setting. For an exposure of 1/60th of a second, the virtual slit is 36mm wide (e.g., the width of the 35mm film frame).

For an exposure of 1/125th of a second, the second curtain begins moving across the film frame when the first is halfway across the opening, and the virtual slit is about 18mm wide. No matter how "fast" the shutter is set, the curtains always travel at the same rate of speed; all that varies is the interval between them, which changes the width of the slit. At 1/1000 of a second, the curtains still move at the same speed, but the second curtain starts following the first almost immediately and the virtual slit is barely a millimeter wide.

The two-curtain shutter has been rotated 90° in recent years, and now travels vertically. In many cameras, the cloth has been replaced by thin metal blades that slide vertically past each other, just in front of the film. These shutters perform in exactly the same way as the two cloth curtains.

The vertical focal-plane shutter requires half the travel time of the horizontal shutter. This is important both because shorter shutter speeds are possible and because supplemental light sources can be used with higher shutter speeds. The focal-plane shutter must be fully open to *synchronize* flash lights, otherwise only part of the scene will be illuminated.

Shutter times were controlled by clockwork mechanisms until the late 1970s, when integrated solid-state electronic circuits became available. Although most cameras now use electronic timing, some professional cameras retain dependable mechanical systems. The electronically timed shutters historically have been very easily damaged by moisture, and they cease to operate when batteries fail (except at a default speed of about 1/60th of a second, on some professional cameras).

## Meters and Exposure Targets

A light meter is a device that measures the light available and has a computer that calculates an exposure based on light intensity and film speed. There are two styles of meters. One measures light falling on the subject before the camera. It is called an *incident light* meter. The incident meter is hand held, separate from the camera. An incident light meter is shown in figure 3.19. The other kind of meter measures the light reflected from the subject and is called a *reflected light* meter. The reflected light meter often is an integral part of the camera.

The incident light meter integrates light falling on the subject through a 180° hemisphere. The meter is held in front of the subject, pointing toward the camera. The incident meter does not indicate to the photographer how much light is reflecting from any particular area in the subject, only how much light is available.

Reflected light meters can measure the light from any part of the subject and tell the photographer how much light is reflected from a dark surface or from a bright, white photographic target. The fact that reflected

Figure 3.19
A hand-held incident light meter measures the light directed toward the subject, rather than the light reflected toward the lens of the camera.

light meters can measure a precise target is important for they can be used to calculate the contrast range of each photographic subject.

All meter readings need to be interpreted, and each reflected light meter integrates the light being measured through the angle of view of the meter. Reflected light meters require careful use to assure that the proper metering target for any given scene is being measured. They are, in effect, miniature cameras without film or shutter.

## Camera as Meter

Almost all contemporary small cameras have integrated light meters. TTL (through the lens) metering is an example of measuring the light reflected from the subject as the meter is located in the path of the light that will actually expose the film. The meter cal-

culations are based on the ISO of the film, which usually is accessed directly from the DX coding stripes on the film canister. In some cameras, the meters even continue to calculate exposure after the shutter has been tripped by measuring the light reflected from the film, and controlling the shutter.

Most TTL meters are *center weighted,* meaning the area near the split-image focusing prism in the center of the field of view has more effect on the meter reading than light at the perimeter of the picture. This metering assumption is valid most of the time because most photographers "center" the subject of the picture. Figure 3.20*A* sketches a typical portrait scene, with light reflected from a dark shadow and brighter skin. Notice that a few degrees rotation of the camera up or down in this scene would significantly change the exposure for a center-weighted metering system.

When the subject of your picture is much darker than normal, the TTL meter will tend to overexpose because it "thinks" the average value should be lighter. In the same way, if the subject near the center is very light (snow, fog, white fabric), automatic TTL exposure calculations will tend to underexpose the film. It is sometimes necessary for you to decide if the subject is markedly lighter or darker than a middle gray. If it is, then point the camera at a midvalue target *in the same light* to determine the exposure.

Because the meter in the camera measures through the lens, the camera can be thought of and used as a spot meter. By pointing the camera at critical subject areas in the photographic scene and noting the exposure indicated for these, exact contrast predictions and development plans can be made for the film.

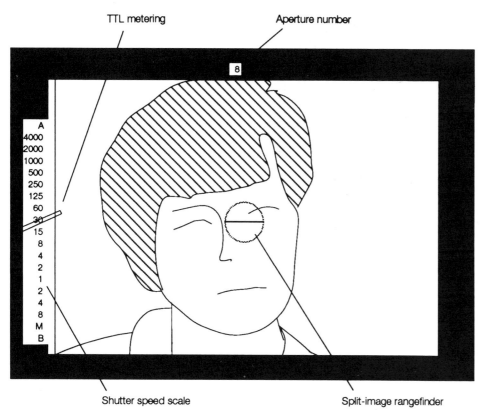

TTL metering        Aperture number

8

A
4000
2000
1000
500
250
125
60
30
15
8
4
2
1
2
4
8
M
B

Shutter speed scale       Split-image rangefinder

Figure 3.20
**a.** TTL metering is the most familiar reflected light measurement. This sketch illustrates how the average luminance is presented in the reflex camera viewfinder as a suggested exposure.

**b.** The incident light meter is held at or near the subject, and it measures the light falling on the subject. Contrast is determined by experience, though measuring the light on the bright and shadowed side of the subject offers some guide.

One way to control exposure overall or to modify it for high- or low-contrast scenes is to target the camera on a standard gray value to determine each specific exposure. Another way is to change the ISO number (i.e., "tell" the meter that the film is more or less sensitive). You can change the ISO number by using the meter override control located near the rewind knob on most 35mm cameras. This allows you to adjust the metering system from +2 to −2 stops of exposure, in half-stop increments (as shown in fig. 3.21).

Experience with your camera will tell you if the ISO value of the film is correct for your photographs. If your negatives are consistently underexposed, a lower ISO number can correct the problem. Changing the exposure from the DX-coded ISO to a greater or lesser exposure in order to create more correctly exposed negatives establishes your own individual *Exposure Index* (**EI**). The EI is a product of

- The metering system in your camera
- The way you meter the subject
- The subject you photograph
- The way the film is developed

Because of metering errors and processing variations, two photographers can use the same film in similar cameras and have personal EIs that differ by a factor of four, and produce negatives with very similar printing characteristics.

## Other Camera Controls

The modern camera offers powered film advance (motor-wind or motor-drive) coupled with the shutter; it is possible with many cameras to expose four to six frames of film each second. This is a remarkable change from the days of wet-plate photography, when each glass plate had to be coated, sensitized, exposed, and developed before the coating had fully dried and changing a plate took as much as twenty minutes.

Figure 3.21
Exposure adjustment settings for a camera with TTL metering allows the photographer to adjust the personal exposure index (EI) from +2 to −2 stops.

Powered film advance is a mixed blessing. It is very useful for sports and other one-time actions. Powered shutters and film advance mechanisms may also be a wonderful way to waste film, permitting you to expose three or four frames, when one well-considered picture would do.

Accidental double-exposure was a constant threat to photographers until the 1930s, when cameras incorporated double-exposure prevention techniques. Contemporary small cameras automatically advance the film as the mirror is returned to viewing position or the shutter is cocked. On most 35mm cameras, double-exposure is still pos-

sible if desired, but the method varies widely from one camera to another and you should consult your operating manual.

Figure 3.22 is an example of deliberate double-exposure, where the two exposures have apparently even value. Double-exposure densities will be *evenly* balanced between the two exposures when the second exposure is *twice* the metered exposure. The reason for this is theoretically complex but can be visualized as the first exposure using the most sensitive silver, leaving only less sensitive silver for the second exposure.

Figure 3.22
Double-exposure on the film can be done despite camera controls designed to prevent it. This is a way of combining or montaging two views in one photograph.
Photo by the author.

## Summary

The simple camera has been replaced with a complex optical-electronic machine that measures the light, computes the exposure, and can be programmed to choose an aperture, shutter speed, or both. The aperture and shutter determine the exposure, and the combination chosen is determined by photographic needs and personal aesthetics. Sharpness or lack of blur in moving objects is controlled by the shutter.

The focal length of a lens controls both the angle of view and the apparent deep space in a picture. Depth of field is maximized by focusing on the hyperfocal distance. For any lens, the depth of field is determined by the aperture, and the smaller the opening, the greater the depth of field.

Light meters measure reflected or incident light. Meters built into the camera are reflected light meters which usually average the light. Multiple exposures are possible on most small cameras.

## Discussion and Assignments

The small camera permits photographing easily almost anywhere, at any time, and makes changing point of view as easy as sitting down or standing up. Contemporary electronic shutter controls linked to an in-camera meter permit exposing film correctly under a wide variety of lighting conditions with almost no risk of failure.

## Assignment 1

Tape a small piece of cardboard over the viewfinder of your camera. Set the focus by placing the ∞ symbol opposite the outermost f-stop line on the aperture control ring. (The ▲ in the center will point at a distance mark around 16–20 feet for a 50mm lens.) Use a piece of pressure-sensitive tape and tape the lens so it will not change focus. You have now reinvented the box camera, except yours has a variable shutter.

Use an aperture priority mode: your camera will now set a shutter speed to fit the lighting of whatever scene you photograph. Go through a day, photographing whatever you want, but accepting the fact that you cannot focus on the scene and you cannot frame exactly what your camera is going to record. Allow yourself to respond directly to what is going on around you, looking over the camera rather than through it.

Deliberately choose to make some pictures in low-level lighting (indoors, late afternoon, etc.) where the shutter speed might well be long enough to cause blur. Follow the action with your camera. Develop the film and compare what you have seen and what the camera created.

## Assignment 2

Load your camera with a twenty-four-frame cassette. After you make the first picture, ask yourself what the subject of that picture was, then allow that subject to suggest the next subject, which you will then seek. For example, if you photograph a cat, then what might a cat seek, or where might it be going? Let each picture direct you to the next.

## Assignment 3

Find several subjects to photograph (a person, object, building, etc.). Photograph it as you normally would. Stop the lens down to the smallest aperture and if the indicated exposure is a second or longer, make a picture, holding the camera as still as you can, knowing you cannot hold it still enough to make a picture without blur. Try to discover how deliberate blur can be used creatively.

## Assignment 4

Look at a subject that is too large to easily frame in your viewfinder. Without moving, make six photographs that break that subject into a horizontal strip picture. Find another that can be broken into a vertical array. Find another that can be photographed only by making a mosaic, a 5 print × 6 print frame array. Develop the film and assemble the contact prints into mosaics. Study them to see how the experiential space and your perception of the subject has been changed.

## Assignment 5

Tape your camera's focusing control (using your knowledge of hyperfocal distance) so the camera is in focus from 5 feet to ∞. Tape a piece of cardboard over the viewfinder. Set the camera's controls to shutter priority. Go for a walk and when you *sense* something happening near you, immediately and intuitively point the camera and press the shutter. The event may be behind your back or over your shoulder. The depth of field will keep *everything* equally sharp, only the shutter time will vary. Trust your responses. Develop the film and make an extra proof sheet. Carefully trim out each frame of the proof sheet and glue these small prints onto 3″ × 5″ file cards. Take some time to study these cards in order to learn what you can about the way you respond and what you intuitively frame in the picture.

# 4 Darkrooms, Workrooms, and Equipment

Figure 4.1
**Street Photographer. Ben Shahn.** Street photographers made a living providing inexpensive pictures through the 1940s using a special camera that not only exposed the picture but contained a miniature darkroom in which a ''direct positive'' print was processed while the customer waited.
Library of Congress, FSA Collection.

## The Darkroom

Basic darkroom needs are light control, safe electrical connections, wet and dry work areas, clean air, and running water (if possible). Dry darkrooms are difficult to work in, but they are practical.

The darkroom is a special work place for photosensitive films and papers. For photo printing, one needs to have controlled, safe lighting, grounded electrical wiring, adequate ventilation, and both wet and dry work areas. For just developing film, one needs only a very dark place for loading a film developing tank; all the actual wet processing of film can be done in a normally lighted room after the film is in the tank.

You may have access to a photographic darkroom at school; however, you can make many other rooms temporarily function as darkrooms. The basic equipment needed to develop film and make enlargements is outlined in table 4.1. A darkroom does not even need to have running water, though water is obviously convenient. A dry darkroom can be in any room and you can wash prints in the sink. A wet darkroom obviously requires plumbing, but with inexpensive plastic pipe, water and drains can be jury-rigged.

Eventually you may wish to create a permanent, personal darkroom. Before that happens, it is wise to work in and experience several different darkrooms and discover what you like and what you find awkward and wish to avoid. Temporary darkrooms can be improvised (from bathrooms, basement wash rooms, closets). Figure 4.3 shows three. One is squeezed awkwardly into a bathroom, with prints washed in a large tray in the tub, the enlarger on the sink, and trays are placed on temporary supports. It is not convenient but it works. The second is more comfortable, but designed to be removed when needed, while the third is permanently built into an attic space. In addition to the darkroom, work space will be needed for print finishing, a sturdy worktable on which to cut mats and finish prints with good light for spotting prints, and a secure dry area (50–80°F and 40–70% relative humidity) for storing prints and negatives.

**Figure 4.2**
**Photo Outfit, 1869. William Henry Jackson.** Early photographers had to carry camera, glass plates, chemicals, a darkroom tent, and even their own water for processing when making photographs before the 1880s. The photographer made this portrait of himself and his loaded pack mule beside a marker cairn in the West. What is not shown is the wet-plate camera making this picture and the darkroom tent in which the negative was developed immediately after being exposed.
National Archives.

## Establishing a Darkroom

A permanent darkroom is not absolutely necessary and much good work has been done in kitchens and laundry rooms. Absolute darkness is desirable but not mandatory for printing. Covering windows at night with a sheet is often sufficient, although street lights close by may present a hazard. Windows may be blacked out (temporarily or permanently) with black plastic vapor-barrier (wrapped around window frames and taped or stapled in place). When making a temporary darkroom, remember that all pressure-sensitive tapes—including masking tape and silver duct tape, sometimes called gaffer's tape—may leave an adhesive residue, and many tapes grip tightly enough to damage paint when removed.

## Table 4.1   Darkroom Equipment

| | |
|---|---|
| Lighttight room with adequate ventilation | 11″ × 14″ glass with sanded edges (to prevent cuts) and foam pad (11″ × 14″ × 1″) for contact proofs |
| Grounded electrical system | Easel for holding photo paper |
| Switches for white light and safelights well separated | Variable contrast filters (for the brand of paper used) |
| Sink with hot and cold water and mixing faucet | Camel's hair brush or Dust Off canister |
| Table for enlarger | Film cleaner |
| Dry work area | Cotton swabs |
| Safelight(s) for enlarger and sink area | Enlarger focusing device |
| Processing timer (with fluorescent dial to measure time in minutes and seconds) | Contact proof and negative magnifier |
| | Dodging tools |
| Enlarging timer (measures time in seconds) | Soft lead pencil for marking prints |
| Enlarger and lens (50mm lens for 35mm negatives, 80mm for 6 × 6cm, 135–150mm for 4 × 5cm) | Printing record notebook |
| Negative carrier | |

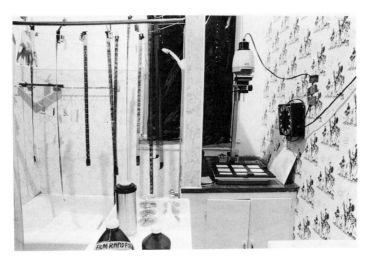

### Figure 4.3

**a.** Bathroom converted into an uncomfortable but usable darkroom. Film (and resin-coated prints) are dried over the bathtub. A vent fan to draw air from the darkroom is in the window to ensure adequate ventilation.

a. Photo by Christine Keith.

**b.** A more elaborate temporary darkroom. The window has been blacked out with black builder's plastic; the cabinets and sink are attached to walls with screws and can all be removed. A U-shaped floor plan is used since the room is almost square. Storage for printing paper is the open shelf. Storage for negatives and prints is under the enlarger on the right.

**c.** Permanent darkroom built into attic space (note the slanting ceilings). This is a traditional center-aisle design with wet and dry areas separated by a narrow runway. Wet equipment storage is under the sink and on the pegboard behind it. Storage drawers for paper and negatives are provided under the enlarger counter.

Screen frames often can be lined with black plastic and put back into place to produce an effective blackout without making the room itself look ugly. Windows without removable screens can be blacked out by cutting a sheet of insulating board to fit snugly in place, and these can be easily removed and stored when the room must be returned to normal kitchen duties.

## Workspace Criteria

An ideal darkroom space is a ventilated, heated, dedicated space with a minimum clear floor area of 7' × 9'. Three-pronged, grounded electrical outlets should exist on three walls. The walls should be painted, rather than papered. If water and drains are not already present, these often can be provided through an adjacent wall. Plastic plumbing has made temporary wet darkroom installations possible. When running water is not available, all work except final washing can be done by using two large plastic buckets, one containing a supply of water for rinsing, the other a waste dump. The wall nearest the sink should be protected from chemical splashing by a high-gloss enamel or a splash guard of builder's plastic.

The walls of a darkroom may be any light color, both to make it a more cheerful place to work and to help you see as much as possible under safelight. However, the wall behind the enlarger may need to be darkened to avoid reflecting diffuse light from the enlarger onto the printing paper; contemporary enlarging papers are sensitive enough to be slightly fogged by enlarger light reflections during printing. A dark rectangle can be painted on the wall behind the enlarger, or a large sheet of black construction paper stapled or taped to the wall.

The darkroom should have a single, well-fitted entrance door that is lighttight and can be locked from the inside. If a ventilation fan is mounted in the door (often the only place), the room outside should be a workroom isolated from the rest of the house and

separately ventilated—all that is needed is a window to remove fumes. An interior closet or some other protected space with constant temperature is very convenient for storing bottles of developer and fixer, and an otherwise unused closet can hardly be bettered for film drying.

In an ideal darkroom, the enlarger sits on a sturdy table or counter, with enough space at both sides for working negatives, fresh printing paper, dodging tools, pencil, timer, and notebook. Safelights should be hung from ceiling or wall.

## Workspace Problems

When a potential darkroom has been located, sketch out solutions to these problems:

- Wet and dry areas
- Water service and drain
- Electrical switches and safelights
- Ventilation
- Film drying
- Print drying
- Print finishing and storage

Wet area locations are often controlled by existing water pipes and drains, but even these can easily be relocated with plastic pipe. However, learn local plumbing code requirements before making decisions about permanent water and drain hookups. When talking to plumbers or building code inspectors, make it clear to them that *no* photographic equipment will be *permanently* connected to the water line, and that all water service will terminate in hose bibs. Even so, many areas will require backflow devices to prevent any possible contamination of the water supply.

Hot and cold water mixing should be available at the sink. You may choose to purchase an expensive temperature regulated mixing unit, or simply use two "cut-off" ball valves (which have straight bar handles that rotate only 90° between being fully open and closed) connected to a "T" joint and terminating in a hose coupling. Either method provides effective control of water temperature.

## Alternative Spaces

A permanent darkroom can be installed in many different spaces, and each offers unique possibilities and problems. Existing bathrooms, kitchens, or laundry rooms can be used both for a darkroom and their original purpose, if the social contracts with other household members can be worked out. Obviously, there is no lack of water in these rooms, and both kitchens and bathrooms often have venting fans. Difficulties arise in that there is usually no storage space in these rooms for the equipment, and time lost setting up and dismantling may be counterproductive.

Basement rooms are usually easy to modify, because they have few or no windows and often are unfinished and ill-defined spaces to start. Raw concrete walls and floors are not easily damaged by splashed photographic chemicals. Electricity, water, and drains are usually available. Temperature variations are minimized by the surrounding earth. On the other hand, attics are difficult spaces to convert unless they are well insulated. They also are less likely to have water or drains accessible.

Ventilation is always a potential problem because air must be either blown into the darkroom or sucked out. Darkroom ventilation should pull chemical fumes away from you and not drag them across your face or body. A careful decision must be made as to which way the air should move. It is usually better to pull heated air from the house, and exhaust this to the outside, especially if you live in a dry or dusty region. Ventilation can be supplied by a lighttight darkroom fan placed in a door or wall. Ventilation fans can be placed in a sheet of plywood, which replaces the glazing in an outside window; this darkens the room and vents it simultaneously. A kitchen vent fan can be used if a light baffle prevents light entering through the fan.

When the basement ceiling is unfinished, a sheet of builder's plastic can be stapled to rafters over the whole photo work area to block dirt, or the ceiling can be covered with drywall and the joints taped. Negatives, paper, and equipment are all quickly damaged by excess humidity, and many basements are damp. Basement moisture can be limited by operating a dehumidifier.

## Darkroom Sinks

The photographic sink is merely a flat, shallow tray with a drain. The size of the sink is determined both by the space available and the maximum print size you want to make. The darkroom sink should be long enough to line up four trays. Sinks are commercially available in plastic or stainless steel, but they can be constructed for much less money. A serviceable sink can be constructed from precut plywood pieces, and requires little woodworking skill. Construction suggestions are offered in figure 4.4.

The height of the sink and dry work surfaces should be set to your own comfort (rather than the "standard" sink heights). Tables and counters that are too low will exhaust you quickly. Standard sink and table heights are established for persons who are about 5'6" tall. If you are much taller or shorter, vary the height to meet your needs.

You can estimate the correct height of the upper edge of the sink (3" to 5" deep) by the following procedure: wear comfortable working shoes, stand with your arms at your sides, elbows bent so that your forearms are parallel to the floor, and hands relaxed. Have someone measure from the floor to your fingers and make this the sink height (unless the sink is more than 24–30 inches across). Plan to make the actual tray surface of the sink 2 inches lower. If a wider sink is planned, it should be 3–4 inches lower, so that as you reach out you can bend into the work slightly.

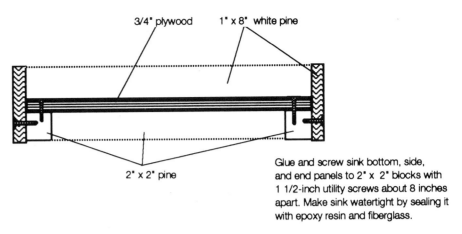

3/4" plywood      1" x 8" white pine

2" x 2" pine

Glue and screw sink bottom, side, and end panels to 2" x 2" blocks with 1 1/2-inch utility screws about 8 inches apart. Make sink watertight by sealing it with epoxy resin and fiberglass.

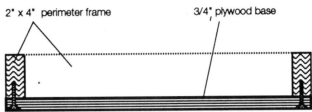

2" x 4" perimeter frame          3/4" plywood base

Either assembly shown will produce a strong, tight sink; neither requires woodworking skills.

a.

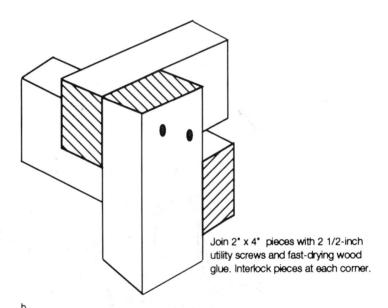

Join 2" x 4" pieces with 2 1/2-inch utility screws and fast-drying wood glue. Interlock pieces at each corner.

b.

Figure 4.4
a. Two methods of assembling a darkroom sink from plywood and standard dimension lumber.
b. Detail of sturdy leg assembly for a darkroom sink.

## Preliminary Floor Plan

The size of the available room, and the location of water and drains, doors, and windows all affect your darkroom plan. Look at figure 4.5 and make a plan to scale on 1/4-inch graph paper. Use a fairly large scale (e.g., 1 inch equals 1 foot). Draw the outline of the room, showing all doors and windows, pipes and electrical outlets—all the things that might influence your design. Cut out colored pieces of cardboard for the sink, enlarger table, etc. Lay these templates on the plan and move them around until the most efficient, logical, and convenient relationship is found.

Dry and wet areas should be determined first. Imagine yourself standing and working in the room: as you turn to pick up a bottle of fixer will it be conveniently at hand? Is a closet door going to open into the enlarger? Take your time, and if you can, actually stand in that space and "play" darkroom.

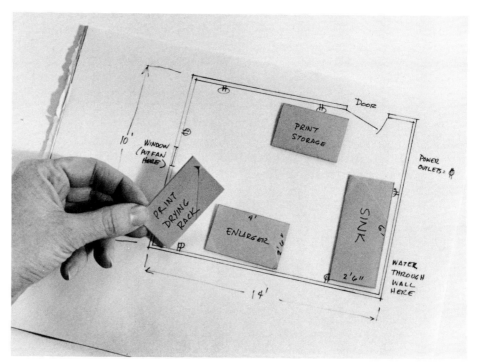

Figure 4.5
Plan a darkroom plan using scale-model cardboard cutouts of sink and enlarger work areas, locating them to make best use of doors, plumbing, and electrical outlets.

Figure 4.6
a. Athens County, Steam Driven Tractor. Julie Elman. b. On the Road, Lancaster County, Pennsylvania (from) Picture America. Jim Alinder.

Photo courtesy of the photographers.

a.

The enlarger, easel, focusing magnifier, timer, dodging tools, pencil, paper cutter, printing paper, and all dry chemicals are stored on the dry side. Any darkroom equipment that touches water is stored on the wet side. Wet objects and chemical contamination are always potential hazards in the darkroom, and you might wish to create a drying area where wet objects are placed to dry and be stored and where chemical measurement is done. This is automatically a danger area, where no paper or negatives can be put down without careful consideration.

There does not have to be a big gap between the wet and dry work area; however, they should be completely separated. No matter how careful you are, eventually a box of hypo crystals or a bottle of fixer will be tipped over. Assume the worst: liquids will somehow eventually leak or spill.

Electrical connections must meet local code requirements, which are established for your physical safety. Have an electrician test your circuits for grounding and replace old-style duplex outlets near the sink with GFI (ground-fault interrupt) outlets. These are expensive but may save your life. Darkroom wiring involves a number of separate circuits, none of them demanding much current. If there are not enough duplex wall outlets, you can extend existing outlets with a power distribution strip.

b.

## Safelights

Safelights and worklights should illuminate trays and prints but not be in your eyes (fig. 4.7). Safelights must be at least 4 feet from the developer tray to avoid safelight fog. The 5 1/2 inch circular safelights (commonly called a "bullet" safelight because of its shape) are convenient: put one by the enlarger, one over the developer tray area of the sink, and an optional one in the storage areas.

An OC filter is the correct color notation for all black-and-white enlarging papers. The filters can be changed easily for other darkroom work, for color printing, or for working with graphic arts films. An economical alternative to separate safelights is a single-tube 48 inch ceiling-mounted fluorescent light with a safelight OC sleeve filter. Because they continue to emit radiation, which can fog film, be careful that all fluorescent lights have been turned off for several minutes before opening film canisters.

If color printing is anticipated, an Osram adjustable filter, which can be converted for either black-and-white or color materials, should be considered. For temporary darkrooms, Jobo makes an elegant battery-operated safelight that may be worn around the neck.

## Film Drying

Film must be dried in a dust-free area where there is little risk of being touched. In climates where dust is a problem, a small recirculating room air cleaner will provide effective dust control and move the air enough to speed drying. The four darkroom dangers to negatives are (1) dust in the air, (2) sediment in the water, (3) an unstable drying line that permits films to

Figure 4.7
Lighting for the darkroom and print finishing area should be arranged so that trays and work areas are well-lit without light being in the photographer's eyes.

fall or touch one another, and (4) touching the wet emulsion with your fingers. Water sediment can be prevented by using a cartridge filter in the darkroom water line. Vacuum cleaner exhaust is a serious source of the worst dust for negatives, and an otherwise appropriate concern for cleanliness can be a source of disaster. Clean the darkroom with a broom and damp mop instead of vacuuming it.

## Print Drying and Finishing

Print drying frames with plastic screens can be built to any desired size (though the most efficient frame size is based on a 16″ × 24″ module). Racks that support a number of frames will fit into many otherwise wasted spaces (e.g., under a worktable or a counter). An alternative to a permanent frame is a screen hammock, consisting of a sheet of plastic window screen stapled to a piece of 3/4-inch dowel (fig. 4.8). When not in use, the screen is rolled up and stored. A 6-foot length of 24″ screen will dry twelve 8″ × 10″ prints at a time.

A sturdy table surfaced with a scrap piece of masonite or heavy cardboard is desirable for print finishing. A solid card table can be used to work on. A very solid worktable can be economically built using the same method as the darkroom sink—merely turn the sink basin upside down.

Prints need to be stored flat. If storage drawers cannot be provided, archival print storage boxes provide an economical, safe environment. Safe print or negative storage requires moderate temperatures and freedom from dust and humidity.

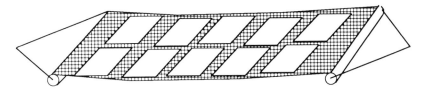

Figure 4.8
**a.** A temporary drying rack can be made like a hammock from two pieces of dowel or aluminum tubing and a length of plastic screen.

**b.** Plastic screen print drying frames tucked under a counter. Using otherwise wasted space, the unattended prints dry safely. This small rack can dry forty 8″ × 10″ prints an hour if a fan is used.

## Basic Equipment Considerations

There are literally hundreds of manufacturers of photographic equipment, but only a few make a quality product that will last, so purchase equipment that is made of the most durable materials. Photo equipment must be able to tolerate the inevitable rough handling that it receives; only well-made gear will survive. Assess your equipment needs by deciding what kind of pictures you want to make and let this decision control kind of cameras, lenses, meters, tripods, lights, and other gear you buy.

As a working professional, in applied or art photography, a balance needs to be maintained between what is owned and what can be borrowed, rented, or leased as needs arise. New models of lenses, cameras, and lights are introduced to the market constantly; in an attempt to sell equipment, ads promise glittering new technical developments, which may not be relevant to your needs.

## Equipment Needed and Wanted

Before investing in a camera system, talk to several professionals and find out what they use, and why they use it. Ask permission to look at their own cameras to see how they have survived professional demands. Ask the owners:

- How often the cameras break down
- How easily are the cameras serviced
- How sharp are the lenses
- How does the camera and lens system handle
- What are known problems with the system they use
- If they were beginning now, would they change?

Compare answers. Professionals buy into fads as often as anyone else, but certain lines of equipment are popular for very good reasons.

Decide what you can afford to buy. Perhaps you cannot get all you need at once; it is usually better to purchase a single item of the best quality and get more when you can afford it. When you purchase the best equipment available, you not only minimize potential down time, but you also protect your investment.

Photographic equipment depreciates at about the same rate as an automobile; it has been jokingly said a camera and a car each lose half their resale value when you take them out of the store. Unfortunately, the joke is true. What is worse, some cameras have a fleeting popularity and cannot be resold easily (or at all). This is certainly true of most amateur equipment, but it does not apply equally to the better lines. Leicas, professional Nikon models, and Hasselblad cameras depreciate slowly, and can usually be resold at reasonable prices.

Camera design has strongly influenced the pictures that are made:

- William Henry Fox Talbot investigated Wedgewood and Davy's experiments with silver salts and made a paper *negative* with a tiny camera obscura in 1835.
- Sir David Brewster describes the *stereoscope* to the Royal Society of Edinburgh in 1849, a device that permitted one to see a three-dimensional effect in the photograph.
- In 1854, Adolphe-Eugené Disderi invents the **carte-de-visite** camera using several lenses to make small pictures on a large plate. These tiny, popular, inexpensive pictures were cut apart after printing. The idea survives in our time as school and baby pictures.
- Eastman's first Kodak marketed in 1889 as a complete photographic system, using the motto: *Pull the string. Turn the crank. Trip the shutter.* The Eastman factory did the rest.
- Reflex cameras with two lenses made in England in 1890. Single-lens reflex cameras made in the United States in 1899. Quality hand cameras begin appearing in 1890. (See Alfred Stieglitz' picture *The Terminal* made in 1892 with a hand-held camera. The picture was made by the photographer in part because his peers considered a hand camera unsuitable for ''art'' photography. Stieglitz called it ''a well considered snapshot.'')
- Oskar Barnack designed the **Leica** between 1911 and 1913, and it was first manufactured in 1923–1924. The camera used standard movie film and cocked the shutter while advancing the film.
- The *Contax* camera manufactured in 1932 with a built-in range finder.
- The *Exacta* camera in 1947 becomes the first popular 35mm single-lens reflex camera with pentaprism and interchangeable lenses.

## Specific Equipment Needs

The work you do will determine what you buy. For example, if you are interested in photojournalism, it is best to have two camera bodies and at least three lenses (covering the range from wide angle to telephoto), or two fixed-focus and one zoom lens. The sepa-rate bodies mean that critical time is not lost changing lenses; when different lenses are mounted on separate bodies, field-of-view changes can be achieved quickly, when there is no time to reconfigure a camera.

Equipment is available in a wide range of prices and styles. Your choice of camera system is affected by what kinds of photographs you plan to make and what camera format is best for those pictures.

There are mechanical criteria:

- Sturdiness of the camera body
- Dependability of shutter
- Quality of lenses

There are money limitations and personal taste:

- Cost of equipment
- Personal response to equipment
- Current professional popularity

Figure 4.9

**a. Untitled. Ezra Stoller.** A wartime photograph of a new event in American industry: a woman handler at a J & L steel mill. The photographer used dramatic lighting to overcome the handicap of slow film (the fastest available was about ISO 64) and a large-format view camera by focusing on her gesture of command.

Beginning photographers often have to "make do" for a time, but in the long run, equipment quality and reliability should have priority.

## Buying Used Equipment

Used equipment in good shape can be purchased for much less money than equivalent new merchandise. Excellent quality used camera bodies and lenses are frequently available in local camera stores (where older models are accepted in trade for new cameras) and by mail from camera brokers (see appendix 4). Used enlargers are harder to find, partly because there have been fewer model changes, and partly because enlargers have changed slowly during the past thirty years and because they are not usually bought on impulse, unlike cameras.

Used equipment can usually be taken home and tried out by signing a purchase memorandum, which is a mutual agreement that if the lens or camera works properly and is in good condition, you have a serious intention of purchasing it. The understanding is that you will promptly expose and process test film used to evaluate the machine. Usually, if you make this kind of agreement, a local dealer will permit you to have equipment for twenty-four hours to make appropriate tests. Reputable camera brokers usually offer similar testing periods for expensive cameras and lenses.

**b. Untitled. Tom Roush.** High-speed film and the 35mm camera permitted the photographer to capture the homely housekeeping gesture and "freeze" the water in mid-flight.

**a.** University of Louisville Photographic Archives.
**b.** Courtesy of the photographer.

## Examining Lenses

Lens and camera always interact, and a test of one is often a partial test of the complete system. Used lenses should be physically examined for:

- Obvious damage to lens barrel or glass
- Mounting flanges that fit snugly and show little wear
- Adapter threads that are clean and accept filters easily
- An aperture ring that moves easily and has clean detent positioning
- An aperture that is symmetrical with blades not shiny at edges
- A lens that is clean internally, without moisture or dust
- Glass elements that are tight in the lens barrel

A simple exposure/development test will *adequately* check these items:

- Accuracy of focus
- Accuracy of exposure with changes in aperture
- Sharpness across the field, corner to corner
- Even covering power
- Absence of obvious flare when the subject is backlighted

Photograph a full newspaper page daily stock report (which provides evenly distributed fine detail with low contrast). The paper must be smooth and flat, carefully and evenly lighted. Use a medium- or low-speed film (for resolution) and develop 20–30% longer than normal to accentuate contrast. Place the camera on a tripod and, if possible, raise the reflex mirror before tripping the shutter. Compare the indicated exposure to that provided by another meter you have come to trust. Make a series of exposures at different aperture and shutter combinations. Expose and develop the film. Make an 11" × 14" full-frame print without dodging or burning, and examine it for variations in sharpness and density (especially at the center and corners).

## Examining Cameras

The brass body beneath the paint will often be revealed at the edges if it has been heavily used. This is not bad; it's only an indication of use. What is important are signs of damage: dents, gouges, or new parts (which indicate rough use or a dropped camera).

A simple mechanical check of the shutter can be done by setting it at a one-second exposure, then cock and trip it several times. The shutter should sound the same every time, and the shutter should remain open for a full second. Change the setting to 1/2 second and repeat. Repeat this for 1/4, 1/8, etc., up to 1/125th of a second. The human ear is a very sensitive instrument, and each shutter speed setting should clearly sound shorter than the preceding one, and every repetition should sound the same. Variations suggest worn escapements or bad electronics; leave the machine in the store.

Repeat the lens test described above, but use a lens you are familiar with and know is in excellent condition. Develop the film and look at it on a light table. Look for variations in density from end to end of the frame to check for shutter drag. Look for variations in density between the aperture/shutter combinations, which *should* have produced similar densities.

## Examining Light Meters

New or used meters should be checked out very carefully before buying. (Read chapter 5, "Meters and Light," before considering any meter.) All meters are easily damaged by rough handling. Meter movements are what rotate the needle that provides the measure of light, and the meter movement is generally more frail than the solid-state circuits that drive it. The needle is supported by an armature with tiny jeweled bearings, which are easily displaced by rough handling.

Solid-state photo-resistive circuits themselves are damaged by excess moisture. The older style photo-generative selenium meter can often be purchased for very little money and will do an excellent job. The significant limitation of the selenium meter is its lack of sensitivity, as compared to the battery-powered resistive meter, and if you are planning on photographing much by low-level artificial light, you will have to stay with the battery-powered meters.

When evaluating a used meter, first open the battery compartment and verify that there is no corrosion. Hold and operate a meter at various angles to verify that the meter armature moves freely and correctly and that the bearings have not been damaged. Then make comparison meter readings, holding it side by side with a meter you know and trust. Make a number of readings in both bright and dimly lighted areas. Not all meters respond the same to different kinds of light, and there may well be differences between meters under fluorescent light and day light.

## Evaluating Tripods

Set up a tripod as though you were going to use it. Study carefully how the legs are adjusted in length, how the legs are attached to the head, how the head rotates and tilts, and how the camera is attached to the head. Try to lengthen and shorten the legs and see if the clamping mechanism releases the legs easily, then holds firmly without having to tighten them excessively. Finally, place a heavy camera on the tripod, and perform the following tests:

1. Rap the camera lens sharply downward with your finger and see how much vertical vibration there is.

2. Rap the camera lens sharply sideways with your finger and see how much rotation or play there is between the head and the legs.

3. Release the head, rotate and tilt the camera, and relock the head. Note how smoothly these things were done and how easily (or hard) the head locked in place.

4. Shorten one leg an inch so that the tripod is leaning slightly, and relock it; let the camera stand on the tripod for twenty minutes. The leg adjustment should not creep.

The adjustable vertical center pole (called an elevator) violates tripod stability. When it is extended, the camera and elevator combine to make an inverse pendulum; the heavier the camera and lens, and the higher the elevator, the more inevitable it will sway and vibrate. Never extend the elevator any longer than absolutely necessary for maximum sharpness. Extend the elevator fully and tap the camera; see how much motion there is and how long it takes to quiet.

Leg attachments strongly affect stability. The best tripods have a crutch construction, in which two widely spaced arms are hinged to the body and join together to meet and form a leg of the tripod. These tripods usually have more positive and dependable adjusting locks for the lower leg than do the tripods with telescoping tubular legs. A tripod that is too light, vibrates, or is not stable is worse than having no tripod at all.

## Assessing Enlargers

As noted earlier, used enlargers are not easily found. Except for development of "color head" light sources, a thirty-year-old enlarger looks much like a new one.

An external assessment of a used enlarger is easy:

- The baseboard must be flat, and not warped.
- Control knobs need to be firmly attached and have no play.
- Positioning clamps must release and grip easily.
- Head positioning levers must not be bent.
- Head assembly must move smoothly along entire track.
- Lamp housing must sit straight.
- Little or no light should leak around negative stage.
- Control switches must work cleanly.
- Wiring insulation must be sound.
- Condenser lenses should have no chips or scratches.

There should be accessory condenser lenses for an Omega enlarger, which needs these to focus light correctly on different sizes of negatives. Beseler enlarger motors must be operated to be sure they are working.

Check the enlarger lenses by rotating the aperture control ring gently from full open to minimum aperture, feeling for clean detents. Remove the lens from the enlarger and look at it for dents (where it might have been dropped) and through it at a piece of white paper to see the aperture blades move smoothly. Verify that there is no fungus or dirt in the lens.

More difficult is determining alignment faults. The enlarger negative carriage must stay parallel to the baseboard. Some enlargers simply do not hold alignment. A simple test is to make and project an alignment test negative. This test does not require a darkroom, but may be done anywhere with moderate ambient light.

Make an alignment negative by using an unwanted negative. Scratch the pattern shown in figure 4.10 into the emulsion with a straightedge and a needle. Place this negative emulsion down in the enlarger and raise the enlarger to project about a 16″ × 20″ image. Focus on a piece of white paper on the easel. Study the torn emulsion lines at the corners and the center to see if they are equally sharp. If they are not, refocus the enlarger slightly to sharpen one corner, then note how much lens travel is required to refocus elsewhere. If more than 1/4 inch of vertical movement is required, the enlarger is significantly out of alignment and may need a lot of work.

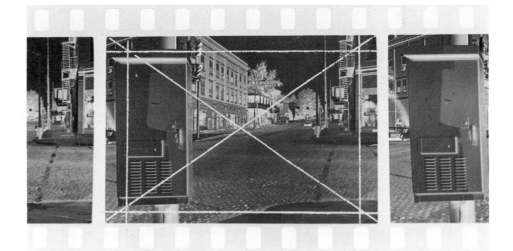

Figure 4.10
Scratching this pattern in the emulsion of an unwanted negative produces an effective focusing target for aligning an enlarger. The torn emulsion pattern is easy to evaluate across the enlarged field without the use of a grain magnifier.

## Summary

Basic darkroom needs are for a light-tight space and safe electrical service. Ventilation must always be provided. Water and waste chemicals can be carried in and out. Kitchens and bathrooms can be converted to temporary darkrooms. Preplan your darkroom's wet and dry areas, ground outlets for safe electrical service, and install adequate safelight and white lights. Print and negative drying areas must be free of dust. Safe print storage requires moderate humidity and temperature.

Equipment needs will vary with professional choices. Used equipment should be considered. Lenses, cameras, and meters can be evaluated with simple tests. Used enlargers are less easily located than used cameras. Enlarger sturdiness and alignment can be assessed without a darkroom.

## Discussion and Assignments

When you are at school, darkrooms are usually not a problem, but when you begin to work by yourself, establishing one frequently presents a challenge.

### Assignment 1

If a school darkroom is available, examine it carefully and learn where the light and water controls are. If your school supplies chemicals, learn what kind of developer and fixer are being used.

If you are planning your own darkroom, find and examine two or three private working darkrooms and see how wet and dry areas are created, how much space is actually needed, and ask the owners what they would keep and what they would do differently were they to start from scratch.

### Assignment 2

Plan in detail how you could convert a space in your present living arrangement to be used as a printing darkroom. Considerations:

- How to achieve darkness
- Where to put an enlarger
- Where to put trays or a tray storage rack
- Where to find electricity
- In a dual-use space (bathroom or kitchen), with limited access times, how and where would you store equipment between printings?

### Assignment 3

Darkrooms can be very unsafe places to work and adequate safelighting will minimize risks. Make the safelight test described in chapter 7 (see fig. 7.3). If the safelight test is negative, increase the brightness of the safelights (by moving the lights or increasing the number of safelights) to a more comfortable level and retest.

### Assignment 4

Carefully tape a daily record of stock prices from a well-printed newspaper onto a sheet of cardboard or masonite. Prepare to photograph it in very even, flat light. Load your camera with Technical Pan film. Mount the camera on a tripod, and frame the sheet of newsprint so that the whole sheet fills the frame. Be sure the back of the camera and the newspaper are parallel.

Expose film at metered exposures, beginning at maximum aperture and decreasing the aperture a stop at a time. Use a cable release to trigger the shutter. If the camera has a mirror release, trip the mirror first, wait a second, and then trigger the shutter. Repeat for other lenses you own or might wish to use. Develop the film for moderate-to-high contrast. Set the enlarger for maximum enlargement, focus carefully, and make 5″ × 8″ test prints from the *centers and corners* of the maximum aperture test, and then repeat at two-stops-down from maximum aperture. (Lenses never produce the sharpest image at maximum or minimum aperture.) Minimize enlarger lens variables by centering the frame dividing line before printing the details of the corners. Compare the different lens resolutions.

# 5 Negative Exposure

Figure 5.1
**Elizabeth Fletcher, ca. 1910. Kate Mathews.** The photographer consistently put aside traditional ways of looking at popular photographic subjects and documented Kentucky community life from 1885 to the 1920s.
University of Louisville Photographic Archives.

## First Exposures

The most exciting pictures are those that reveal your own daily life; they are the pictures no one else can make. Your first pictures "should" include different subjects in different scenes: some may be dark, some bright, with subjects close to the camera or far away, with light coming over your shoulder or from behind the subject. Try photographing many different things, in different ways. Put aside thoughts of right and wrong ways of seeing and doing. Photographic problems inevitably will arise, but they can be solved.

If you are unsure of where to begin photographing, you can give yourself assignments—find interesting patterns, concentrate on special events (county fairs, street scenes, people at work in professional costumes), relationships (large-and-small, near-and-far, light-and-dark), make pictures of people on the street. (Several *subject* assignments are offered at the end of this chapter.)

Most films are now described as having **latitude,** a term used to describe photographic materials that are forgiving of most errors of exposure or development. Today's high-speed 35mm films are also moderately fine-grain films that will produce a fully detailed 8″ × 10″ print with excellent separation of values in shadows and highlights. Any of the standard films are suitable to begin photographing: Kodak T–Max 100 or 400, Tri–X, Ilford FP4 or HP5, or Fuji Isopan 100 or 400. You may wish to use your camera's automatic controls to set shutter and/or aperture adjustments by using a hand-held or internal light meter. The camera's internal, automatically coupled meter permits and allows you freedom to simply point the camera and shoot.

Many cameras require you adjust the meter in the camera to the correct film speed, but almost all the newer 35mm cameras have connectors at the edge of the film compartment inside the camera that are used to sense the pattern of silver lines on the cassette, which is the **DX** coding. This automati-

Figure 5.2
**Untitled. Jim Zietz.** This street scene illustrates the kind of picture that happens only for an instant, and is an ideal subject for 35mm camera photography.
Courtesy of the photographer.

cally adjusts the meter in the camera to the film you are using.

Photographic film's ability to respond to light, or film speed rating, is indicated by the **ISO** number. Moderately slow, or less sensitive films like Kodak Plus–X, T–Max 100, or Ilford FP4, have an ISO rating near 100. Tri–X, T–Max 400, and Ilford HP5 have ISO numbers of 400, which indicates they are very light sensitive. Slower films provide finer detail; faster films permit photographing with less light.

Manufacturers suggest shutter and aperture combinations for common outdoor lighting conditions. If you do not have a meter (either hand-held or in the camera), use the exposure guide data printed on the inside of the film carton or on a sheet packed with the film.

Start photographing in daylight by setting the shutter at 1/125th of a second and allowing the camera to choose the aperture. This is called *shutter priority.* Light meter and exposure calculating systems inside the camera will adjust the size of the lens opening to make correct exposures. Later, you may wish to change to *aperture priority,* where the shutter speed is varied according to the light that is available, but this is risky at first because shutter speeds longer than 1/60th of a second often produce visible blur unless special care is taken to keep the camera still during the exposure.

Your camera may have different programming possibilities (i.e., aperture priority or shutter priority, or be fully automatic and offer you no individual control). Most cameras permit the operator to be in control, but if your camera is fully automatic, begin by making pictures, see what happens, and concentrate on discovering *how* the camera's pictures differ from your anticipated image.

Assignments are a way of getting started and loosening up, but photograph everything that interests you: don't feel constrained by assignments. Photography challenges your seeing, and the most moving photography is often made by discovering commonplace events through the eye of the camera.

## Basic Principles

Silver process photography is based on the fact that some silver chemicals called **silver halides** are very sensitive to light.[1] Contemporary photography is based on dispersing silver halides evenly in a gelatin emulsion, which is then coated in a thin layer on either a transparent (film) or opaque white (paper) support.

Exposing any silver halide to a great deal of light will cause it to change color by the action of the light alone, from a white salt to brown or red. This was the basis of photographic printing in the nineteenth century, although today this effect is no longer used. Something different happens when a silver halide is exposed to a little bit of light: the light produces an invisible, but real **latent** image. The latent image can be made visible by chemical development.

Exposing a silver halide emulsion to a little light and then immersing it in a developing solution causes a rapid and dramatic visible change. Where light has touched the emulsion, with development the silver salts darken from a pale pink to a deep, satiny black. The discovery of the latent image and subsequent chemical development is the base on which all contemporary silver process photography has been built.

## Film Types Available

Different abbreviations that indicate how sensitive photographic emulsions are to light have been used. In recent years, ASA (American Standards Association) was replaced by ANSI (American National Standards Institute), and that in turn by the ISO (International Standards Organization) numbers. European films are marked with DIN *(Deutsche Industrie Norm)* numbers. The American numbering system is arithmetic (e.g., an emulsion marked 200 is twice as sensitive to light (or "fast") as one marked 100). A DIN marking of 21 is the same as an ANSI or ISO of 100. The European system is logarithmic, which means a DIN of 24 is twice as fast as a DIN of 21.

Many excellent and competitive black-and-white films are now available, and they all have these characteristics in common:

- *Sensitivity:* Films are evaluated according to how little light is needed to produce a usable image. Films with standard or experimental ISO ratings from about 25 to 3000 or more are now available. The ISO rating for the film is a starting point for exposure, but you may need to establish a personal **Exposure Index (EI)**, to compensate for variables of exposure and development in your system.
- *Contrast:* The density range a film produces from being exposed to a given luminance range and given standard development determines the film's inherent contrast. All general-purpose 35mm films now are very sensitive to development contrast control, by increasing or decreasing developing time, dilutions, or developer formula.
- *Acutance:* Film is graded according to how many lines of information per millimeter it can **resolve**. The resolving power of a film is also called **edge sharpness**,

which is a measure of the diffusion of light within the emulsion. Slow films have higher acutance than fast films, but acutance is also affected by development: developer formulas with large amounts of sodium sulfite produce images with lower edge sharpness. High acutance developers produce negatives with more obvious grain but less acutance, compared to "fine-grain" developers. The physical distribution of silver halide grains in the emulsion controls the acutance.

- *Color sensitivity:* Most contemporary 35mm films are **panchromatic**, meaning they respond well to all colors of visible light. The principal exception is infrared film, which is sensitive both to visible light and infrared radiation (the long-wave radiation just beyond the visible spectrum, which we perceive as heat). Ektagraphic HC film is **orthochromatic**, (not sensitive to red or yellow light), as well as having very high contrast (though it can be processed for more moderate contrast by using a very dilute, or specially formulated developer).

## Latent Image, Light, and Film

Light from the lens enters the emulsion when film is exposed and encounters silver halide particles. A large amount of the light is merely reflected back from the film and must be absorbed by the black interior body of the camera. Some of the image light passes on through the emulsion and is absorbed at the back of the film. If there is enough light to create a latent image, the larger silver halides react and tiny areas become unstable, breaking down into silver and gas components. These unstable areas are used during development to make the entire crystal revert to silver metal, producing the dark image we see.

Figure 5.3 partially illustrates the complexity of contemporary films. The base is a gray-dyed plastic support. The emulsion may consist of two or more layers of gelatin. A very thin "super" coat of chemically hardened gelatin (with no photosensitivity) protects the emulsion from abrasion. The back of all but a few scientific films are coated with a darkened **antihalation** layer of gelatin to prevent a secondary image being formed by light reflected from the back of the film. The dark, colored dyes in the antihalation layer are absorbed during processing. The gelatin in the antihalation layer also helps keep film from curling and makes it easier to handle.

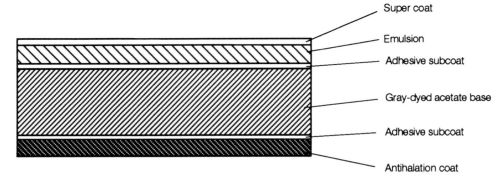

Figure 5.3
Schematic drawing of a cross section of typical black-and-white film (not to scale).

## Meters and Light

In order to make accurate predictions of the exposure needed to make a picture, one must know the **intensity** of light. Photographers had few dependable metering devices before photocells, which created an electrical energy when light touched them, became available in the 1930s. Before that time, most photographers made an educated guess about the exposure needed, or estimated the amount of light by the time of day, the season, the weather, and the latitude. These all factored into the f-number and shutter speed to be used.

Light reflected from a subject can be electronically measured as **luminance,** a term that describes light energy in terms of candelas per square meter.[2] The physics of light measurement are beyond the scope of this text, but luminance is a precise way to describe the intensity of light sources in the photograph, whether they are reflected or self-luminous (flames or electric lights). Luminance range is an objective measure of the brightness range of a subject, which appears to the eye (and eventually in the print) as contrast. The luminance range of a subject provides a measure of con-

trast, as a given film and development will create *printable* negative densities for only a certain subject luminance range.

Most contemporary photo meters use arbitrary number scales (rather than offering a direct measurement of light in standard laboratory units like the candela). Because of this, a meter reading of 10 on one meter does not always equate to a 10 on another meter. However, all meters do use a log exposure scale, which means that a meter scale change from one number to the next (e.g., 10 to 11) indicates an increase of twice the light energy. Likewise, a change from 10 to 9 means that half the light is available. This 2:1 ratio between meter numbers parallels the change in intensity created by rotating the aperture ring and changing the f-number a full stop, which also produces a 2:1 change of intensity. Because of this, it is often more convenient to speak of the meter measurements in terms of the number of **stops** from one meter reading to another in the same scene.

Light meters are either photo-generative (i.e., generate electrical energy when light impacts on them), or they are photo-resistive. The photo-generative meter is still found in hand-held meters. It is inherently bulky but is also mechanically dependable and requires no batteries.

The photo-resistive meter works because it restricts the flow of elec-

tricity in a circuit as a function of the light striking the photosensitive device. Power for the circuit is provided by a small battery. Photo-resistive meters are sensitive to battery voltage changes, and as the battery ages, meter indications will err toward overexposure.

The photo-resistive meter can be made very sensitive to light, but it also can be temporarily desensitized by exposure to very intense light (being pointed at the sun). On the positive side, it can be made small enough to be placed inside the camera. Sensitivity and size advantage have made the battery-powered photo-resistive meter standard, because by placing it inside the camera, it can measure light being used to form the picture on the film itself.

The **reflected light meter** measures the light reflected *from the subject toward the camera.* The reflected light meter is the kind incorporated in all contemporary cameras. In cheaper cameras, it may be located on the front, pointing toward the subject. In single-lens reflex cameras, it is located inside the camera.

It is important to realize that the hand-held reflected light meter measures light reaching it through a given angle of view—in this sense it resembles a small camera in that light is focused on a photo-sensitive area. The size of metering target is dictated by the physical design of the meter. Most

Figure 5.4
**The Town School. Sarah Tarnoff.** An everyday scene rediscovered through the eye of the camera.

Courtesy of the photographer and Agfa-Beseler.

hand-held meters have a wide-angle view, and integrate light through the same angle as a 35–40mm focal length camera lens. These meters are often improperly used to measure reflected light from metering targets that are too small to be accurately metered, producing exposure errors.

A typical hand-held meter measures light from a rather large area, and the smallest target where one is sure to measure only light from the target area is at least 5″ × 5″; it is safer to use a larger metering target, and the most common is a **standard**

Gray Card, which is 8″ × 10″. Some reflected light meters have lenses that measure only a 1° or 2° field of view and are called **spot meters**. A spot meter can measure the light from very small target areas.

The **incident light meter** measures *light falling on the subject*. The incident light meter does not provide accurate indications of how much light is available to the lens from any given part of the photographic subject. This meter was invented for use in film studios where the lighting was totally controlled and the range of light intensity

falling on the subject being filmed was constantly measured to determine the overall effect of the light.

Although either kind of meter can be used to accurately calculate the exposure required to make a picture, experience and common sense are required to translate the meter readings into working exposures, or in more advanced photography into a development plan for controlling negative contrast. Correct metering allows you to both determine correct minimum density exposures and also to predict suitable negative development.

a.

b.

Figure 5.5
Two examples of difficult light metering subjects. The forest floor does not have a "safe" metering target. Adequate detail is retained in the dark tree trunks to keep those areas visually interesting. Scattered light illuminates the face of the standing child and softens the edges of the dramatic window light on the children. Because exposure is correct for the skin and clothes and the vivid figure/ground relationship, the lack of background detail is acceptable. a. Untitled. Jeanne Hankins. b. Untitled. Julie Taylor.

Photos courtesy of the photographers and Agfa-Beseler.

With a reflected light meter, you can meter **shadows** (to estimate correct exposure) and then you can also meter **highlights** (to estimate the luminance range, or contrast). Reflected light meters can measure the actual luminance range of the photographic subject; incident light meters cannot. Yet either kind of meter can provide excellent exposure and development guides if the character of the meter is understood.

## TTL Metering

Through the lens (TTL) meters are reflected light meters. Some cameras have different modes of operation for their TTL meters, to allow the photographer to determine which part of the scene will control the exposure. Most, however, show the photographer (or directly control both aperture and shutter) an indicated exposure, which assumes light from all the shadowed and highlight areas (including direct light sources) will *average* to produce satisfactory densities on your negative. This assumption is generally true only if the scene is of normal contrast (i.e., the luminance range from the darkest area to the brightest is suitable for the film being used and for normal development). Often it is necessary to adjust the indicated meter exposure to a greater or lesser value, because the meter fails to provide right information for contrasty or flat scenes and you wish to expose more or less.

Consult your camera instruction manual for detailed operational instructions, because some popular small cameras do not allow exposure manipulations except on a "manual" mode. While this mode will inevitably permit you to make more mistakes, it also allows you the chance for creative exposure control, and to learn how the photographic system really operates.

## Film Density Defined

*Density* is a commonly used term that is often misunderstood. Beginners often confuse density and contrast. Density is a logarithmic measure of how much passes through the negative as compared to how much light is shining on it (i.e., a comparison of the transmitted light to the incident light). If the film absorbed no light at all, it would have a transmission of 100%, or a zero density and an opacity of 0%.

When the film absorbs half the light, it has a transmission of 50%, and an opacity of 50%. Properly exposed and developed negatives have limited densities, and should have some opacity even in very dark shadows while remaining fairly transparent in brightly exposed areas (like cloudy skies or white sand beaches). Opacities important to the photographic negative generally lie between above 50% and well below 100%.

Mathematically, the relation between the light available to the negative and the light allowed to pass through it is expressed as:

$$T \text{ (transmission)} = \frac{\text{transmitted light}}{\text{incident light}}$$

And the opposite of **T** is opacity:

$$\text{Opacity} = O = \frac{1}{T}$$

*Opacity* is a term that describes **absorption** of light.

Few photographers are comfortable with mathematics, but a brief refresher is needed because density numbers have some special properties one needs to know. Opacity and transmission are plain arithmetic numbers, but density is described in logarithmic notation: Density is the logarithm to the base 10 of **O**, the **Opacity**.

Logarithms provide a mathematical means of expressing large numbers in a very compact form, and logarithmic numbers have some special relationships that are important to remember even if you do not fully understand the mathematics. For an example of how large numbers are compressed when stated as logarithms, while a density of 1.0 is equivalent to a transmission of only 10%, a density of 2.0 is a transmission of 1.0%, and a density of 3.0 is a transmission of only 0.1%.

The important thing to remember about logarithmic density numbers is that a density *change* of 0.30 means that the transmission of light possible has been doubled or halved (depending on a decrease or increase in density). This simple relationship is of practical importance if you have a **densitometer,** a special meter with which to measure the transmittance of a negative, or if you are using neutral density filters (described in chapter 10).

While you need not know logarithms, there are common density numbers that occur frequently in the photographic literature that are conve-

nient to know. These are the most important density numbers for 35mm negative films:

- 0.30 = Typical minimum density
- 0.80 = Typical middle gray density
- 1.20 = Typical detailed highlight density

## Estimating Density

You can train your eye to estimate appropriate negative densities quite accurately. First, it is important to understand you cannot accurately evaluate negative printing densities by looking through the negative directly at a light source. What you see through the negative itself becomes a distraction, but more important the amount of information your eye can see does not relate to what is usable in printing. View a negative by reflected light.

---

A century ago, Ferdinand Hurter and Vero Charles Driffeld exposed photographic emulsions to calibrated light sources and then developed the negatives carefully, controlling time, temperature, and agitation. They discovered that *silver emulsions respond predictably,* and that the density produced by a given exposure can be predicted when a standard development is used. They described this relationship between exposure, development, and density as the **characteristic curve.** The characteristic curve is also called the density versus log exposure curve (or D log E curve, or the H & D curve).

---

The first impression when one looks at the negative this way is that you cannot see it. That is absolutely correct: you cannot see all highlight detail in a typical negative because most beginner's negatives are overdeveloped. But what you can see *is what can be printed on a normal print.* Also, study the shadows by looking through the negative at *reflected* light, though you may wish to use a piece of plain white paper. In any case, the shadows should have detail.

Correct negative highlight densities examined by reflected light are very slightly transparent. Hold a negative as shown in figure 5.6 so that you look *through the negative highlights* at the print of a book or magazine (printed on white paper). Try to make out the shapes of the letters on the page. You should be *just able* to see text through the dense highlights. (Note: the figure shows a Technical Pan negative. This film has a very clear film base.) Should you be printing with a diffusion enlarger (and many of the new color enlargers have diffusion heads), an ideal negative will have highlight areas that are more dense than when printing with a condenser enlarger. Using this empirical density evaluation method, diffusion enlarger negatives will be more nearly opaque and the printed page will not be visible through the highlights: it is more difficult to visually estimate such densities correctly.

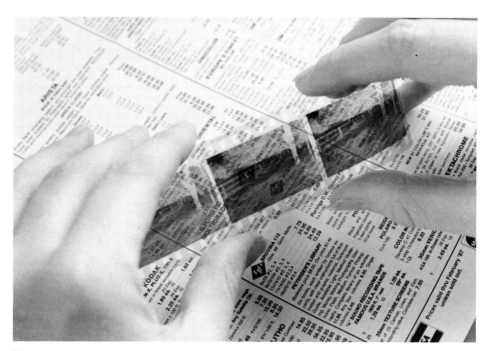

Figure 5.6
Examine negatives to discover what highlight details can be printed easily by looking through the negative at printing on white paper.

## Exposure and Reciprocity

When making a print, one has a constant light source (the enlarger lamp). The intensity of the light reaching the print is easily controlled by the aperture; exposure is controlled easily by the timer. A film exposure made with a camera uses varying light intensities: the aperture controls the intensity of light passing through the lens while the shutter controls the time.

In general, exposure can be described by this equation:

$$E = I \times T$$

where E is exposure, I is intensity, and T is time. This is called the **law of reciprocity.**

This is a *reciprocal* equation (e.g., as intensity increases, the time must be decreased proportionately). If the intensity of light is doubled and the time is halved, the exposure will stay the same. If the light level falls to a quarter, then the exposure time would have to be four times as long.

Within wide limits, the reciprocity law equation is true. However, reciprocity fails when light intensity is very weak and the exposure long (generally, when the exposure is longer than a second). Reciprocity also fails when light intensity is great and the indicated exposure time is very short (less than 1/1000 of a second).

Reciprocity failure means the exposure necessary to produce adequate minimum density will be larger than calculation from a light meter reading indicates because of the **reciprocity effect.** Additional exposure is needed to correct for reciprocity failure. The correction is surprisingly large, and it varies with the kind of film used; T-Max films, for example, are less sensitive to reciprocity failure than earlier Kodak films. Although table 5.1 only indicates reciprocity effect corrections for low-intensity light that causes long exposures, similar multipliers of exposure are required when very short exposures are encountered. Normally, these are rarely met except in scientific and industrial photography.

Table 5.1  Long Exposure Reciprocity Corrections

| Metered Exposure | Actual Exposure | | Development Decrease | |
|---|---|---|---|---|
| | *T–Max* | *Other Film* | *T–Max* | *Other Film* |
| 1 second | 1 second | 2 seconds | none | 5% |
| 10 seconds | 15 seconds | 50 seconds | 10% | 20% |
| 30 seconds | 1 minute | 3 minutes | 10% | 20% |
| 1 minute | 1 minute, 30 seconds | 10 minutes | 15% | 25% |

## Metering Assumptions

TTL meters generally assume the target is a middle gray.[3] This value is *photographically* halfway between a paper white and paper black. It is also what is seen when one looks at a flat surface that reflects 18% of the light falling on it.

When you point a camera with TTL metering at an all gray area with 18% reflectance, the indicated exposure is close to what you will meter if you point the same camera with a normal (i.e., 50mm) lens at an average landscape or portrait, and this is how we generally make pictures. The metering assumption is that the darkest and lightest areas and intensities in the picture will average out to an 18% equivalent. Problems arise when parts of the picture are much brighter than expected, because then the average light from the scene is more than expected and the indicated meter exposure is less than actually needed to produce good shadow detail.

You can use the camera's TTL meter to determine correct exposure for important shadows by coming close to the subject, pointing the camera at the shadows, and using the *indicated* shadow exposure to calculate the *actual* exposure.

The exposure indicated when you meter a shadow is greater than what the actual exposure should be. The shadow area is not a middle gray, 18% reflectance value. If you expose the entire scene at the indicated shadow exposure, the scene will be overexposed. One needs to know or guess *how much darker* than a standard middle gray is the shadow area you meter.

Figure 5.7
**Untitled. Amy Engelskirchen.** A scene where highlights and shadow areas are averaged by TTL meters.
Photo courtesy of the photographer and Agfa-Beseler.

## Metering Light to Determine Contrast

There are two ways to estimate correct exposure for high-contrast scenes. First, one can simply name it a high-contrast scene and arbitrarily expose more than the indicated exposure. Second, one can meter the important shadow areas and use that meter reading to *place* the exposure for adequate shadow detail on the negative.

A hand-held reflected light meter or an in-camera TTL meter permits precise estimations of contrast. You do this by:

1. Locate the brightest subject areas with detail. These highest textured highlights **(HTH)** are the brightest areas that must have detail in the print (i.e., be printed as a pale, detailed gray).

2. Locate dark areas with important shadow details. These important shadow areas **(ISA)** can be defined as large, dark areas that should retain rich detail in the print (e.g., dark blue jeans, black leather jackets, and the bark of darker trees in open shade).

3. Locate meterable targets within these defined values.

Meter both critical highlight and shadow areas and write down the indicated exposures. Count the number of stops between the important shadow (ISA) and the highest textured highlight (HTH) areas to determine the scene's contrast. Look at figure 5.8 to see the relationships between the exposure range and estimated contrast, keeping in mind the following:

- A scene is **flat** when there are only *three* stops range between the ISA and HTH.
- A scene is **normal** when there is a *four* stop range.
- A scene is **contrasty** when there is a *five* stop range.

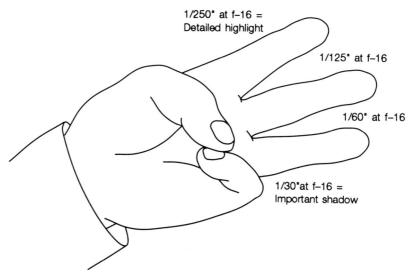

A three-stop range between important shadow and detailed highlight

Figure 5.8
**a.** Three-finger rule: the scene is flat when there is only a three-stop range between important shadow area meter reading and highest textured highlight area indicated exposure.

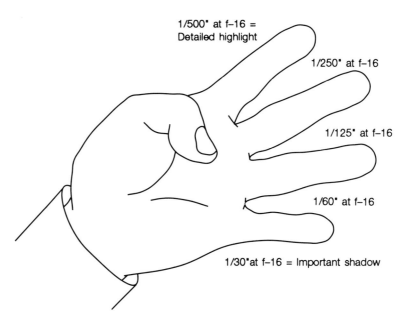

A four-stop range between important shadow and detailed highlight

**b.** Four-finger rule: the scene is normal when there is a four-range stop between important shadow area meter reading and highest textured highlight area indicated exposure.

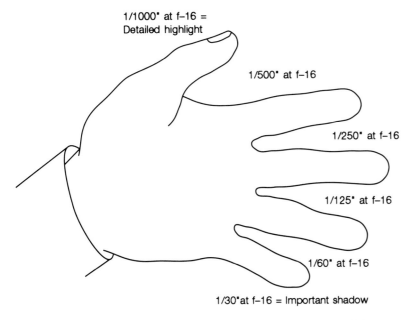

1/1000" at f–16 = Detailed highlight

1/500" at f–16

1/250" at f–16

1/125" at f–16

1/60" at f–16

1/30" at f–16 = Important shadow

A five-stop range between important shadow and detailed highlight

**c.** Five-finger rule: the scene is contrasty when there is a five-stop range between important shadow area meter reading and highest textured highlight area.

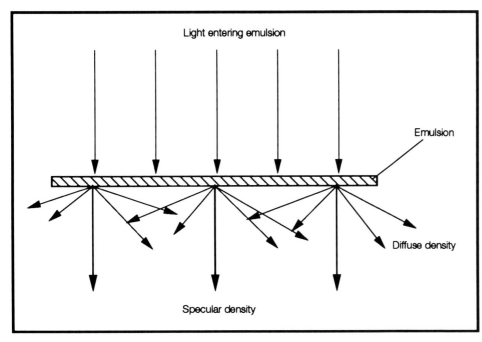

Light entering emulsion

Emulsion

Diffuse density

Specular density

Figure 5.9
Specular and diffuse effects in photographic emulsion.

Major errors are often made when one begins placing exposures by metered shadow reflected light readings rather than using an average indicated exposure. First, many incorrectly exposed negatives are the result of trying too hard to locate the "darkest detailed shadow." Beginning photographers consistently choose very dark subjects to meter because your eyes can see selectively and it is easy to "look into" shadows. Our eyes see detail in the scene where there will be little or none in the photograph. Second, the darkest detailed shadows are physically too small to meter accurately with a hand-held, or even a TTL reflected light meter.

Metering errors interact with a natural tendency to push the limits of the medium. Use the important shadow area (ISA) as a metering target. It is safer than searching for the *darkest* detailed shadow, both because of errors in choosing the right value to meter and size of metering target. This method does not violate anything you will find in publications on the Zone System. It does change the interval between low- and high-value meter readings because the difference between these is one stop less.

## Density Effects

There are two ways to describe and measure density. The apparent density is affected by *how* the light passes through the emulsion when a print is made, as shown in figure 5.9. The *same negative* has a different density range depending on how it is printed. *Parallel* light rays (typically used to provide the exposing light in a well-engineered condenser enlarger) are used to measure **specular density**. *Scattered, nondirectional, or diffused light* is used to measure **diffuse density**. This is the kind of light used in contact printing or available in enlargers with color heads and "cold light" heads.

In other words, a print made by a condenser enlarger is more contrasty than a print from the same negative printed by contact, or with a diffusion enlarger. This contrast effect can be anticipated when developing the negative. Unfortunately, *Kodak consistently recommends diffuse density developing times, which are much longer than condenser enlarger developing times,* and correct developing times are 10–20% less than the published Kodak recommendations to produce an ideal negative (for printing with a condenser enlarger).

## Ideal Negative Defined

An *ideal negative* can be defined as one exposed to produce adequate density to provide printable shadow detail, and developed to correct highlight densities that print easily on a "normal" paper grade. Correct exposure and development are both required to produce such a negative. If a brilliant print is an aesthetically important consideration, then an ideal negative can also be defined as one that permits making a *full-substance* presentation of the subject and a *full-scale* print. A full-substance presentation is one that adequately suggests *all* the surfaces in the original subject, from dark, shadowed leather to brilliant white shirts. Full scale means that the full-reflective range of the print is used, from paper white to the richest black possible with the silver in that paper. Full-scale, full-substance printing is an ideal that may not be suitable for all photographs: the decision to use this criteria is both technical and aesthetic.

## Pushing Film

Film sensitivity (or film speed, or ISO) is determined by physical qualities of the silver halides in the emulsion. Increasing developing time ("pushing" the film) will not significantly increase the amount of usable silver density in the darker shadows. **Push development** or using a stronger developer will usually produce more silver only in the fully exposed areas. Pushing film in-

creases contrast in the middle and high values and when printed produces a picture with very dark shadows. Figure 5.10 shows a typical "pushed" Tri–X negative print, with visible grain and good contrast in the middle gray values, but little or no separation in dark shadow areas. Pushing T–Max does cause more increase of midshadow densities, compared to other films, but also inevitably raises highlight densities sharply and easily increases contrast to an unprintable level.

## Characteristic Curve Defined

The gelatin of the emulsion, the plastic film itself (and the dye it often contains), the subcoatings, and the antihalation layer all absorb light. These become the **film base** density. Further, even without deliberate exposure there is always some developed silver density because of heat, X ray, and other radiation exposure. This non-image density is called **fog**. The sum of these is the *film base plus fog (FB+F)* density. Modern 35mm films have a FB+F density of about 0.28 to 0.30, which means that 50% of the light is absorbed by the film base plus fog.

Figure 5.11 shows how a typical silver halide emulsion responds to increasing exposure and standard development. There are five areas of this curve one needs to understand:

- **Threshold** is the minimum exposure required to begin an increase in density above FB+F. The threshold determines the ISO number of the film as it reflects the absolute amount of light required to produce a density change above FB+F. A very weak light source may be measurable (by eye or by using a very sensitive light meter) and not be strong enough to expose the film to threshold.
- **Toe** is the nonlinear part of the curve where density increases above threshold, but the density changes are unequal. This is the critical area that defines how the darkest shadow subjects will be

recorded. A one-stop increase of exposure at the toe will produce a density increase as little as 0.02 with a high-speed film or as much as 0.06 with a low-speed film. A "long" toe will tend to crush shadow values together but also permits some latitude in estimating exposure. A "short" toe will require more precise placement of exposures. The toe may be as much as three-stops exposure range (for the typical high-speed film like T–Max or Tri–X) or as little as one-stop with a slower film like Pan F.

- **Straight line** describes the important large midsection of the H & D curve where all but the darkest shadow subjects will be recorded, plus the middle and high values of the scene. Each stop increase of exposure will produce a density increase between 0.08 and 0.12 for a 35mm negative. The straight line portion of the H & D curve extends about 8–12 stops exposure range. The slope of the straight line section of the curve can be easily changed by varying development. Increasing development will make this slope steeper, or increase contrast.
- **Shoulder** is the area of decreasing sensitivity found in any silver emulsion where an increase of exposure does not produce an increase of density. The shoulder also reveals the maximum density a given film and developer will produce. Tri–X shoulder values are typically about 1.90–2.10; T–Max shoulder densities will rise much higher, approaching 3.0. Like the toe, this may be gentle or sharp.
- **Reversal** (solarization) occurs with all silver emulsions, which can be so heavily exposed to light that the latent image is actually reversed and *less density* is produced with *increased* exposure. This effect was common in the nineteenth century, and there are many pictures from that time that show the sun itself as a black disc, hence the term *solarization.*

Figure 5.10
**Untitled. Blake Madden.** Photograph made with Tri–X rated at EI 1600, developed in Edwal FG7 with sulfite. "Push" development produced contrast and grain and vigorous tonal separations.
Courtesy of the photographer.

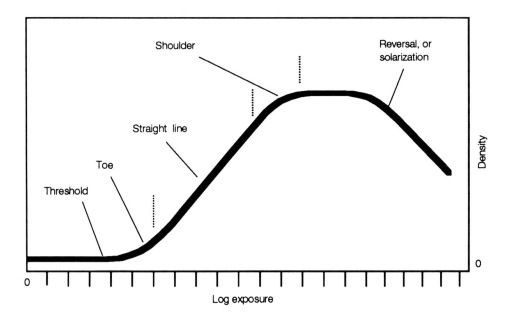

Figure 5.11
The *D log e* or characteristic curve, which describes the developed response to light exposure for all silver halide emulsions.

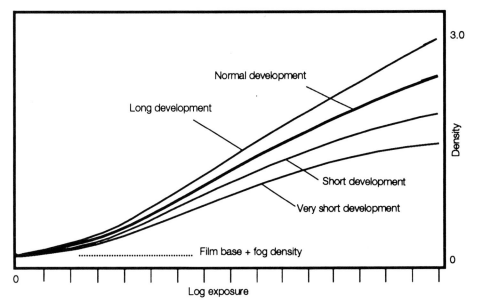

Figure 5.12
A *family of curves* reveals how films exposed identically produce much different highlight densities by changing the developing time.

What a characteristic curve does not reveal clearly is that it is the result of various exposures but only *a single developing time.* As developing time is changed, important density variations appear in the curve, as shown in figure 5.12. This curve reveals that density in areas with little exposure (shadow values in the negative, or highlights in the print) does not increase much with increased development compared to heavily exposed areas.

A film's characteristic curve is always a sum of the emulsion used, the developer formula, and developing time, temperature, and agitation. Figure 5.12 illustrates how the density of an emulsion changes as developing time is changed. Notice that all four curves originate together at FB+F. The units of exposure are each twice the previous one. If the initial exposure or *basic* unit of exposure is one second, then the *second* unit would be two seconds, the *third* unit would be four seconds, the *fourth* unit would be eight seconds, and so on. These exposure units can be related to opening the lens of a camera a full f–number (or stop) for each new exposure, or doubling the exposure shutter time.

Increasing developing time always increases contrast (overall density range), but does not usually significantly increase useful shadow detail. The tabular grain technology of the

Kodak T–Max films seem to provide *some* increase in lower densities with increased development, but the overall density range, or contrast change, is still proportional to the development.

A problem with metering darkest detailed shadow values to determine exposures (as described earlier) is that 35mm films tend to crush shadow details. Shadow separations are lost because of interaction between the soft toe in the characteristic curve for high-speed films, the desire for minimum density negatives to minimize grain, and the characteristic curve of contrast grade 3 paper (normal grade for 35mm enlargements). Other film formats (2 1/4 × 2 1/4 and sheet films) have inherently better shadow separation; this (in combination with the different tonal scale of grade 2 paper) produces richer shadow details, which in turn justify the metering of darkest detailed shadows to determine exposure.

---

- Talbot's experiments with tiny ''matchbox'' cameras in 1835 eventually led by 1839 to a **negative-positive** process where a paper negative was used to make many similar prints in what he later called the **calotype.** This is the beginning of photography as we know it.
- Other photographic processes were also discovered or publicized in 1839,

Figure 5.13
**Height and Light in Bruges Cathedral, 1907. Frederic Evans.** The original print is on platinum paper. This historically important printing process used a very slow iron salt, which required a printing exposure of twenty minutes or more in direct sunlight and therefore could only be used to make contact prints. The long tonal scale preserved detail in very contrasty subjects with dark shadows and intensely lighted highlights.
Library of Congress.

including Bayard's direct-positive photographs and Mungo Ponton's bichromate prints.
- Frederick Scott Archer's wet-plate process using collodion on glass invented in 1851. Glass eliminated the texture of the paper negative, and the wet-plate negative printed on albumen paper became the fatal competitor to the daguerreotype.
- Wet-plate chemistry was modified to create tintypes; cheap photographs flooded the market in the 1860s and effectively devalued photography.
- Flexible dry film invented in 1887 by Hannibal Williston Goodwin; this freed the photographer from the fragility and weight of glass plates and encouraged the development of hand-held cameras.
- **Kodachrome** marketed in 1935. It was a three-color process that used *dye-*

*coupling development,* in which a dye image was created during development of the silver metal image.
- **Polaroid** diffusion process announced by Edwin Land in 1963, permitting anyone to make prints without a darkroom or handling of photographic chemistry.

All contemporary high-speed films have a gentle slope of toe, which is significant in that a soft toe minimizes shadow detail separation. The only way to avoid this (which may be seen as a problem of aesthetics) with high-speed films is to *increase exposure* when dark shadow details must be clearly separated. Increasing exposure moves important shadow details up the curve, beyond the toe. It must be remembered that *any* extra exposure also increases grain size.

## Matching Negatives to Paper

Each contrast grade of printing paper is designed to make the best prints from negatives with a matching density range. Figure 5.14 shows typical characteristic curves for enlarging paper. Note how these rise from near zero reflective density (where almost all the light is reflected) to a density of about 2.0 (the maximum black that most papers produce). The figure also shows density ranges for high-, normal-, and low-contrast 35mm negatives.

Correct highlight and shadow values in a print are produced easily when the negative density range (contrast) matches the paper's characteristic curve. If the negative has a longer density range (is more contrasty), then you must print either to retain highlight details or shadow details or manipulate mechanically by burning and dodging or chemically by special developing to retain detail. For a straight print from a flat negative, either the highlights are correct and the shadows are weak, or the shadows have the correct darkness and the highlights are gray.

Figure 5.15 suggests the compromises for printing mismatched negatives and paper contrast grades. Given a high-contrast negative, either the highlight details may be printed correctly, and the shadows fall into black,

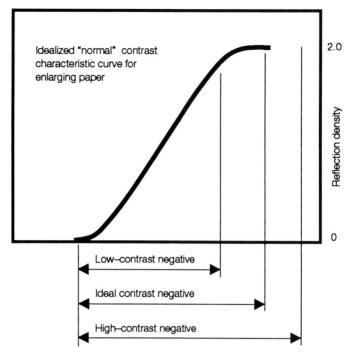

Figure 5.14
Prints look best when negative densities match paper contrast. Idealized density correspondences between 35mm film negatives and printing paper contrast grades are shown.

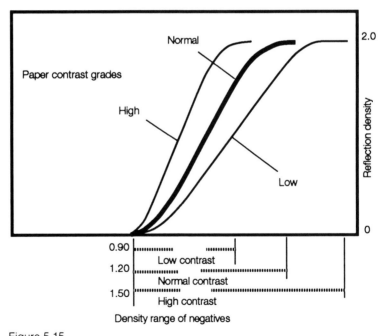

Figure 5.15
Compromises must be made when printing negatives of different density range with only one contrast grade of paper: either the print will appear flat or detail will be lost, depending on the contrast of the negative.

Figure 5.16
**Marvin Hagler in Training. Ben Brink.**
Dynamic graphic separation of middle gray
values results from moderate increase of
development time for Tri–X film, although
tonal detail is minimal in both the very low
and the light gray tones.
Courtesy of the photographer.

or the shadows may be printed correctly and the highlights lose detail. This is not always bad. In figure 5.16, a slightly contrasty negative clearly separates the three runners from the background; the photographer chose to print for shadow detail and let the distant shoreline blend into the sky.

## Contrast Control
## Exposure/Development

Neither the shadow (ISA) nor the highlight (HTH) meter readings produce the actual shutter and aperture settings used for contrast control exposure and development. If the indicated ISA exposure were used, the film would be overexposed because the meter "thinks" it is measuring a middle gray

value. The actual exposure given the film is usually a stop less than the ISA-indicated exposure.

The meter readings are taken to calculate the luminance range, or contrast. The ISA is one stop darker than the Gray Card. Converting the ISA-metered exposure to the actual exposure means setting the shutter or aperture *one stop less* than the indicated ISA exposure. Simply remember that correct film exposure is determined by the scene's shadow areas.

Look at the characteristic curve in figure 5.12 again and observe how middle value and shadow densities (just left of the midpoint of the curves) also decrease as development time is decreased. Contrasty scenes require shortened development and the re-

duced development time will somewhat thin even important shadow densities.

A contrasty scene will require less highlight density, and negative highlight density (and contrast) can be reduced by shortening the developing time. This is called **compression** development.

Compensate for reduced shadow density in contrasty scenes (caused by shortened development) by increasing exposure slightly (reducing the EI). When contrasty subjects are photographed, the EI reduction can be done either by resetting the ISO number of the camera manually, or changing the DX adjustment to a minus number.

When flat scenes are photographed—and the development is increased to compensate—*less* exposure is needed. Flat scenes can safely use one stop less than the ISA-indicated exposure. Put another way, a flat scene requires less exposure and more development than a normal scene, while a contrasty scene requires more exposure and less development.

## Estimating Contrast by Eye

Nothing can replace the accuracy of a precision meter measuring light from the subject when estimating contrast, but the educated eye can approximate the results of shadow and highlight metering. When the subject is lighted by daylight, contrast can be adequately estimated by examining the quality and sharpness of shadows cast by the subject:

- Normal scenes have visible, but soft-edged shadows.
- Flat scenes have shadows with little or no definition.
- Contrasty scenes have wire-sharp shadows.

Figure 5.17*A* is a normal scene and the shapes of shadows are just visible. Figure 5.17*B* shows the exposure indicated by an incident meter. The meter does not indicate contrast; the photographer must make that decision. Subjects of differing contrast often have identical incident light meter exposures.

The same scene is shown in figure 5.17*C* later, when the light direction changed and the contrast increased. The contrast in the foreground is flat—as determined by the absence of well-defined shadows—and the overall contrast is normal. The *same exposure* was indicated by incident-light metering. The resulting negatives were printed for similar middle gray values.

a.

b.

Figure 5.17
**a.** Defined shadows with soft edges suggest a normal contrast scene. **b.** A digital-display, silicon-cell, battery-operated incident light meter. A shutter speed is chosen and the meter indicates the appropriate f–stop. **c.** As light changes, contrast changes: the foreground is now flat, without well-defined shadows, but the overall contrast (including the background fence) is normal. Developed on the same roll as **a,** the scene was printed for similar middle gray values, resulting in darkened shadows.

c.

## Grouping Exposures for Contrast Control

Compromise development (table 5.2) will allow negatives from a variety of lighting situations to print easily, even though roll film does not permit developing each negative to fit a different luminance range. When you begin photographing with a roll of film, make a note of the starting contrast conditions and expose the complete roll of film with a choice of similar contrast-range scenes (i.e., ones that are within one contrast grade either way). Develop the film for the *average* condition.

Keep careful notes on exposure ranges and contrast predictions until your system is working correctly. Perfecting contrast control with 35mm film also requires you to keep developer temperatures and agitation patterns the same from one roll to the next. It may take several rolls before you begin to be comfortable with the selection demands that utilizing contrast control imposes on you, because one cannot shoot "any old thing" without regarding the contrast as well as the minimum exposure.

## High-Contrast Scenes

Contrast evaluation is complicated by scenes that appear contrasty but in fact are composed of two normal (or even flat) scenes: one brightly lit, the other in shade. Both the brighter and darker scenes will suffer when a compromise development is attempted. The best solution is to recompose the picture, separating bright and dark areas into separate photos.

Figure 5.18
**Untitled. Paul Teeling.** Before Ellis Island was rebuilt by the National Park Service, the long-abandoned immigration center was photographed and this decaying flag was discovered. A hand-held reflected light meter measured shadows at the left to determine exposure, and the film was developed in less than the manufacturer's recommended time to limit highlight density and retain detail in the sunlit patch in the foreground.

Courtesy of the photographer.

---

**Table 5.2    Small Camera Contrast Control Compromises**

Scenes of similar contrast can often be clustered on a single roll of film; a compromise development (see chapter 7 for development notes) will permit good prints to be easily made. *Use the first development ratios for T-Max films, and the second for other films.*

| Description of Scene | Development Ratio | Paper Grade |
|---|---|---|
| Very flat | | 4 |
| Flat | 110–125% normal | 3 |
| Normal | | 2 |
| Flat | | 4 |
| Normal | normal | 3 |
| Contrasty | | 2 |
| Normal | | 4 |
| Contrasty | 80–90% normal | 3 |
| High contrast | | 2 |
| Contrasty | | 4 |
| High contrast | 70–80% normal | 3 |
| Very contrasty | | 2 |

Many scenes are more contrasty than the eye sees. Almost all indoor scenes illuminated by artificial light are quite contrasty. Likewise, most outdoor scenes under direct sunlight and with sharp shadows are contrasty. High-contrast scenes require *more* exposure than flatly lit scenes.

## Summary

Meters are used to evaluate subject luminance range (or contrast) and this data suggests development. Both reflected light and incident light meters are useful. An incident light meter may often suggest more accurate overall exposures, given the fact that the reflected light metering must be interpreted. Reflected light meters can be used to separately measure shadow and highlight luminances and these readings used to calculate contrast by counting the difference between indicated exposures, stated in f–stops. Contrast may be estimated without a meter when the subject is in daylight by studying the quality of cast shadows.

Negatives exposed for adequate shadow detail and developed for correct highlight densities enable one to produce acceptable prints with little manipulation during printing. The ideal 35mm negative is defined as having minimum density while retaining shadow detail, and a detailed highlight density that is just translucent when viewed by reflected light. Such a negative will print easily on contrast grade 3 paper and produce a full-scale, full-substance transcription of the original scene.

Negative shadow densities are determined by exposure, and typical highlight densities are subject to the brightness range of the subject (and are modified by development, as outlined in chapter 7).

## Discussion and Assignments

Choosing a subject, finding the best moment, getting an effective angle of view, exposing and developing the film correctly—these are basic problems in black-and-white or color photography, small camera or view camera, photojournalism or art photography.

Many exposure errors blamed on light meters are in fact errors of interpretation, or errors in using the meter. Most errors are caused by metering targets that are too small or by accidentally including light sources in the meter's view. Unfortunately, some photographers cannot learn to use a reflected light meter and produce accurate exposures, while others have similar problems with incident light meters.

Some TTL metering systems will underexpose high-contrast scenes because the bright light sources in the picture overwhelm the meter's light averaging calculations. When photographing indoors or in very contrasty outdoor lighting, and a full-scale, full-substance photograph is desired, reduce the EI setting by half (i.e., when using an ISO 400 film, set your meter at 200 or adjust your DX control to +1). This one-stop correction will usually provide a minimum safe exposure, and compensate for metering error.

### Assignment 1

Work with a friend or another student. Take a picture of her/him as your first picture. Now trade cameras and photograph your partner again. Feel the difference the camera makes in finding the picture, choosing the moment to make the exposure, and how that "feels," especially when the other camera is a different make or model.

### Assignment 2

Without going more than 50 feet from the front door of your house, dormitory, or classroom, find examples of these five photographic subjects:

- Patterns of light and shade
- A subject close to the camera relating to another subject far away from the camera
- A central, visually isolated subject
- A person photographed with the sun over your shoulder, from one side, and from behind the subject
- Something photographed *out of focus* on purpose

### Assignment 3

Photographic subjects exist everywhere. Make note of what time you get up in the morning and what time it gets dark at night. Calculate the number of minutes between these (in the winter it may be as little as 600, in the summer as great as 900); divide time by 36. This number will vary from about 15 to 25 and will be the time in minutes between your exposures.

Load your camera with a 36-exposure roll of T-Max 400 or HP5. Expose a frame every unit time (15 to 25 minutes) for the entire day. This means that wherever you are when that unit of time is up, look around you to find a photograph. It may be an object, or a discovery of form, or a relationship between things (people, objects, light and shape, etc.). Avoid saying to yourself "that's a good subject," or "that's a dumb thing to photograph." Discover what can be seen in the time and place where you are.

### Assignment 4

Meters vary in their sensitivity to kinds of light. Compare Gray Card and white card readings using your TTL meter and at least one other, different reflected light meter. Compare the meters under sunlight, tungsten, and fluorescent light. Make careful notes of the indicated exposures, and analyze which meters indicate greater or lesser exposures.

### Assignment 5

Use TTL metering, an incident light meter and a hand-held reflected light meter. Find a scene of normal contrast, one which has large, easily meterable target areas, and reasonably stable light (where light conditions are not changing minute by minute). Using the TTL meter, calculate an exposure for the scene the way you normally would, and expose two identical frames. Cover the lens and expose a blank frame. Use the incident meter and calculate a new exposure *without referring to your previous exposure calculations.* Expose two identical frames and one blank frame. Finally, using the reflected light meter, calculate a new exposure, and shoot two frames and one blank. Repeat this with contrasty and flat scenes. Develop the roll normally (as described in chapter 7) and examine the developed film.

Refer to your exposure notes and see which metering method produced the most accurate exposures for each of these scenes. When there is an error, analyze what you did and why that result occurred.

## Notes

1. A halide is a compound of metal and certain gases. When exposed to light, the bond between these elements is weakened; in the developing solution, the weakened bonds are destroyed. The result is an image composed of silver metal, held in place by the gelatin of the emulsion. 2. **Candela** is a scientific term that has replaced *candle* in defining light intensity. Light intensity used to be defined by the amount of light that a candle (of a specific size and material) produced when burned under specific conditions. 3. *Middle gray* refers to the Kodak 18% reflectance neutral Gray Card, which has a psychological value of appearing midway between black and white. It has a reflective density of 0.74. The *18% reflectance Gray Card* and *middle gray* terms are interchangeable. This card offers a repeatable standard metering target, especially useful where there is no meterable subject. A problem is that some TTL meters produce correct exposures (with EI equal to ISO) when the camera's meter is measuring Caucasian skin (with an average reflectivity of about 32%) rather than an 18% Gray Card. This is almost a full stop difference of exposure.

# 6 Negative Development

Figure 6.1
**Portrait of a Signpainter in His Office.**
**Arnold Gassan.** An example of exposing
much more than TTL metering suggested
(to retain detail in the furniture) and
using shortened development
to keep contrast down.

## Darkroom Clothing

Before beginning any darkroom work, you need to obtain starting equipment (table 6.1) and you need to consider your work clothes. Use a chemist's apron to protect good clothes. Photographic chemicals stain easily and fixer creates brown stains: the silver salts dissolved in fixer discolor and are set by heat and light. Do not wear wool, polyesters, or other synthetics in the darkroom. They generate large electrostatic charges that attract dust, which will cling to the film.

## Preparing Chemicals

You will need film developer, stop bath, film fixer, and water. The basic photographic solutions are outlined in table 6.2. Developer chemistry is described in detail in chapter 11.

No photographic chemical is benign; any of them will cause discomfort if splashed into the eyes, or if the fumes are inhaled. Avoid breathing chemical dusts! Powdered chemical dusts are also dangerous to all photographic papers and films.

Photographic developers and fixers are compounds of several different chemicals and parts of the compound may dissolve at different rates, so stir the solutions steadily until you are sure *everything* is mixed. A plastic bucket may be used to mix powdered developers or fixers. The powders should be poured smoothly into the water and stirred continuously until everything is dissolved. When mixing liquid concentrates, be careful to avoid splashing them.

Many standard developers are sold in concentrated solutions that are diluted when used, but a number of popular formulas are available only in powder. Fixers are sold in both liquid and powder versions. Both the liquid and the powder compounds store well at room temperature if they have not been opened or mixed with tap water. The solutions should be mixed in rooms with good ventilation, but not in the darkroom itself.

Most photographic chemicals dissolve best in warm water, but some of the components may be weakened if the water is too hot. The best temperature for dissolving most powdered photographic chemicals is 100–125°F. If the water is colder, the chemicals will dissolve much more slowly, and may be reluctant to dissolve at all. Mix all powdered developers twenty-four hours before you expect to use them, to be sure they are fully dissolved. Because hot water is needed to dissolve the dry chemicals, mixing ahead of time also lets them cool to working temperature before they are used.

Start mixing with about two-thirds the total volume of liquid desired. For example, if a gallon package of D–76 is being mixed, begin with 70–80 ounces of water at 125°F. Cut open the chemical package, pour in the powder in a smooth stream, and stir constantly until it is dissolved. Adding chemicals too fast often will produce insoluble lumps (which means something is missing from the final solution).

Liquid concentrates should be mixed in a similar way, except the water should be at working temperature. Liquid concentrates also need to be stirred well, to ensure that they are evenly dispersed.

**Table 6.2   Photographic Solutions**

**Dilutions and Use**

Photo chemicals are sold in liquid concentrates or as dry powders that are mixed to prepare **stock** solutions. Concentrated stock stores well and is diluted with tap water to *working strength* just before being used. Most contemporary developers and some other solutions are dumped after being used once, a process often referred to as "single shot" use.

Dilutions are always indicated as a ratio of *stock to water*. D–76 developer, for example, is usually used 1:1 or 1:2, meaning one part developer to one part water, or one part developer to two parts water. Edwal FG7 developer is most often used 1:15, meaning one part developer to fifteen parts water.

**Developer**

All powdered silver process film (and paper) developers begin to decay soon after they are mixed with tap water. Aging is slowed if the solution is kept in the dark, at moderate temperatures (55–70°F), and away from air. Store developer stock solutions in brown bottles in a cool place (clear bottles may be used if stored in the dark), and try to keep the bottles full. A partial gallon of a developer will last much longer if divided and stored in quart bottles, each full to the top.

Many excellent film developers are sold. Kodak D–76 (sold in powder form), T-Max and Edwal FG7 (in liquid concentrate) are suggested. These are very stable, dependable, and generally available, with excellent properties. D–76 is probably the most widely used film developer formula available.

T-Max is a high-energy developer for both normal development and for "pushing" film. Edwal FG7 is a concentrated liquid developer with excellent storage properties and is both a "high-energy" developer (for pushing development) in strong dilutions and a "fine-grain" developer in weaker dilutions.

**Stop**

Acetic acid is used with film and prints to stop the developing action. The acid is sold in concentrated forms and is diluted when used. The most popular stop has a yellow pH indicator added, and is sold by Kodak as *Indicator Stop Bath.*[1]

**Fixer**

Fixer is a mild acidic compound that removes the unused silver halides left over from making the negative or print image. Fixer is made in powder and liquid forms. The powder uses sodium thiosulfate, and the liquid version uses ammonium thiosulfate, which takes the silver halides into solution more quickly. Therefore, the liquid concentrate is called **rapid fixer**.

Rapid fixer concentrate is diluted with less water when used for film, or with more water to make a more dilute solution for prints. Fixers may also contain hardening chemicals that tan the emulsion, making it more resistant to scratching. Because hardener cannot be premixed with the concentrated rapid fixer, a separate solution is provided (in a little bottle); this must be thoroughly and carefully stirred in when the working solution is mixed.

Figure 6.2
**Untitled. Alison Lake.** A graphic scene where the absence of shadow details enhances the distortion of space in the photograph.
Courtesy of the photographer and Agfa-Beseler.

### Health Hazard

Avoid prolonged contact with all photographic solutions to minimize damage to your hands. Rinse your hands in running water after each immersion, and dry them frequently. Use lanolin-rich hand creams after handling photo chemicals to restore skin oils.

If small white blisters appear on your hands, you may be *Elon sensitive*, and you will have to avoid contact with developers that contain it. Elon is a chemical in the developer that causes skin rashes in about one in eight people.

Hydroquinone may produce a *contact dermatitis*. If skin rash or chapping occurs, then protect yourself by using disposable surgical gloves.

Elon: Kodak D–76 and most other developers in powder form use Elon. The same chemical is sold by others as **Metol.**

Acetic Acid: The fumes of concentrated acetic acid (sold both as **glacial acetic acid** and as **Indicator Stop Bath**) may cause severe irritation to your nose and mouth. Avoid splashing it as direct contact with the liquid could damage your eyes. Do not breathe fumes from the concentrate.

Note: Never touch your contact lenses while working with any photographic solution until you have washed your hands thoroughly with soap and hot water.

## Handling Film, Reels, and Tanks

Exposed film must be handled in total darkness. Special small darkrooms for removing film from cassettes and loading on developing reels (separated from the safe-lighted printing darkrooms) are provided in most schools. When working at home, it is possible to use an ordinary closet. An alternative is to use a photographic **changing bag.** This is a lighttight cloth bag with short sleeves through which your hands enter a work space. Changing bags can be used anywhere and eliminate the need for a film-loading darkroom.

If you try using an ordinary closet as a film-loading darkroom, close the door and stand inside for several minutes, until you see where light enters. Usually, this is only under the door and, in older houses, through the keyhole. Mask keyholes with duct tape; place a rolled towel at the foot of the door to block light. If light leaks around the edge of the door itself, hang a blanket over the frame.

Prepare to develop film by locating electrical switches so you can find them in total darkness (because you will have to turn on the lights after your film is loaded). Arrange your film and developing equipment safely and logically on a dry work space so all of it can be found in the dark.

Contemporary films are too sensitive to light to be handled under any visible safelight. You will find you need practice in handling film in the dark and getting it smoothly onto the developing reels. The film must be removed from the protective canister, loaded onto a reel, and put into the developing tank in complete darkness. Experiment with a test roll before you start working with your "real" film. Buy a 24-exposure roll of the cheapest film you can find (sometimes photo stores have special sales of "out-of-date" film) and use it for trial loading.

Figure 6.3
a. **Untitled.** Three men in the 1870s commemorated a special time together on a "tintype," which was a cheap small (2″ × 3″) piece of black lacquered metal with a grey-brown image on it. Special cameras were used that had several lenses because there was no negative and each tintype was unique.

**b. Untitled. Reni Zietz.** The 35mm camera
allows the photographer to abstract
culturally revealing moments without the
subjects ever being aware of being made
part of another's vision.
Courtesy of the photographer.

If you have never worked in total darkness before, try putting out everything you need, then close your eyes and pick up and put back each piece of equipment until you can do it easily. There is hardly anything more heartbreaking than to get the film out of the cassette and fumble around in the dark only to knock the reel and tank off, be unable to find them in the dark, and in a thoughtless panic turn on the lights before you find a safe place to put the naked film. Finally, be certain no one can open the door to your film darkroom before you have the film fully protected from light.

Stainless steel reels and tanks are best. The metal tank permits easy adjustment of the solution temperature when it needs to be warmed or cooled. The reels have the least contact with the film and do not inhibit developer flow during agitation. Plastic reels almost always produce density variations when vigorous agitation is attempted, and most plastic tanks prohibit agitation by inversion.

Use a bottle opener to pry off the end cap from the film canister. See figure 6.4 for details. Remove the plastic spindle with the film curled around it, find the tapered end of the film, and remove it (either tear it off or cut it off). Place the end of the film carefully in the center of the developing reel, holding it in place with the clip provided or with pressure from your thumb.

Film is often damaged when being wound on developing reels. Take a moment and be sure the film is centered between the wire spirals and then wind it smoothly onto the reel. A strong, straight pull on the film after it is hooked at the center of the reel will "seat" the film in the spiral and get it flowing correctly onto the developing reel.

The first quarter-turn of the film onto the reel is critical. When it is correct (the film is aligned with the reel), the rest of the loading will follow smoothly. Improper starts cause film to buckle and stick to itself two or three turns later. Creases in the undeveloped film act just like an exposure to light and cause changes in the emulsion, which develop as crescent-shaped marks that show as white in the print.

Figure 6.4
**a.** Before turning out darkroom lights, measure developer temperature. The developer can be brought to temperature in the tank and placed in a water bath until the film is in the tank and the lid closed.

**b.** The metal end cap on the Kodak cassette is easily removed with a standard bottle opener.

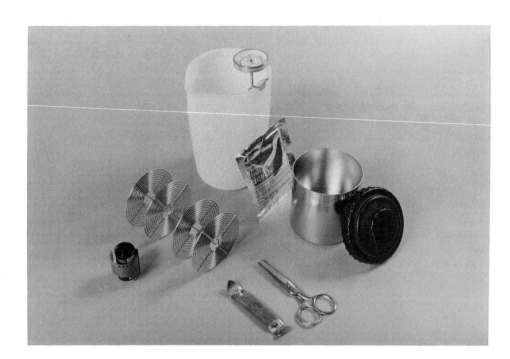

**c.** Film, scissors, metal reels, daylight developing tank, film developer, graduate, thermometer, and bottle opener are equipment needed to develop film. Both reels should be used and the tank filled—even if only one roll of film is being developed.

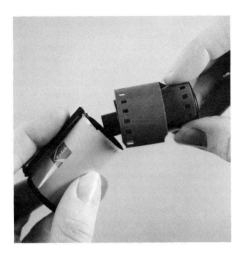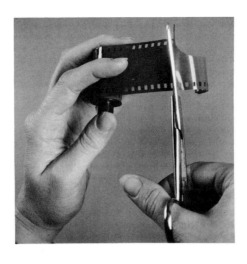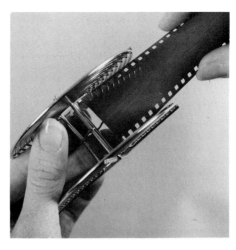

d. Remove film from the cassette but keep it furled.

e. Remove the tapered film.

f. Locate the center of the reel (either an opening or a clip) and feed film into it. Hold film tightly in place with your thumb while starting the film straight.

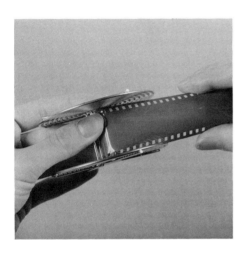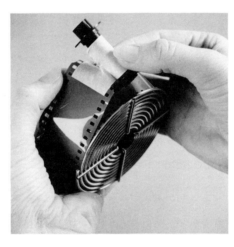

g. The first quarter-turn is critical: if not centered and straight at the start, the film will buckle within two or three turns.

h. When film is on reel, tear off the spindle and discard it.

i. Place loaded reels in tank with developer at working temperature. If it is not practical to have developer in the tank then prewetting with plain water will maintain tank temperature and prevent streaky development.

j. Water, developer, stop bath, and fixer can be poured into the tank through the lighttight top. Developing can be done in ordinary room light.

## Prewetting Film and Developer Temperature

It is best to place the film directly into the tank containing developer. The development temperature is more precisely known if the developer is measured in the tank, rather than in a graduate and then poured into the tank.

Fill the tank with developer (fig. 6.4*B*) and, if necessary, bring it to the correct temperature by running hot or cold water around the outside of the tank. Then—*in the dark*—load the film on the developing tank reels and put the reels in the already filled tank. Put on the lid and agitate the tank.

When you do not have a wet darkroom, the film can be placed in a dry tank and the developer poured in through a lighttight opening in the lid (fig. 6.4*J*). Irregular development often occurs when the developer is poured onto dry film. It is best to **prewet** the film by filling the tank with tap water at the desired developer temperature. Prewetting also eliminates risk of air bubbles forming on the film—these retard development and produce small black spots on the prints. Agitate vigorously by continuously inverting the tank for thirty seconds, then pour out the prewet water without removing the lid.

Figure 6.5 is a blank processing record sheet to use for your own system.

## Development and Contrast Controls

Different developers often produce slightly different results. All films respond to these controls:

- Developer formula
- Time
- Temperature
- Agitation

Each of these affect negative development. Increased strength of the developer, increased developing time, increased temperature, and increased agitation cause increased contrast.

### Table 6.3   Film Processing Time Table

This table outlines typical step-by-step times. Times will vary for each film/developer combination. The table illustrates T–Max 400 35mm film in Kodak T–Max developer. Kodak data guides offer times for both 68°F and 75°F; the 75°F is chosen because that is most popular with professionals. If Kodak D–76 is used, the solution made from the powder should be diluted with equal parts of water shortly before developing the film, and the developing time should be increased to eight minutes. All processing steps other than developing time will remain the same, no matter what film or developer is used. T–Max film requires double the fixing time of other films. Use Edwal Hypo Chek every three or four rolls to insure fixer strength.

| Step | Time | Process |
|---|---|---|
| 1 | 1 minute | Prewet: water at 75°F; agitate continuously |
| 2 | 4–7 minutes | T–Max developer at 75°F (shorter time = less contrast). Initial agitation 8–12 sharp inversions of tank. Rest until start of second minute, then 8–12 inversions each minute. |
| 3 | 30+ seconds | Stop bath or water rinse, with continuous agitation |
| 4 | 2–4 minutes | Fix, with continuous agitation—T–Max requires twice the fixing time as other films, and *rapidly* exhausts the fixer. |
| 5 | 30 seconds to 1 minute | Fixer remover solution: use continuous agitation |
| 6 | 1–2 minutes | Fill developing tank, agitate, dump. Repeat ten times. (Alternative: use negative washing tank and wash at 75°F for 1 minute.) |
| 7 | 1 minute | Fill tank with distilled water and wetting agent: rock tank gently |
| 8 | | If necessary, squeegee film. Hang to dry |

Developing time starts when you *begin* pouring the developer in, and ends when the last of the developer pours out of the tank. Place the developing tank and all storage graduates (with stop and fixing solutions) in a **water bath,** a photo tray two-thirds full of water at the working temperature, which will keep all of the solutions at the same temperature.

Agitation is the process of moving the developer in the tank in a controlled way. Hold the tank and invert it about its own center as shown in figure 6.6. This produces very even development. Plastic reels and other kinds of tank agitation often produce uneven density streaks across or along the film.

Agitation should be done for short times, at regular intervals, and in exactly the same way each time. There are subtle differences in the film image if agitation is done for ten seconds each minute, or five seconds each half minute. Either is acceptable. There is no need to begin agitation by banging the tank on the sink to displace bubbles even when not prewetting because the vigorous, controlled motion of the developer destroys bubbles.

Correct agitation replaces the developer in the film emulsion at regular intervals, but does not create excess turbulence around sprocket holes or reel wires, or permit continuing currents in the developer. Correct agitation also avoids turbulence near the edges of the film, which will appear later in the print as light and dark scallops related to the film sprocket holes.

Some film and developer combinations do not respond well to vigorous agitation. Kodak's Technical Pan film in Technidol developer and *any* high-speed film in Acufine developer require *very gentle* agitation (one to four inversions of the tank each minute, rather than eight to twelve). If more agitation is used, the result will be very high contrast, streaks, and—with Acufine—very large grain.

Film Processing Record:

Date  _____

Film  _____

Developer (note dilution):  _____

Agitation: Normal  [     ] Notes:

---

| Step | Time | Process |
|------|------|---------|
| 1 | 0 to 1 minute | Prewet (water at _____ °F) |
| 2 | _____ | drain prewet |
| 3 | _____ | developer ( _____ °F) |
| 4 | 30" minimum | stop bath |
| 5 | 10" | drain stop bath |
| 6 | _____ | fix (open tank after 1 minute to check clearing, fix for <u>twice</u> clearing time) |
| 7 | 30" | rinse (fill and dump twice) |
| 8 | 1 minute | hypo clearing solution |
| 9 | _____ | final wash |
| 10 | 1 minute | wetting agent |
| 11 | _____ | dry |

Figure 6.5
A film processing record that can be
photocopied and used to keep track of
your own film processing.

Figure 6.6
Small tank film agitation is best when the
tank is inverted sharply about its own
centerline, back and forth. This motion stirs
the developer but does not allow
continuing movement.

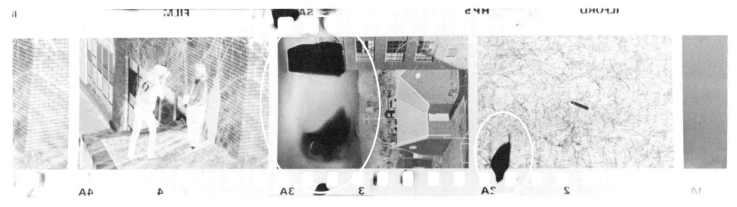

Figure 6.7
A bad start in the film track will cause the film to buckle and touch: patches will not be developed or fixed. These unprocessed spots are opaque and pink or gray to the eye (the color of unprocessed emulsion).

Agitation and development problems are shown in figures 6.7 and 6.8. The effect of development on film is shown in figure 6.9.

Increased contrast will happen when the frequency of inverting the tank during agitation is increased. Decreasing the vigor or frequency will decrease contrast. When lower contrast is desired, it is correct to agitate less (either by inverting the tank fewer times each minute, or by agitating less frequently, or both). The effects of a particular agitation method are best decided by examining your pictures.

Solarization is commonly (although incorrectly) used to describe partial tonal reversal of prints or negatives, caused by re-exposing them to light after partial development. This apparent reversal should be called the Sabbatier effect (discovered in 1862). Partly developed emulsion is desensitized by the developer itself, and re-exposure fogs only the original shadow areas; as development is continued, partial reversal of the original density scale is achieved.

## Stop Bath and Fixing Film

Prepare to stop development by opening the small lid of the developing tank; you should begin draining the developer ten seconds before the developing time is finished. The tank will be empty when the timer reaches zero.

Figure 6.8
Film not exposed (usually because it was not correctly engaged in the take-up reel) will be clear but have edge frame numbers and emulsion identification. (These are printed with light at the factory.) When the processed film is totally clear and *does not* have edge numbers, fixer has accidentally been used instead of developer. (Sooner or later, it will happen!)

Development should be halted by soaking the film in a very weak acetic acid solution, called **stop bath**. The stop bath is prepared from concentrated acetic acid and it overwhelms the basic pH developer solution. The film stop bath may be reused until the pH indicator color turns from yellow to purple, which indicates that it is exhausted, but often it is discarded at the end of each developing session. When the stop bath has been drained, fill the tank with fixer. No rinse is needed between the stop and the fixer, as they are both acidic.

The film is no longer sensitive to light after the film is fixed because image silver has been developed and the remaining silver has been removed.

Fixer dissolves the unused gray silver halides in the emulsion. Removing these prevents the developed image from changing after development. Removing the unused silver hal-

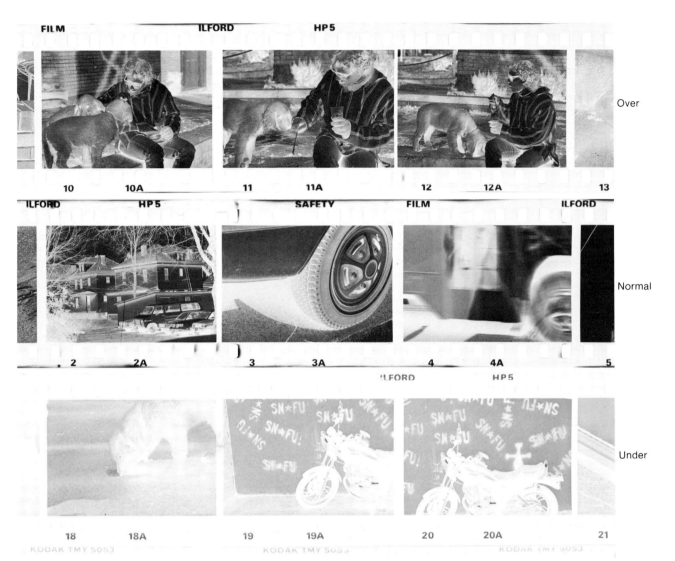

FILM          ILFORD          HP5

10  10A          11  11A          12  12A          13

Over

ILFORD  HP5                    SAFETY          FILM          ILFORD

2  2A          3  3A          4  4A          5

Normal

18  18A          19  19A          20  20A          21

Under

KODAK TMY 5053          KODAK TMY 5053          KODAK TMY 5053

Figure 6.9
Effect of development on film: under-, normal, and overdeveloped film. Overdeveloped film has more obvious shadow details and opaque highlights. Correctly developed film has shadows that are a little darker than the unexposed edges of the film and highlight areas that can *just* be seen through. Underdeveloped film has no *printable* detail in shadow areas and highlights that should be dense can be easily seen through.

ides is called **clearing,** and the film should be fixed for *twice the clearing time.* The clearing time will vary from one film to another. A **hardening fixer** is used for film because the negative is less easily scratched. Besides removing the unused silver halides, film fixer dissolves the antihalation dye in T–Max films.

- Hurter and Driffeld in 1888 complete primary research into how photographic materials respond to light and how the *actinic* quality of light can be measured and predicted. The work results in *sensitometry* in photography and in the first dependable photographic exposure meters, called *actinometers.*
- **Autochrome** color transparencies marketed in 1907.

- Simple silver salts are not really sensitive to anything but blue light, making color photography a futile dream until color sensitivity of silver salts was created by Hermann Wilhelm Vogel in 1873 by adding dyes to the emulsion.
- **Technicolor** developed in 1915. It was a three-color print and/or transparency process using both silver and bichromate technology, where colloids are hardened by exposure to light.

## Film Washing Aids and Film Washing

The fixer itself would eventually destroy the silver image if left in the emulsion. After fixing the film, rinse it once with plain water by filling the tank with water, dump it, and then refill the tank with a hypo clearing solution. Though often referred to as a "fixer remover," the clearing agent does not remove the fixer from the emulsion, but chemically transforms it into a compound that will wash out easily. Without this, wash times are quite long, and even extended wash periods will not remove all sodium thiosulfate.

You may efficiently wash negatives by using a washing aid and a negative washer (a plastic cylinder with a hose, which injects water at the bottom) for one to two minutes. A tested, safe alternative is to repeatedly fill the film tank with water, agitate, and dump it. As little as ten fill-and-dump cycles will safely wash film. This method is the most economical for water consumption. Putting the tank under a faucet and letting water pour into it (even for a long time) *is not* a safe washing technique and is also very wasteful of water.

## Final Rinse and Drying

With wet film, the least handling is the best, but water must be removed from both sides of the film to prevent spotting. This can by done by rinsing it with a wetting agent before hanging the film to dry. As a water drop dries, a varying pattern—which cannot be removed—is formed in the emulsion. A wetting agent breaks the surface tension and allows the water to drain smoothly from the film, minimizing the risk of water drops standing on the emulsion. If there is sediment in the final rinse water, it also may be necessary to wipe (or squeegee) the film (fig. 6.10).

Prepare final rinse by adding a wetting agent to water, per the instructions on the bottle. If you have hard water or dirty tap water, use bottled or distilled water for the final rinse. Pour

Figure 6.10
The blank end of the wet film can be folded over a drying line and held in place safely by an ordinary clothespin. When local water conditions require film be wiped, a plain viscose sponge is wet with the final rinse and squeezed dry. The sponge is then dragged gently down the film to remove all surface water and dirt.

the wetting agent into the final rinse water and stir gently, then pour the rinse over the film in the tank and agitate gently (to avoid foaming) for thirty seconds. Dump the tank. (Be sure to wash the reels in hot water after the film has been removed for the wetting agent will coat the reels and make it hard to load film.)

The film may be dried on the reel in a forced air dryer, but it will be easier to store if hung straight. Hang your film in a dust-free place for drying. Ordinary snap-type clothespins will hold the film securely if the top of the film is wrapped over the drying line. If your wash water is quite clean, nothing further is needed.

Many city water supplies have some fine suspended solids, and buildings with iron plumbing also generate fine particles that will adhere to the wet negative. These later appear on the print as white spots. Although there is some risk of scratching, each side of the film should be carefully wiped down with a clean, damp sponge, fresh Chem–Wipe, or Photo–Wipe to remove excess water.

Figure 6.11
Cut film into 5- or 6-frame strips, and trim the corners at one end of each strip.

## Store and Identify Negatives

Take film from the line as soon as it has dried. Hold the film by the edges; never touch the image area (on either side). Dirt and skin oils damage negatives.

The film base often has a pale purple color. This is the remaining traces of the **antihalation** dye from the back of the film, which is put there to improve tonal quality. T–Max film may have some color after processing, but the dye has no noticeable effect on the print.

Carefully cut the film into strips of five or six frames (fig. 6.11). The image is contained in the emulsion, a thin layer of gelatin and silver. It is less reflective than the film base, or support side, of the film. To see the picture "correctly," the film should be viewed from the base side, with the emulsion held away from you.

Place the film strips in plastic storage sheet slots (fig. 6.12). Plastic protective sheets are a convenient way to store film and are punched to fit regular three-ring binders. The storage sheets are thin and transparent enough that good proof prints can easily be made without handling the negatives individually. Contact proof sheets made from the plastic storage sheets can be three-hole punched,

**Figure 6.12**
With sharp corners removed, the film strip slides easily into a slot in the protective plastic film storage sheet. Caution: the plastic storage sheet can cause scratches to the film if roughly handled.

**Figure 6.13**
Film storage sheets and contact proofs can be kept in storage boxes to keep both negatives and proofs together and safe from dust.

filed in a three-ring binder with the negatives, and stored with the negatives in a storage box (fig. 6.13).

Identify negative sheets as they are created. Descriptive titles are useful, and dates are usually important. A simple, but useful, filing system is to date all negative sheets (and their proof prints) chronologically. For example, 01–14–91–A–32 would identify frame 32 of the first roll developed on January 14, 1991.

**Table 6.4  Recommended Film Developers**

| General Use Developers | Fine Grain Developers | High-Energy Developers |
|---|---|---|
| Kodak T-Max: med/fine grain (high energy and fine grain) | Kodak Microdol-X (half ISO film speed) | Kodak T-Max: fine grain, high energy |
| Kodak D-76: med/fine grain (similar to Ilford ID-11) | Edwal FG7[a] (1:15 w/ sulfite) | Acufine Acufine[b]: medium (2–4 × ISO) |
| Kodak HC-110: med/fine grain (high acutance) | Edwal Super 20 (best for Panatomic-X) | Acufine Diafine[b]: fine (3+ × ISO) |
| Kodak Hobby-Pac: med/fine grain (similar to HC-110) | Kodak Technidol[b] (for Technical Pan only) | Kodak Hobby-Pac[a] medium (w/ sulfite: grain, speed = Acufine) |
| Edwal FG7: med/fine grain (dilution 1:3) | | |

[a]To prepare 500 ml of developer, almost fill a 35mm film plastic canister with sodium sulfite.
[b]Reduced agitation is used: invert tank three or four times in the first thirty seconds, then invert gently from one to four times at the beginning of each minute of development.

## Choosing a Developer

There are general purpose, fine-grain, and high-energy developers (table 6.4). There are many good developers available, but most photographers settle on one or two. Experiment carefully with a new developer by exposing test rolls on subjects that interest you. Developers differ in subtle ways in how they transform silver halides into images.

Make a five-frame test section; expose the rest of the film on typical subjects. Process the film and determine that it is, in fact, exposed and developed correctly, then print it. Compare grain produced by the new developer and your old standby. Compare the prints with prints made from negatives developed in your standard developer for differences in shadow area details, middle tone separation, highlight details, and overall contrast.

Finally, when you experiment with a developer, make test exposures of "unimportant subjects." Beginning photographers often expose important pictures based on hearsay, and are disappointed at what actually develops.

## Compromises in 35mm Contrast Control

The 35mm camera offers the photographer great freedom in being able to make pictures easily and almost anywhere, and to carry great quantities of film in a small space. In exchange, exposure-development or contrast control over individual pictures is compromised. Small camera photography almost always involves compromises between quantity and quality of exposures.

Imagine that you have exposed thirty-two frames of photographs of the beach, where the sand and the water reflect light into the shadows, limiting the brightness range of the subject. You leave the beach, but pass through woods, where you photograph something in deep shadow.using dappled light coming through the branches. Even though the exposures are longer, the *brightness range* is much greater than on the beach.

In the darkroom, you must decide whether to develop the film for the beach scenes (low contrast) or for the wooded area (high contrast) in order to make the best possible prints. Which to preserve; which to sacrifice? The high-contrast scenes are together and at the end of the roll, so they *could* be cut off and developed separately. But what happens if some of the scenes in the deep wood were made on the way to the beach, more were made after exposing six or seven frames on the beach, and the rest of the roll is exposed near sundown when contrast may be high or low?

## Questioning Negative Developing Times

The following experimental tests require print-making skills. Work through chapter 7 and then come back to this section.

Manufacturer's recommended film developing times are only suggestions, although they are based on rigorous testing. As mentioned earlier, the recommended negative development times provided by Kodak are for diffuse density printing, and are usually 10–20% *longer* than needed to produce correct condenser enlarger printing densities.[2]

Because a poorly exposed and developed negative will hardly ever yield a good print, despite the variety of printing controls that are available, it is better to test a developer or film for yourself than unquestioningly accept data sheet recommendations. This is in part because there are many variables your processing provides. Small differences in agitation technique or developing temperature have significant effects on film contrast.

Expose and develop at least one experimental test roll for any new film and developer combination to find a suitable developing time for your negatives. Laboratory correctness is not the goal, but finding a negative that fits your personal criteria is. Work to discover the degree of contrast you find pleasing in your prints, and don't forget that the type of enlarger you use will affect negative development.

## Film Exposure and Development Test

Any combination of film and developer can be easily tested and evaluated. A simple but adequate test (see figure 6.14) requires using only five consecutive frames of film on several rolls. Expose these as follows:

1. Hang a large piece of white paper where it is evenly lighted. This may be in open shade or direct sunlight, pinned to a wall, or hung from a clothesline.

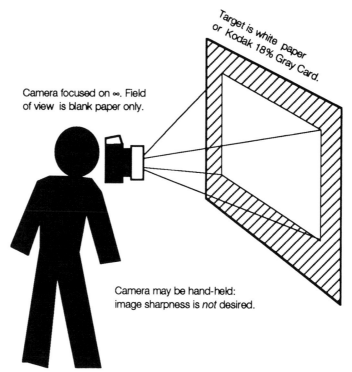

Camera focused on ∞. Field of view is blank paper only.

Target is white paper or Kodak 18% Gray Card.

Camera may be hand-held: image sharpness is *not* desired.

Figure 6.14
A target sheet of white paper (or a standard 18% reflectance Gray Card) is used to find your personal Exposure Index and developing time. The camera is focused on ∞ to avoid recording smudges and dirt on the target.

Table 6.5    Five-Frame Test Analysis

| Negative | Print | | Corrections |
|----------|-------|---|-------------|
| *Exposure* | *Development* | *Shadows* | |
| 1:  under | under | weak | intensify negative<br>increase paper contrast |
| 2:  under | over | too dark | decrease paper contrast |
| 3:  over | under | weak | reduce negative densities<br>increase paper contrast |
| 4:  over | over | too dark | reduce negative densities<br>decrease paper contrast |

Corrections for Future Negatives*

1: increase exposure 1 stop, increase development 15–25%

2: increase exposure 1 stop, decrease development 10–20%

3: decrease exposure 1 stop, increase development 15–25%

4: decrease exposure 1 stop, decrease development 10–20%

*For T-Max developer, use the smaller corrections; for D-76, use the larger corrections.

2. Stand close enough to the target so that pictures can be made of only the paper; do not photograph your own shadow.

3. Focus the camera on infinity, not on the paper; photograph only the reflected light, not the smudges and imperfections of the target sheet.

At the beginning of photography in 1835–39, the only subjects that could be photographed were those that could hold still during the very long exposures. The time required to make a photograph changed very quickly (even from the first days after Daguerre announced his process to the end of the year 1839), became steadily shorter until the end of the century, then shortened dramatically during this century.

An implied history of what could be photographed is suggested in the following average exposure times (calculated for bright sunlight and an aperture of f–16):

- 1839—2,400 seconds
- 1854—120 seconds
- 1856—30 seconds
- 1880—5 seconds
- 1910—1/10th second
- 1930—1/25th second
- 1960—1/250th second

When the camera is pointed at the paper, write down the indicated meter exposure (just to have a record in case you make a mistake), but actually expose the five test frames as follows (table 6.5):

1. 5 stops *less* than indicated

2. 4 stops less than indicated

3. at the indicated exposure

4. 3 stops *more* than indicated

5. 4 stops more than indicated

Use the rest of the roll of film to expose pictures you want, then process the new film and developer combination, using the manufacturer's recommendation. The film should resemble figure 6.15. If there is no recommended developing time available

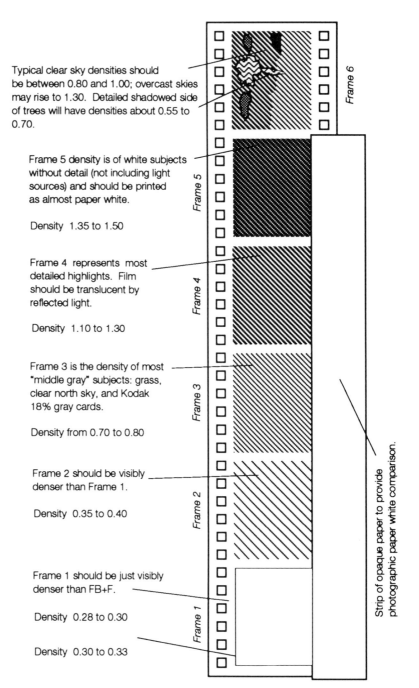

Typical clear sky densities should be between 0.80 and 1.00; overcast skies may rise to 1.30. Detailed shadowed side of trees will have densities about 0.55 to 0.70.

Frame 5 density is of white subjects without detail (not including light sources) and should be printed as almost paper white.

Density 1.35 to 1.50

Frame 4 represents most detailed highlights. Film should be translucent by reflected light.

Density 1.10 to 1.30

Frame 3 is the density of most "middle gray" subjects: grass, clear north sky, and Kodak 18% gray cards.

Density from 0.70 to 0.80

Frame 2 should be visibly denser than Frame 1.

Density 0.35 to 0.40

Frame 1 should be just visibly denser than FB+F.

Density 0.28 to 0.30

Density 0.30 to 0.33

Strip of opaque paper to provide photographic paper white comparison.

Figure 6.15
This drawing illustrates what one should find in an ideal five-frame exposure and development test film.

(this is the usual case when using an Ilford film with Kodak developer, for example), look for instructions for similar film/developer combinations.

Films of similar speed usually respond in similar ways. An ISO 400 film from Ilford or Fuji often makes usable

first-try negatives when developed like a Kodak ISO 400 film. Making a guess at a correct development will at most "ruin" a roll, but the over- or underdeveloped film that might result can provide useful information for deciding what is the correct development range.

Figure 6.16

**a.** Underexposed and underdeveloped film: no separation between first two frames. The contact proof is exposed for correct highlight values (the most dense frame) and FB+F density does not approach the maximum black paper density available.

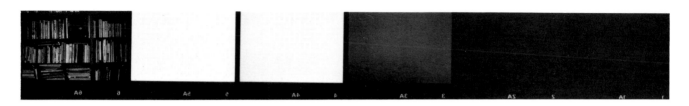

**b.** Underexposed and overdeveloped film: highlight density frames printed for paper white and first visible separation, but underexposed film produces little or no visible separation between the first exposed frames and FB+F.

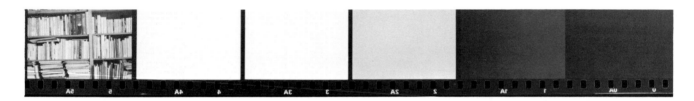

**c.** Overexposed and underdeveloped film: there is more density in the shadows; this would be right for some scenes but may also produce more visible grain.

**d.** Overexposed and overdeveloped film: more contrast and more visible grain.

Make a careful contact proof of the film and dry it. Expose the contact proof so that frame 5 is *just visible* (off-white) on the print. Because the wet emulsion will prevent you from seeing small differences in these gray values, rinse the print to remove fixer, and dry it quickly to evaluate the print exposure before continuing. See figure 6.16 for examples of printing errors that can mislead you in making a correct exposure-development assessment.

## Negative Exposure Checks

Any exposed area on the film itself *should* have slightly more density than the unexposed (FB+F) film surrounding it. It should be slightly more dense because a small error on the side of overexposure is better than a little error on the side of underexposure. It is better to have printable negative detail than to have a negative with minimum grain but no printable shadow detail. But the most common error is to have correct negative density range *and also have overexposed film.*

Examine the film itself. Compare it to figure 6.16. Frame 1 should be just visible when compared to FB+F. If it is *fully* visible, then the film is *overexposed,* and future rolls should be given *less exposure.* To correct this problem, increase your camera EI one half stop: if you were using 400, reset it to 600. If your camera is DX-coded, change the meter adjustment ring to decrease exposure 1/2 stop.

When frame 1 shows *no change* from the surrounding density, the film is *underexposed* and future exposures must be *increased*. Reset the camera meter EI from 400 to 300, or change the DX adjustment +1/2. When frame 1 and frame 2 are the *same value* as the surrounding film, you are *underexposing* a stop or more. *Decrease* the meter EI by half, or change the DX adjustment +1.

## Final Note on Contrast Control

Contrast is determined by the lighting and subjects in the scene, but can be controlled by choice of the developer formula, time, temperature, agitation used, and the developer dilution. Decreasing time, temperature, or agitation, or increasing developer dilution will decrease contrast.

Reduce contrast by lessening the negative development time or agitation, or use a more diluted developer to limit development of highlight densities. Reducing development time will usually cause some loss of density in the middle-value shadows. T–Max developer can be diluted to 1:6 (with developing times approximately doubled) to achieve normal shadow detail while retaining printable highlights.

Longer-than-normal, or extended, development is suggested for low-contrast scenes, and shortened development is suggested for contrasty scenes. Either lengthening or shortening development time suggests inverse changes in exposure. Contrast grouping is suggested as a means of producing 35mm negatives that print easily and well though differing scenes have different contrast.

Negative contrast and overall density may be increased by chemical intensification or reduced by chemical removal of silver. These processes are included in chapter 12.

Figure 6.17
**Morning Light, Denver.** High-contrast scene exposed one stop more than TTL meter indicated and developed 20% less than manufacturer recommended produced a negative that retains printable detail in both shadows and highlights.
Photo by the author.

## Summary

Wear cotton clothes in the darkroom to avoid static charges, which will attract dust to the film, and wear a darkroom apron to protect clothing from chemical stains. Photographic solutions begin to decay soon after they are mixed with tap water. Ageing is slowed if the solution is kept in the dark, at 70°F or below.

Acetic acid is used with film and prints to stop the developing action. Fixer is a mild acidic compound that removes the unused silver halides. Photographic chemicals dissolve best in warm water (not above 125°F). Elon sensitivity is an allergenic reaction to a developing agent, and if rash or blisters appear, you will have to avoid contact with developers that contain Elon.

Exposed film must be handled in total darkness. Stainless steel reels and tanks are best for developing film. The metal tank permits adjustment of the solution temperature when it needs to be warmed or cooled. Loading the metal film reels may be difficult at first, and the first quarter-turn of the film onto the reel is critical.

Developer strength, developing time, temperature, and agitation affect contrast. Although contrast in a scene is determined by the lighting and subjects, it can be modified. Increasing time or agitation increases contrast. Agitation is the process of moving the developer in the tank in a controlled way. The clearing agent does not remove the fixer; it merely makes fixer easier to wash out. After washing, water must be removed from both sides of the film to prevent spotting. Take film from the line as soon as it has dried.

Experiment carefully with a new developer. Hold the film by the edges; never touch the image area (on either side). Compromises between quantity and quality of exposures are inevitable. Manufacturer's recommended film developing times are only suggestions. Use the five-frame test to learn what a film-developer combination might produce. When examining the test film, remember that any exposed area on the film itself *should* have slightly more density than the unexposed (FB+F) film surrounding it.

## Discussion and Assignments

### Assignment 1

Investigate effects of varying development time. Carefully expose a roll of film that has subjects with similar gray values in similar lighting, and then, in the darkroom, remove the film from the cassette and cut it with a scissors into three pieces about the same length. (Yes, you will probably destroy two frames by cutting through them while doing this, but you may save a lot of more important frames later for having done this test.) Store each third of the roll in the plastic film canister that the cassette comes in. (The Kodak canisters with the gray lids are lighttight; unfortunately, the Ilford canisters with the colored lids are not.)

Prepare to develop the film. Develop the three pieces separately, one at a time, at the same temperatures and for exactly the same times. Agitate the first strip of film as suggested in the text. Agitate the second strip by inverting it only twice (instead of ten to twelve times) at the beginning of each minute. Agitate the third strip using another agitation technique (twisting the tank, pumping it back and forth, etc. Ask around—you will get lots of suggestions).

Fix, wash, and dry the films. Contact proof all of them together. Look for differences in contrast (separation of light and dark values), and in uneven densities near the edge of the film (especially near the sprocket holes). Try to figure out what effects are the result of the variations in development technique.

### Assignment 2

Cut off the tapered end of an undeveloped roll of film and place it directly in the film fixer in ordinary room light. Agitate it frequently and keep track of the time while watching the fixer remove the gray undeveloped silver halides in the emulsion. Note the time when the last of the gray is dissolved. The correct fixing time for that kind of film and developer is *twice* the observed clearing time. T–Max films will take much longer than other Kodak films or the Ilford films.

Exposure and development interact and affect grain structure, density, and contrast. The following assignments investigate these relationships.
NOTE: All following assignments require print-making skills described in chapter 7.

### Assignment 3

Photograph a scene at four different exposures:

- 1 stop under the metered exposure
- At the metered exposure
- 1 stop over the metered exposure
- 3 stops over the metered exposure

Finish the roll of film and develop it for the contrast of the majority of the scenes on the roll. Carefully enlarge and print for identical highlight gray values an 8″ × 10″ section from the biggest enlargement you can produce of the full frame of each of the four test exposures. Compare the prints for grain size in the highlights and for useful detail and correct blackness in the shadows.

### Assignment 4

Expose a roll of film to similar scenes of moderately high contrast, using your usual metering method. In the dark, cut the film in half. Store both pieces.

Develop one piece in your regular developer, but for 20% less than your normal developing time. Develop the other piece in your regular developer, but agitate by inverting the tank sharply *only* twice at the beginning of each minute. Fix, wash, dry, and print scenes from both strips of film and compare them for adequate shadow detail and printable highlight densities.

---

## Assignment 5

Expose a roll of film of normal scenes. Cut the film in half and develop one half in your usual developer for the normal time. Develop the second half in a developer that has been suggested by another photographer for a "best guess" time. Enlarge and print similar scenes and compare them for grain, contrast, shadow detail, and shadow separation.

---

## Assignment 6

Ansel Adams popularized the **Zone System** as a way of previsualizing the final print while in the presence of the photographic subject. Subject luminances, negative densities, and print values are linked by "zones." There are eleven, from 0 (black) to X (white). In 35mm photography, zones 0 and I are effectively the same, and these two differ only with large format, contact prints. These names suggest a mental image of *equal density* steps: black, almost black, dark gray, and so on to almost white and white. But the actual gray values created by equal changes of exposure are not like that. Instead, they are crushed together in the shadows and in the highlights, and are very widely separated in the middle values.

Pin a large sheet of plain paper to a wall or hang it from a line. Illuminate it with very even light. Focus the camera on infinity, not on the paper (you are only interested in the light from the paper, not the paper itself). Expose ten consecutive frames on a roll of film. This is an extension of the five-frame test done earlier. (You might wish to expose eleven frames, exposing the first frame at the metered exposure just to create a definite starting place on the film for the test strip.)

The first frame is exposed five stops less than the indicated meter exposure, the second four stops less, etc. Continue until you have exposed ten frames, the last being exposed five stops more than the original indicated exposure. These exposures will produce printing densities that photographically define Zones I through X *in your photographic system*. Use the rest of the roll for other photographs and then normally develop, fix, wash, and dry the film.

Use a mat knife and straightedge to cut off the perforations and unexposed film along both sides of the test frames. Carefully separate the individual frames and reassemble them with their long sides together, taping them neatly together at the edges with Scotch Magic tape. (This tape has very low printing density, compared to glossy acetate tapes.) This assembled strip of film is a negative Zone step tablet, created by your photographic process.

Make a contact print of the Zone density strip, exposing it and developing it for two minutes in normal concentration of developer at your regular working temperature, with continuous agitation. If the exposure is correct, the most dense film (Zone X) will remain paper white, and the next strip (Zone IX) is a just visible gray. There should be a barely visible separation between the black of the "clear" (i.e., film-base-plus-fog frame) and the frame with -4 stops of the indicated exposure. A trial print exposure for most contemporary enlargers (set to illuminate an 8″ × 10″ print) should be between ten and fifteen seconds at f–16.

The differences in value between the two highest zones and the two (or even three) lowest zones are so slight that they probably will not be visible on a wet print. The test exposure should be rinsed and dried before proceeding. When a correct exposure is found, make a finished print.

Examine your dried Zone test strip. Compare the total range of physical steps (black to white) to the range of useful, or dynamic, print values your camera, film, and processing system actually produces. Discover by looking that most of the tonal information in your photographs is found between Zones IV and VII. The darker and lighter values give the midvalues substance and light, respectively. You will find little or no separation between Zone I and III, and very little between Zone VIII and X.

---

## Notes

1. Chemists use *pH* as a shorthand indication of the percentage of hydrogen ions in a solution, which is an index of acidity or alkalinity. The scale is from 0 to 14, and 7 is neutral. 0–7 is acid, 7–14 is alkaline. Strong acids burn skin by combining with the water and then carbonizing; strong alkali damages skin by combining with the fats. Most photographic chemicals are weakly alkaline or acid and will not do immediate damage, but *all photo chemicals* will irritate the skin over time. 2. Kodak technical literature states that reducing contrast for printing with condenser enlargers through shortening their recommended developing time requires "an increase in exposure of one stop" (Current Information Summary, CIS–88, October 1986, p. 11). This implies that the ISO number of a film should be reduced by half when developing for printing with a condenser enlarger if full shadow detail is to be retained in the print.

# 7 Making Contact Prints and Enlargements

Figure 7.1
**Untitled. Reni Zietz.** The gesture of the child echoes that of the statue, and as it is seen by the photographer's eye it is captured by the 35mm camera.
Courtesy of the photographer.

## Contact Print as Record

The contact print is made by laying a set of negatives on the photographic printing paper (emulsion to emulsion) and exposing the paper to white light through the negatives. The most convenient light source in most photographic darkrooms is an enlarger.

A contact print is an economical way to discover what your camera has recorded. The contact proof sheet describes all the photographs on a roll of film. These are easier to examine than the negative images and they present alternative information.

One can study the contact proof to discover which frames have the best exposure, and to evaluate contrast prior to using large sheets of paper. *Contrast* is a term used to describe the range of values from the brightest to the darkest area of a print or a negative.

## Photographic Papers

Today's papers are either **fiber-based** or **resin-coated** (fig. 7.2). The resin-coated (RC) papers have a plastic seal that keeps processing chemicals from reaching the paper base, so that only the emulsion gets wet. The plastic also changes the way the print looks and feels.

Processing time is short because chemicals enter the emulsion only and are washed out quickly because they do not penetrate the paper base. The total wet time for RC papers should be kept short, preferably under ten minutes. Long wet times will allow liquids to penetrate, however, and this will affect longevity and also change the base color slightly. Resin-coated papers are commonly used when production speed is important.

Fiber-based papers lack the plastic seal but have a more "papery" feel, which many photographers find pleasing. Washing chemicals from these prints takes longer. The different brands of papers each has its own look and feel, and each type has special uses.

Table 7.1 Contact Printing

**Standard Darkroom Equipment**

Photographic safelights with Wratten Series OC filter: (OC filter is recommended for most enlarging papers)

Contact print frame: 10" × 12" piece of 1/4" thick plate glass and a sheet of low-density foam

Print tongs (reduce contact with photographic chemicals)

Clean, small towels

Photographic trays: four 8" × 10" or 11" × 14"

Automatic tray siphon or other print washer

Rubber squeegee or viscose sponge

Photographic printing paper: contrast grades 2, 3, or 4; or Kodak or Ilford variable contrast paper and a set of printing filters for that brand of paper

Processing chemicals: Paper developer, Indicator Stop Bath, Rapid Fix diluted for use with print-washing aid

Drying screen for prints

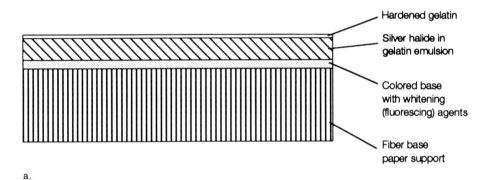

a.

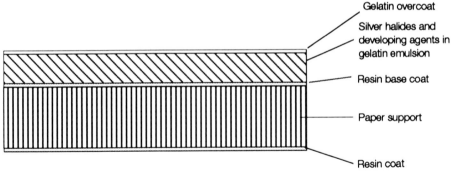

b.

Figure 7.2
**a.** Cross section of typical fiber-based photographic paper.
**b.** Cross section of typical resin-coated (RC) photographic paper.

Photo print papers (both fiber-based and RC versions) are made in **graded contrast** and **variable contrast**. Contrast grades generally available are numbered 1 through 4, with 1 being a very low contrast and 4 a very high contrast. Contrast grade 3 is generally recognized now as being the normal grade for printing 35mm negatives.

Variable-contrast papers consist of both high- and low-contrast emulsions that are sensitive to different colors of light, coated on the same support. They are exposed by coloring the light from the enlarger with colored filters, which are capable of producing different contrast prints from a single sheet of paper, equivalent to printing with several graded papers.

Variable-contrast papers can be used like a graded paper when making a print of an overall contrast—or they permit one to print negatives with areas of differing contrast, such as open shade and direct sunlight. The RC papers and fiber-based papers respond nearly identically to filter controls, but an advantage to fiber-based paper is that they are more responsive to development manipulations.

## Safelights

Photographic papers are very sensitive to light: open all photographic paper packages and handle the paper only under **safelights**. Photo papers are not equally sensitive to all colors of light. Suitably colored filters are made to provide safe lighting for various kinds of film and print handling; for example, correctly filtered yellow-orange light of low intensity will usually not produce unwanted exposure on either graded or variable-contrast papers.

Do not assume a safelight will not cause unwanted value changes. Under some conditions, even safelights will affect the paper—if it is exposed for a long time or if the light is too intense. Use the low-wattage lamp suggested by the safelight manufacturer.

No darkroom should be used extensively without evaluating the safelights as they are used. Like all silver

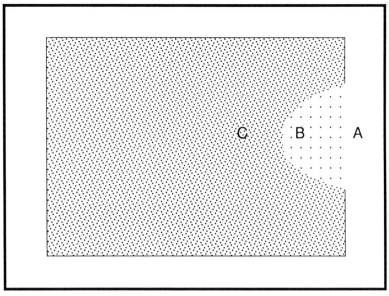

Figure 7.3
Fog paper with a minimal exposure under the enlarger to produce a very pale gray when developed (area B). Area A is protected by the easel frame and will be a *maximum white* reference. On a second sheet exposed the same as the first, place an opaque object on the paper and allow two to three times normal safelight working time before developing. If lighting is *not* safe, area C (the sum of controlled threshold exposure and fog exposure) will differ from area B and then the safelight must be dimmed or relocated.

emulsions, photo paper emulsion has a threshold exposure that must be met before a latent image is produced. Merely laying a piece of paper on the enlarger easel for several minutes and then developing it cannot properly evaluate the risk of fog by safelights that are too bright or placed too close to the work area.

Study figure 7.3 to help visualize a safelight test that works by establishing a threshold exposure with the enlarger as a calibrated source. Set up the darkroom for processing prints. Adjust the enlarger as though you are going to make a contact proof, focused but without a negative. Place a piece of print paper in the enlarger easel and adjust the easel frame so a 1/2″ band of paper is protected from *any* exposure.

Expose the paper to white light for no more than a second under the enlarger set at the smallest aperture possible. Leave the paper on the printing easel and lay an opaque object on the paper as shown in figure 7.3. Leave this assembly for the *maximum time* you would normally be handling paper under the safelight. Develop the paper for two to three minutes; stop, fix, rinse, and dry the print.

There should be a slight, but clear, difference between A and B (see fig. 7.3) because B is a minimum, controlled exposure that created a density just above threshold. If the safelights are too bright or too close to the work area, there will be a small, but definite, difference in density between areas B and C. If area B is not visible, the safelights are appropriate to the working space.

| Table 7.2 | The Enlarger |
|---|---|

**Purpose**

To project light through a negative to form an image on another photographic emulsion

**Components**

Support: a rigid frame to position the head

Head: contains the lamp house, negative stage, light diffusion or condensing system, focusing controls, and enlarging lens

Lamp house: contains an electric light

Diffuser or condenser lighting system: condenser produces more contrast; diffusion requires more contrasty negatives

Filter drawer for printing contrast control filters

Negative stage to hold the negative carrier

Elevation lock for the enlarger head

Focusing control to adjust the enlarging lens

Enlarging lens: controls brightness of projected light

Baseboard: flat platform.

## The Enlarger

The enlarger (table 7.2) is an electrical machine that, for safety reasons, must be well-grounded (through a three-wire power connector). Any enlarger can be damaged by rough handling. Never force controls, overtighten locking knobs, or let the lamp house fall shut. The enlarger should be on a firm table or bench, well separated from the "wet side" of the darkroom in order to avoid damage to negatives and prints when liquids are spilled.

## Preparing the Darkroom

The darkroom can be made ready in white light. As a matter of safety, be sure that light switches for both white and safelights are located away from wet areas. Safety aside, when your enlarger is electrically grounded you minimize dust on negatives.

When working in the darkroom, it is better to have only the chemicals and equipment actually needed out on the working space. This prevents damage by inadvertent spills to lenses, films, and papers. Remember that photographic papers will be damaged by even momentary exposure to ordinary room lights. Turn on the safelight and turn off the white light before opening paper packages.

Figure 7.4
**The World in a Crystal. Bill Andrews.**
Photographing the image of the world made by another lens, the photographer transforms our vision.
Courtesy of the photographer and Agfa-Beseler.

Dust control is always a problem when enlarging small negatives. Darkroom preparations are the same for making the contact proof print and the enlarged print. The clothes you wear can minimize dust: synthetic fabrics generate large electrostatic charges, so wear cotton clothes when handling negatives or making prints.

Set up the darkroom trays for printing (fig. 7.5). Place four photographic trays in the sink if you are printing with fiber-based papers; five if using RC paper. Remember, when using RC paper, the *total* wet time should be kept short.

The first tray is for developer. Although 8″ × 10″ trays can be used for 8″ × 10″ prints, many photographers find prints are easier to handle and there is less risk of damage while agitating them during development if a larger tray is used. There should be at least thirty-two ounces of developer in the tray. Dektol is a popular print developer, usually used in a dilution of 1:2 (although it may be used in greater dilution or at full strength), which means twelve ounces of Dektol stock and twenty-four ounces of water are used.

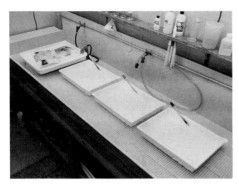

**Figure 7.5**

**a.** Photo trays arranged for printing. The far tray is for storing and washing prints. The near tray has developer, the middle tray stop bath, and the third tray fixer. RC prints would be processed straight through and dried. Fiber-based prints would be stored in the wash tray. All trays are supported on a plastic grid, which allows spilled chemicals to drain away. If wash water runs underneath, it will cool the developer: wash temperature should be at or above desired developer temperature.

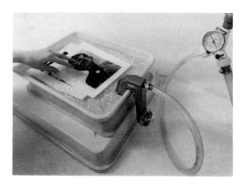

**b.** The inexpensive print-washing siphon works well for washing RC prints (which should have limited wet time) as well as fiber-base prints.

**c.** A plastic slot washer is expensive but washes prints to "archival" standards for maximum permanence.

**d.** RC prints should be squeegeed and hung to dry after a short wash.

Print developing times and print contrast are affected by temperature. As temperature increases, the developing time needed decreases. Most photographic solutions function most predictably at 68–70°F. As the temperature decreases, so does the print contrast. Below 68°F, print developer contrast decreases rapidly. It is better to have the developer be a little too warm than too cool.

When print wash water drains past the developer tray, adjust the wash water temperature to 70°F before starting. The wash water can be used to control the developer temperature, and when it is cold you will make prints that are gray where there should be black.

When getting started, especially in a new darkroom, keep a photo thermometer in the developer tray or beside it and measure developer temperature frequently. If the developer temperature drops, it can be warmed back to correct working temperature by setting that tray in a larger tray half full of water that is 10–15° warmer than the developer.

The second tray contains stop bath, a mild acid solution that neutralizes the print developer and prevents the image from developing further. Stop bath for prints is prepared by adding 1/2 ounce of Indicator Stop Bath to one quart of water. (This quantity can be approximated by filling the bottle cap four times with the concentrated yellow stock.) The stop bath is colored with a pH indicator that changes from yellow-orange to magenta when the tray solution absorbs too much developer; under the darkroom safelight, the stop bath will suddenly appear cloudy and dark and should be dumped and replaced.

The third tray contains print fixer. The liquid rapid fix concentrate can be mixed with differing amounts of water to produce either a film or paper fixer. The print fixer is much more dilute than film fixer, and *does not need* the emulsion hardener contained in the small supplemental bottle of chemicals that is provided with the fixer concentrate. Do not use film fixer with prints as it will tend to bleach them, and do not use film fixer with prints because dyes from the film are absorbed by the fixer.

The fourth tray is either a final rinse (for RC) or a water storage when processing fiber-based paper. RC prints should be washed and dried immediately after fixing. When a number of fiber-based prints are being made, rinse each print with running water for thirty seconds after fixing, and then store the print. Several fiber-based prints can be stored in the fourth tray prior to final washing. Eventually, the print storage tray water becomes a very dilute fixer because each print carries some fixer, and it should be dumped and refilled after every eight to ten prints.

At the end of the printing session, complete the processing of all fiber-based prints by cycling them through a print-washing aid for two to four min-

Figure 7.6
**Untitled Photogram. Marianne Kelley.**
Photograms are created in the darkroom.
They are images made without using a
camera and also show how photographic
paper responds to light. Lay transparent or
opaque objects on print paper. Use the
enlarger or a flashlight to expose the paper.
Objects and light may be moved during
exposures.
Courtesy of the photographer.

utes. Then wash all prints thoroughly
before drying. Washing time is controlled by the thickness of the print
paper, the washing technique, and the
longevity desired. The print washing
times recommended by the manufacturers of the print washing aids are
suggested. These are reasonably short
and are water conserving.

In summary, the fiber-based paper
print is fixed for a total of two minutes
in rapid fixer after development and
stop bath, rinsed for thirty seconds
and stored in water—or agitated in
fixer remover in the fourth tray for one
minute, washed for at least five minutes in a print washer and put to dry.
The RC print is fixed, washed for the
time recommended by the manufacturer, and dried immediately.

## Expose a Contact Print

The enlarger is a calibrated light
source (i.e., provides a repeatable exposure) for making contact proof
prints. Plug the enlarger into a
*grounded* power outlet. Prepare to
make a proof print by putting an empty
35mm negative carrier on the negative
stage, with a 50mm lens in the enlarger.

A cautionary note: when the enlarger is turned on and the negative
stage open, light spills out, which
might fog photo paper left out of its
package in your work area. Fog is non-
image exposure of the photo emulsion,
caused by light and heat. To avoid this
risk, lift the enlarger head, place the
negative carrier onto the negative
stage, then close the enlarger and turn
it on.

Most black-and-white enlargers
now on the market create a field of
light of about equal brightness. Correctly exposed and developed negatives require approximately the same
exposure whether one is making a contact proof or an enlargement (with the
enlarger illuminating an 8″ × 10″ area
on the **baseboard**). Knowing these
facts, one can easily make a usable
8″ × 10″ print from most enlargers on
the first try.

Turn on a correct safelight for the
paper you are using; turn off the white
lights. Find the *focus* and *time* switch
on the enlarger timer and turn it to
*focus*. Open the lens to maximum aperture by turning it gently. Raise the
head of the enlarger along the vertical
support track until there is a rectangle
of light on the baseboard just a bit

larger than 8″ × 10″ paper. Focus the enlarger by moving the lens up and down with the focus control until the edges of the rectangle of light are sharp.

Dim the light by "stopping down" the lens to f–11. A contact proof exposed on contrast grade 3 fiber-base paper for fifteen to twenty seconds at this aperture will usually produce usable contact or enlarged prints from properly exposed and developed negatives.

When making a contact proof, you want to:

1. Expose the paper enough so that there are details in the light gray areas of the picture when it is developed

2. Choose the right contrast grade of paper so that dark areas in the picture have some visible detail

It is tempting to buy "cheap" paper for proofing, but this is a false economy. It is best to use the same kind of photographic paper for the proof print as for the enlarged print because exposure and contrast estimation can then be made from the contact proof.

Open the photo paper package and remove a sheet of the paper. The emulsion side is smoother than the back, and the paper will normally curl slightly toward the emulsion. You may use a soft lead pencil to write the exposure, aperture, and exposure time on the back of each print. Write lightly and stay near the edge of the print. (Too much pencil pressure will change the emulsion and cause a pale image of your writing to appear in the picture.)

Place the paper emulsion up on a plastic foam pad on the enlarger baseboard. Cover the paper with the negatives, placed emulsion down (fig. 7.7). You may wish to use a plastic storage sheet to hold the negatives, but as you gain more experience with these materials you will find a better quality proof can be made without the storage sheet.

Cover the negatives and paper with a heavy sheet of glass, which is used only for making contact prints.

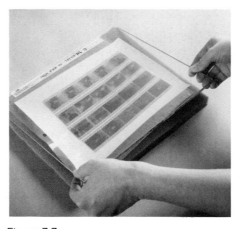

Figure 7.7
**a.** An excellent inexpensive contact printer made from a piece of 1/4″ plate glass with ground edges and a sheet of plastic foam. Put the foam on the enlarger baseboard, place paper emulsion up, and lay a sheet of negatives on the paper, emulsion down.

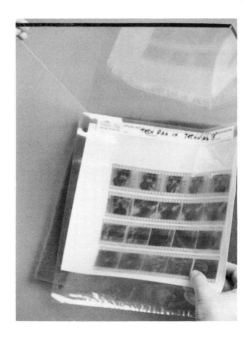

**b.** Place the glass firmly on the negative and print paper. The weight of the glass is sufficient to hold the negatives in close contact with the printing paper, producing a sharp, clear proof.

Set the enlarger timer to expose the paper for fifteen seconds. You can use variable-contrast paper with no filter for proofing, but the advantage of using a numbered filter is that both exposure time and contrast are known when you plan your enlarged prints.

Place the correct contrast-numbered filter in the enlarger (if you are using variable-contrast paper). Start the timer to supply directed light of repeatable intensity exposing the paper through the glass and negatives. When the timer turns off the enlarger light, remove the glass, store the negatives safely, take the paper from the enlarger to the sink, and develop it.

## Develop the Contact Print

Normal developing time varies with the paper used: for most RC papers it is from thirty seconds to one minute. Do not try to guess developing times: use a clock with a second hand or a lab timer to measure development.

Slide the paper smoothly into the print developing solution, wetting it evenly and quickly. Fiber-based papers respond well to development time controls and may be usefully developed as little as one minute or as long as four or five minutes. However, many RC papers have developing chemicals in the emulsion and consequently these papers are not very responsive to development time changes (though some new RC emulsions will produce richer blacks if developed longer).

Agitate the print during development. Agitation should be done constantly. In general, print agitation cannot be overdone. Inadequate agitation produces dull prints, with little contrast and a brownish color.

Print agitation *can* be done by rocking the tray constantly from side to side and end to end. Rocking the tray means to lift one edge of the tray sharply, then put it down. This creates a wave that scrubs the emulsion, replacing old developer with new. Lift all four edges of the tray in rotation. Mild back-and-forth rocking is not enough. More vigorous agitation consists of lifting the print, allowing it to drain for a second or two, and then rewetting it.

Tongs can be used to handle the paper in solutions. An advantage of tongs is that they keep your hands out of the chemicals. A disadvantage is that tongs easily scar or crack print emulsion.

Watch the photograph emerge from the blankness of the paper during development and watch what time it takes for the first hint of dark shadows to appear and for the image to *seem* complete. Compare this to the standard development time. Until you have had a lot of experience, develop your print for a standard time (1 1/2–2 minutes), unless it is obviously so dark or so light that you cannot see important detail.

The print is overexposed if an overall image appears in less than fifteen seconds. If there is no detail within individual frames after forty seconds, the proof sheet is underexposed and will need at least another half stop of exposure.

Evaluating wet prints takes a lot of practice. Do not try to judge exposure or contrast under safelight in the darkroom. Fix and rinse the print, then examine it under white light before presuming to make a correction.

## Stop, Fix, and Rinse the Print

After development is complete, lift the print and let developer drain back into the tray as long as the developer runs off in a steady stream. It takes about five seconds to drain an 8″ × 10″ print. Lay or slide the print carefully into the stop bath. Agitate it there for twenty to thirty seconds. Lift and drain the stop bath from the print, and place it in the fixer.

Fiber-based prints should be agitated for the first thirty seconds, and then every twenty to thirty seconds until fixing is complete. Do not exceed maximum fixing times recommended by the maker of the fixer. Rinse off excess fixer and store it in a tray of water until printing is done. RC prints should be agitated continuously in the fixer, removed after a minimum fixing time (as suggested by the paper manufacturer), washed, and dried.

The minimum fixing time recommended by the manufacturer is best for all prints. The reason for this is that after the correct minimum fixing time,

no additional silver salts are removed from the print, some insoluble chemical salts often are added to the print, and with extended fixing, some of the image itself is bleached out by the fixer. The longer the print is in the fixer beyond the necessary fixing time, the weaker and more unstable the remaining silver print image.

## Chemical Use

About fifteen prints of good quality can be developed in a quart of working-strength, diluted developer. Many more prints *can* be made from the developer, but they will progressively use less of the silver available, producing prints with weaker shadows, and there is also often a real color change and the print takes on a brownish cast. In addition, there is an increasing chance of stains (unfortunately, these often are visible on the print only after it has dried).

Stop bath exhaustion is known when the pH indicator changes color from yellow to purple. The "feel" of the print also provides an effective estimate of stop bath strength. The freshly developed print feels slippery; the acid stop bath changes this within three to five seconds to a crisp, rubbery feeling. When this fails to happen, replace the stop bath.

Fixer removes the unused silver salts. A quart of fresh fixer will safely fix about twenty-five 8″ × 10″ prints. As seen in the darkroom, there is no obvious color change as the fixer becomes exhausted (although if examined in daylight, the absorbed silver salts make it look pale yellow). Using Edwal Hypo Chek is an economical way to determine if the fixer is effective without affecting the fixer itself. Detailed instructions on the bottle describe how to take a sample of the hypo and add a drop of the testing fluid and observe the change that occurs to measure fixer exhaustion.

Prints treated in exhausted fixer will produce irregular tan spots within a few days where the silver salts that

were not removed discolor in the light, and the entire print often will turn pale brown within a few months. Prints that are improperly fixed and then heated in a dry-mounting press (see chapter 4) will usually show tan or brown spots immediately.

Fiber-based prints are interleaved—pull a print from the bottom and lay it on top—for the recommended time in the fixer clearing solution and then washed. Although the fixer clearing bath has a pale purple color when exhausted, it is ultimately more economical to use it once and dump it: the solution is less expensive than remaking prints that develop hypo stains. When the prints are thoroughly treated, drain each carefully and place it in the print washer.

When printing is done for the day, dump the working-solution developer in the tray. It is both partly exhausted and heavily oxygenated and does not keep well. (If you are going away from the darkroom for some time and plan to return to work, float a clean, empty tray on the developer solution to prevent contact with the air and it will be usable when you return.)

Dump the stop bath—like the print washing aid, it is inexpensive and more easily remixed than stored and reused. Keep track of the number of prints that have been fixed because it is usually worth saving. A gallon of fixer can be used for about a hundred 8″ × 10″ prints before it is unsafe. Keeping a record of the number of prints processed will let you know when it is necessary to replace the fixer.

Brown spots on clothing used in the darkroom are assumed by beginners to be "developer stains" because they have the color of exhausted developer. They are, in fact, spots of silver-laden fixer that has been splashed (usually when the fixer is being poured back into a storage bottle). These spots are invisible when the clothing dries; the complex silver and sulfur compounds do not wash out easily and the chemicals turn brown after the cloth is washed and dried.

Figure 7.8
**Untitled. Michelle Kindel.** Careful posing and use of environmental lighting are essential to this record of an introspective and self-conscious moment.

Courtesy of the photographer and Agfa-Beseler.

These washers are also expensive and bulky.

The active chemical in fixer suggested by John F. W. Herschel in 1839 was called **sodium hyposulfite** and was given the nickname *hypo*. Although the correct chemical name was **sodium thiosulfate**, the nickname is still commonly used.

With the help of print washing aids and interleaving prints every minute, the washing time for adequate permanency of prints can be reduced to five minutes, but for archival storage longer times are used. At the end of the wash, drain each print, place it face up on a smooth sheet of plastic (you can use the bottom of a smooth tray), and wipe off the surface water with a squeegee or sponge.

A simple test can be made at this time for residual fixer, before the print is dried. Place a drop of undiluted Kodak **Rapid Selenium Toner** on the white border of the print emulsion. The toner itself has a pale tan color, but there should be no significant color change in the spot after two to three minutes. If the spot darkens or changes color, the fixer remover and wash steps were inadequate. The print should be treated with print washing aid again and rewashed. Prints fixed and washed even for the short times suggested here will last for many years.

Prints must be dried in a dust-free place to avoid having dirt embedded in the emulsion. Fiber-based prints can be dried face down on clean nylon screens, or even on a clean, lint-free bedsheet. Photo grade blotters are sold for drying fiber-based prints, but eventually any blotter will become contaminated with fixer, and that destroys any hope of permanency. Resin-coated prints can be dried (face up) on nylon screens or hung to dry on a line.

Fiber-based prints will begin to curl as they dry. However, they can be flattened and then kept flat if they are taken from the drying rack as soon as they are dry to the touch, before they curl a lot. Place them face down on a glass or Formica surface and cover with a moderate weight for a day or two and they will stay flat.

## Washing and Drying Prints

A useful and inexpensive print washer is the **Automatic Tray Siphon.** This simple device vigorously washes prints by jetting water across the top of the tray, swirling the prints around and drawing it from the bottom of the tray, maintaining a constant water level. The washer's limitation is that no more than five or six prints should be washed at a time. There is no obvious physical reason more prints cannot be put in the tray, and it is tempting to add more, but they simply will not wash thoroughly. For thorough washing, they must also be interleaved frequently, moving the bottom print to the top.

Each print added to a wash tray brings new fixer with it. Safe print washing time when using a tray is counted from the moment when the *last* print is placed in the wash water. Batch washers, where a large number of prints tumble together in a drum, cannot be trusted to provide thorough washing. The best print washers consist of vertical slots in a plastic frame, with water entering at the bottom. Prints are isolated from each other and water flows upward past each print.

## Using the Contact Proof Print

When the contact proof is too dark, too light, or sloppily made, it fails to provide much information and is both expensive and useless. The individual frames will be similar in value if your original negative exposures were correct. Take some time and study the pictures.

The properly made contact proof has several uses. It is:

- A record of your pictures
- An exposure guide for making enlargements
- A predictor of printing contrast grade
- A record of how you saw the subject then
- A guide to the way your vision of the subject changed

A unit exposure increase is called *opening up a stop,* a photographic shorthand term meaning to increase the lens opening so that twice as much light passes through. Doubling the exposure time is the same as opening the lens a stop. If the highlights are almost visible, try increasing the exposure time by 50% (e.g., from fifteen to twenty-one seconds for the second proof print). A full stop increase is often not needed, and if not it is easier to change the exposure time than to find a place on the aperture ring that is "half-way" between stops.

The brightest subjects in your photographic scene had some visible detail (which only disappears in direct light sources), and this detail should be apparent in the print (fig. 7.9). If proof print image of clouds, light concrete, white houses, or white shirts lacks detail, the print does not have enough exposure (fig. 7.10). If there is no detail at all in these highlights, you may wish to make a second print and allow more light to pass through the negative. Increase the exposure by opening the lens to the next aperture (e.g., from f–11 to f–8), and expose another sheet of paper.

Figure 7.9
Contact proof is exposed enough to reveal highlight details, and that exposure is noted on the back of the print. The contrast of the negative and paper match, and the film sprocket holes are just barely visible against the black background. When enlarged on the same contrast grade of paper, these negatives will produce a print of correct contrast.

Figure 7.10
Underexposed proof print lacks detail in highlights and has a gray (rather than maximum black) sprocket pattern.

When highlights are dark gray and shadow areas are black, the proof has been overexposed (fig. 7.11). Expose another sheet of paper, but *stop down* (reduce the lens opening) to the next aperture setting to decrease the amount of light onto the printing paper. Cutting the exposure time in half is the same as stopping down a stop. It is useful to think of a half-stop change as a 25% reduction (in this example, from fifteen seconds to about eleven or twelve seconds).

## Contact and Enlarged Print Contrast

The contact print is an example of diffuse density printing. When a negative of correct density range is printed by contact and correctly exposed and developed, the visual separation between FB+F density and the sprocket holes (where there is no density) should be slight, but visible. The sprocket holes in the print should be *just visible* when viewed in good light.

The contact proof print has inherently *less* contrast than an enlarged print from the same negative would have—when it is printed with a standard condenser enlarger. The difference is close to, though not quite, a full paper contrast grade. The enlarged print from a correctly exposed and developed negative—printed on the same contrast grade paper—will have more contrast; when exposed for correct highlight detail it will show *no separation* between negative FB+F and maximum black in the contact proof.

Overdeveloped negatives have increased contrast; these will produce proof prints in which shadow details and the film perforations are black (fig. 7.12) when the print is correctly exposed (i.e., *when the highlights have detail*). They may be saved by using a contrast grade 2 paper (or filter).

Figure 7.11
Overexposed proof has dark highlights and the sprocket holes have merged with the unexposed FB+F.

Figure 7.12
High-contrast proof has highlight values that are okay, but the sprocket holes have merged with FB + F film. There is *nothing wrong* with prints that look like this, but a proof print is always less contrasty than an enlarged print made on the same contrast grade paper and this proof suggests the negatives themselves are overdeveloped.

Underexposed, underdeveloped negatives (or both) have diminished contrast. When printed for correct highlight details, the print will show the unexposed edge of the film as a clearly visible gray band. The holes and the space between the film strips are the only areas of the proof print that approach a maximum black (fig. 7.13).

Underdeveloped negatives produce a proof that is flat and gray: remake the proof using a contrast grade 4 paper (or filter).

## Expose and Develop an Enlargement

### Table 7.3  Enlarging Equipment

**Standard darkroom equipment plus:**

Magnifier to study contact proof sheet and negatives

Easel to hold printing paper on baseboard

Sheet of plain white paper for focusing

Camel's hair brush, or air burst cleaning product

Focusing magnifier for enlarger

Cardboard, masking tape, stiff wire, and scissors to make dodging and burning tools

## Choose a Negative

Examine the contact proof sheet to find a frame of film that interests you and that also has good printing possibilities. Using the contact proof sheet is easier than looking directly at the negatives because you can see the picture rather than the reverse pattern of densities in the negative.

When first learning to print, you might wish to consider these when choosing a negative:

- Sharpness of focus
- Correctness of exposure (adequate shadow detail)
- Correct development (translucent highlights)

None of these are *necessary* for an interesting photograph, but when you are beginning to print, the choice of a correctly exposed and developed negative will facilitate learning and understanding printing controls.

**Figure 7.13**
Low-contrast proof has adequate highlight detail but lacks density, and FB+F (around the sprocket holes) is gray rather than black. This proof is also usable. When enlarger settings, exposure time, and paper contrast grade are noted on the print, the proof becomes both a record of images and a predictor of enlarged print exposure and contrast.

### Health Hazard

Air-burst cleaning products are pressurized containers that must be handled and used with care. Never puncture one, and dispose of them carefully when they are used up. Avoid breathing the fumes. Spraying onto a hot surface can create toxic vapors.

Dust-Off is made in two versions: Product #1 is flammable and should not be used near an open flame. It contains 65% chlorodifluoromethane and 35% dimethyl ether. Product #2 is 100% chlorodifluoromethane. Prozone is 100% chlorodifluoromethane. These compressed gases are advertised as being environmentally safe. If released quickly, however, these can cause damage to skin, due to freezing. All gases under extreme pressure chill as they expand to normal atmospheric pressure. The gas in these containers has been pressurized until it is a liquid. If a container is tipped so that the liquid is released onto the skin, freezer burns may result. The negative can also be damaged by the liquid.

## Make an Enlarged Full-Frame Print

Remove the negative you are going to print from its protective sleeve, holding it by the edges. Turn the enlarger on and use the light coming through the lens to examine both sides of the negative for dust, which must be removed before making the print. Dust on the negative will make shadows that appear as white spots in the enlarged print. Use either a soft brush or compressed gas to blow off the dust (fig. 7.14A–C).

Place the negative in the negative carrier, emulsion toward the lens (and the print paper). The carrier both holds your negative flat during printing and it also masks out light from around the image. Masking unwanted light reduces the flare of unfocused light within the enlarger, and this helps make a sharper, more tonally rich print.

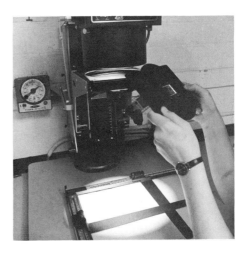

**Figure 7.14**
**a.** Remove surface dust by blowing it off. It is very important to avoid touching the image area of the negative strip with your fingers.

**b.** Use a soft brush to pick up surface dirt. The bulb handle blows the brush clean again.

**c.** Place the cleaned negative in the film carriage and examine it by the enlarger's own light to be sure it is clean.

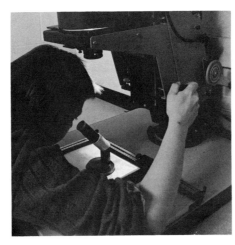

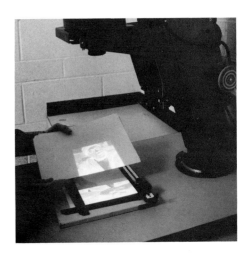

**d.** Adjust the enlarger head and focus the image on scrap paper in the printing easel.

**e.** Use a focusing magnifier to focus on the silver grain.

**f.** Test exposure strips can be made on a full sheet of enlarging paper in the printing easel. Use a piece of cardboard to cover all but an inch or two. Be careful to not move the easel, uncovering more of the paper to give an additional exposure. Repeat this until the entire sheet has been exposed.

**g.** Strips of enlarging paper can be exposed to the same part of the picture for different estimated exposure times.

Turn on the enlarger and center the printing easel under the projected image. Put a piece of plain white paper the size of the print you want to make in the easel to make a brighter image with which to focus. Raise or lower the enlarger head until the full frame of the negative appears on the easel (fig. 7.14D). Frame the negative image on the enlarging easel. For your first print, it is always best to use the entire negative area, without cropping or eliminating any of it so that you see *what you saw when you made the picture,* rather than presuming you know what you want the picture to be.

Gently open the lens to full aperture, and carefully focus the negative. You may wish to use a focusing magnifier to focus on the "grain," which is the pattern of silver particles that form the image in the negative (fig. 7.14E).

## Trial Exposures

Trial exposures require making a guess about the exposure, from under- to overexposure of the print. There are two different traditions in exposing test prints. One is to use the contact proof sheet exposures as a guide and proceed directly to a trial exposure. The second is to expose a trial print in bands or strips.

The first method uses the contact proof as an exposure guide: set the **enlarger lens** to the same aperture that was used for exposing the contact print (which you wrote in pencil on the back of the contact proof print), and set the enlarger timer to the same time and aperture. Under safelight only, open the package of printing paper. Put a sheet of the same brand and contrast grade of printing paper used for the proof sheet in the easel, with the emulsion side toward the enlarger. Use the timer to turn on the enlarger and expose the paper.

The second method—making exposure strips—can be used to discover correct exposure for any negative, whether it has been proofed or not. All contemporary enlarger lenses have aperture control rings with *detents,* mechanical stopping places that indicate a full f–number change in opening. Focus the negative and close

the aperture three detent "clicks" or three f–stops. Place printing paper on the easel.

## Contact Print as Exposure Meter

A well-made contact print is a useful exposure guide when making an enlargement. Compare the contact print of the negative you have chosen to print to the other frames on the proof sheet. Figure 7.15A illustrates a typical proof sheet; the picture to be printed has been boxed.

Print exposure is determined by *highlight details* in the negative. These will appear on the print as light, textured gray values. In figure 7.15A, the contact proof images have adequate highlight detail, with the sense of being light and open. Seeing this on the print means the exposure for the contact proof was correct; therefore, the proof print's exposure time (fifteen seconds at f–11 for this picture) can be used for a trial enlargement.

Dark shadow areas in the proof will show *some* detail in the shadows when a correctly exposed and developed negative is printed on a normal contrast grade of paper. But the shadow areas will be a little less dark in the contact proof print than in the enlarged print.

Since the boxed print in figure 7.15A has about the same values as any other on the page, and since it has adequate shadow detail, one can assume that the trial exposure for a full-frame enlargement on an 8″ × 10″ sheet will be about the same as the contact proof print exposure. In fact, the enlarged trial print shown in figure 7.15B was printed at the same exposure as the proof.

Before the enlarger is turned on to expose the test paper, mask off all but an inch or two of the test sheet with a piece of cardboard (see fig. 7.14F). Expose the uncovered area for three seconds. Without moving the printing easel, uncover another inch or two. Repeat the exposure. Uncover another interval and repeat the three-second exposure. Continue to the end of the sheet.

The strips have been exposed for 3, 6, 9, 12, 15, etc. seconds. After they are developed, one of these strips will

probably show reasonably correct densities. If your negatives are much more dense, a larger lens opening will have to be used. A variation of this test is to expose two- or three-inch wide strips of paper, one at a time (see fig. 7.14G). Place them sequentially on the easel so that each captures the same important light, middle-gray, and shadow tones (sky, textured highlights, important skin tones, and shadows).

After you do this several times you will discover that your print exposures cluster around certain values (e.g., 20 seconds). When this happens, make the test strip exposures at one or two second intervals (i.e., 16, 18, 20, 22, 24 seconds).

## Processing the Test Prints

The test prints are developed just as the contact proof sheets were developed. Develop the strips all together for 1 1/2 minutes. After fixing the print or the test strips, wash in running water for a minute, long enough to remove the surface fixer, then squeegee the water off and examine the tests in white light.

Do not try to evaluate the exposure or contrast of a print under safelight. Wetting temporarily thickens the gelatin emulsion and the wet print looks more glossy, contrasty, and lighter in value than the same print will look when it is dry. This darkening of the print as it dries is called **drying down,** and it takes much experience with printing, and with different papers, to predict how much change will appear. Test prints can be dried with a blow dryer to speed up evaluation.

Blanquart-Evrard developed the **albumen print** in 1847. Smooth paper was coated with egg albumen sensitized with silver salts. The albumen produced a print as rich in detail and tone as the daguerreotype. A waxed paper negative was initially used. This recorded detail well, even though the exposures were long. Commercial production of quality prints became possible, and photographic prints became cheap.

Experience will indicate how much exposure reduction is needed to com-

Figure 7.15
a. Proof sheet with the picture selected.
b. An enlarged full-frame proof print of the selected picture.

**Photographs by Sarah Kracke.**

a.

b.

pensate for drying down. Many contemporary papers respond well to an 8–10% reduction. This means that if the wet print has correct highlights and the exposure is 20 seconds, expose another print for 18 seconds, develop it the same way as the first, and when it dries the highlights will be correct.

The correctly exposed and developed wet print will have only a trace of detail in highlights. If you *can* see full highlight detail in the wet print, *it is already overexposed* and when the print dries down it will appear gray: what were sparkling highlights will be dull. Shadows in wet prints are often richly detailed, and have a lustrous black-on-black quality, but that is lost when the

print dries down and shadow details merge. The correctly made wet print looks a bit "thin" and "flat."

Complete the fixing and washing if you wish to keep the full-frame test print after you have examined it in white light; otherwise, throw it away. Never save partially processed prints as the chemicals they contain will contaminate print dryers and other prints.

## Making the Trial Enlarged Print

Examine highlights first (table 7.4); if you decide the print is too light, then increase the exposure. If it is *very* light (fig. 7.16*A*), increase the exposure a full stop by opening the aperture to the next number (or by doubling the exposure time). When the highlights are too dark, decrease the exposure by a stop. When negatives are correctly exposed and developed to fit the lighting on the subject, they should produce adequately detailed shadows in the print when printed for correct highlights (fig. 7.16*B*).

Until you have a lot of experience, you will not know how much change in value will result from changing an exposure. A small correction may not be enough and a big increase may be too much. Making calculated and deliberate errors either way is called **bracketing** and it speeds up accurate printing. If you find you are making several trial prints with small increases of exposure in an effort to "creep up" on the correct exposure, then try bracketing. Deliberately attempt to *overcorrect* the second print. If the first is too light, deliberately attempt to make the second a little too dark. If successful, the third (correct) exposure can be accurately guessed. In the same way, if the first print is too dark, try to make the second a little light. A third print exposure can be placed within the framework of the first two and produce good highlight values.

Shadow values in the print are controlled by the exposure and contrast of the negative and the contrast grade and development of the paper. When print shadows are gray instead of near-black, increase print contrast by using a higher contrast grade of paper or by using a higher number filter for variable-contrast papers. If the shadows are overwhelmingly black and reveal no detail, use the next lower filter, or the next lower contrast grade.

**Table 7.4  Exposure and Contrast**

Examine highlights first:

| Highlights | Problem | Correction |
|---|---|---|
| Dark | Overexposure | Close aperture or decrease time |
| Light | Underexposure | Open aperture or increase time |

If highlights are correct, examine shadows:

| Shadows | Problem | Correction |
|---|---|---|
| Dark | Excess contrast | Use lower filter or lower contrast paper |
| Gray | Low contrast | Use higher filter or higher contrast paper |

a.

Figure 7.16
**a.** First trial print: obviously too light (by about a stop). Even though it was evident after 20″ development that it would be light, the print was developed for one and one-half minutes to help estimate the needed exposure change.

**b.** Second print. A full stop exposure increase created highlight densities that were about right.

**c.** Third print: developing time increased to three minutes to raise contrast (darken shadows in rocks). The edges of the picture were darkened by burning-in for a stop.

b.

c.

Exposures will vary slightly from one paper grade to another because each graded paper emulsion has a different sensitivity to light. (The actual sensitivity is indicated by the ISO number on the package.) Also, the more contrasty the paper, the more critical the exposure. You usually have to make a new highlight exposure test when you change from one contrast grade to another. This is true for either variable-contrast or graded papers, though Ilford and Kodak variable-contrast papers now have approximately the same printing speeds for filters 1–3, and though a stop increase is suggested for filter grades 4–5, a test will probably be needed because highlight exposure needs to be very accurate with the higher contrast papers.

Before developing a print, you may wish to preserve a record of your test exposures and development times as you work: use a soft lead pencil and write the contrast grade, exposure aperture, and exposure time on the back of the proof print near the edge. This information can be used later to predict printing times and paper contrast grades to use when making enlargements.

## Print and Negative Problems

Handling problems may appear in the full-frame enlarged print:

- Water spots or stains from chemicals
- Creases from handling
- Fingerprints
- Dust spots

Print cropping and dust spots can be corrected after the print is made, and the methods for correcting these are described in chapter 8; other errors may require remaking the print.

## Negative Faults

An unmanipulated, full-frame enlarged proof print helps in discovering most negative development problems (table 7.5). These include:

- Irregular densities near the edge of the frame. These are usually caused by improper agitation and can be avoided by changing the agitation method.
- Pinholes (small black spots in the print). Sometimes caused by small bubbles if the developer does not immediately wet the negative, but more often caused by inadequately dissolved sodium sulfite when powdered developers (D–76, or FG7 with added sulfite) are used. Sulfite dissolves poorly below 110°F, and partially dissolved sulfite in solution etches tiny holes in the silver during development.
- Scratches on emulsion or support sides of the negative. Short, intermittent scratches usually are caused by dirt on the squeegee or wiping sponge when the negative was dried. Long, straight scratches extending over several frames are usually the result of dirt in the camera or the felt light-trap of the film cassette through which the film passes.

## Evaluate the Print

Examine the overall picture only after the print has dried. Ask yourself how changing values might change the meaning of the picture. You have the choice to make individual parts of the print lighter or darker during printing.

Make final prints only after examining the trial print and estimating the corrections you think are needed (fig. 7.16C). You may wish to make other changes, such as cropping the picture to clarify the content, darkening the corners, and changing the tonal range slightly (i.e., making the print slightly more or less contrasty).

Table 7.5  Printing Problems

| Problem | Causes | Cures | Discussion |
|---|---|---|---|
| Small white spots on prints | Dust on negative | Use spotting brush to paint dyes on emulsion | Dusty negative drying area; sediment in wash water; failure to sponge negative; failure to wipe or blow dust off negative before enlarging; dirt in enlarger head (on the condenser lenses); enlarger not grounded; wool or polyester clothes worn when printmaking. |
| Irregular, blotchy gray areas | Water spots on negatives | None | Wetting agent not used; negatives not sponged; water drops allowed to dry on film. |
| Streaky, gray, or mottled print shadow areas | Uneven, short print development | Remake print | Agitate print vigorously; develop at least one minute. |
| Gray edges of paper outside image area on print | Fogging | Remake print | Paper exposed to white light from open enlarger head; development too long; excessive exposure to safelight; white light turned on before print is fixed; paper old or storage temperature too high. |
| Fingerprints | Touching negative; fixer or developer on hands when touching print | Cleaning negative with film cleaner may help; wash hands, use clean darkroom towel and remake print | Skin oils etch film base: clean negatives promptly after they are touched. Wash hands frequently and use a clean darkroom towel. Brown stains result from developer; white fingerprints on prints are caused by fixer. |
| Brown or yellow stains | Exhausted stop bath; long development in exhausted developer; exhausted fixer; dirty drying racks; spilled chemicals | Use fresh chemicals; clean hand towel; wash all prints thoroughly; keep darkroom clean | Image color changes with developer exhaustion; chemical spills must be cleaned up immediately; exhausted fixer leaves silver and sulphur compounds that will not wash off but will discolor the print; drying racks must be kept clean of all chemicals. |
| Negative sharp, print not sharp | Negative "popped" from heat; enlarger head moved; enlarger bumped | Check focus just before printing; do not lean on enlarger table | General blurring often is caused by enlarger heat, which expands the negative so that it bows out of the plane of focus in the negative stage; a smeared or double image is caused by the enlarger table being moved during the exposure. |

Study the contrast of the enlarged print. Beginners tend to make pictures that are very contrasty or very flat. Too much contrast often makes a picture look harsh, when a soft, luminous darkness is actually desired. Prints that are flat and gray show all the details but are usually dull. Not all the tones in the gray scale are needed, and a print may need only two or three well-placed values to be complete, as illustrated by figures 7.17 and 7.18.

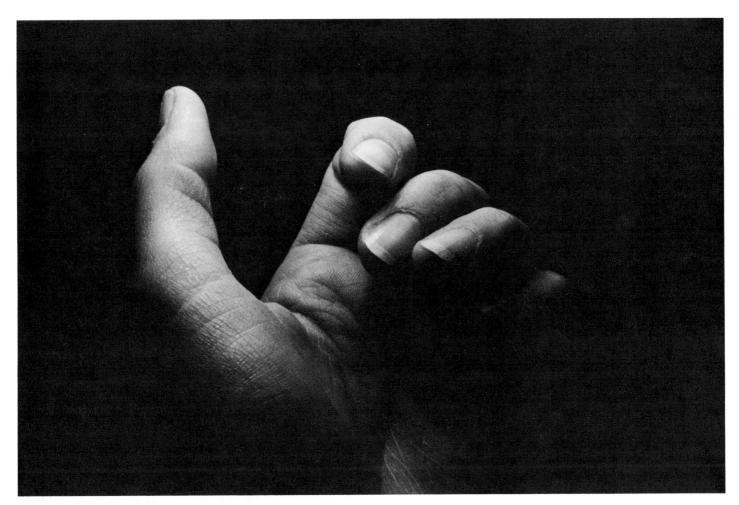

Figure 7.17
**The Photographer's Hand. Kate Keller.** The intimate insight into the power of one's own hand rising out of the darkness.
Courtesy of the photographer.

Figure 7.18
**Untitled. George McGreer.** A sparse forest seen in fog is described in subtle values.

Courtesy of the photographer and Agfa-Beseler.

## Print Contrast Control

Paper contrast grades are numbered from 0 to 4 to indicate increasing contrast. A contrast grade will produce maximum black in the print from FB+F when highlight densities are exposed to produce textured highlight values in the print. The contrast grade does not indicate specifically how a given paper will respond to small variations in shadow or highlight areas.

Print contrast changes can be made in large steps by changing grades of paper (compare fig. 7.19A, contrast grade 2 paper, with fig. 7.19B, contrast grade 3 paper). More subtle changes can be produced by varying developing time, or using a different developer when using fiber-based papers. If the RC paper you are using contains developing agents, contrast control is limited mostly to changing filter numbers.

A "normal" paper contrast grade from one manufacturer may be more appropriate for your negatives than another. Figures 7.19A, B, and C show a negative printed to illustrate the change in shadow values when the print is exposed to produce similar highlight values on contrast grades 2, 3, and 4. Contrast grade 3 is the *normal* grade for small camera negatives because of differences in the shape of the negative characteristic curve and the shorter density range used in 35mm photography (though the "normal" grade for large camera negatives is grade 2).

The apparent contrast of a print is determined to some degree by the lighting environment in which it is viewed. There is a real risk of overprinting (making a print too contrasty and dark) if the darkroom white light used for viewing wet prints is too bright. Wet prints seen under darkroom work lights always seem to have lustrous shadows, but they dry down into dull prints without much shadow detail and with gray highlights when viewed under ordinary room light. This loss of brilliance is exaggerated when a print is seen framed under glass. A more brilliant and contrasty print may be desired when it is to be framed than when the print is intended for a hand-held portfolio.

a.

b.

c.

Print contrast can be decreased in any of the following ways:

- Developing for less than thirty seconds (RC paper only)
- Diluting developer stock with twice the recommended water
- Using Kodak Selectol Soft

Contrast can be increased by:

- Developing fiber-base paper longer (up to four to five minutes)
- Using paper developer diluted less than recommended
- Raising developer temperature to 75° and developing fully

Fiber-based paper developing time can be decreased to as little as one minute to decrease contrast, or increased to as much as four minutes to increase contrast. The risks associated with shorter times are uneven development and washed-out, watery shadow values. With extended development, there is an increase in contrast, and also a risk of graying the highlights (though this is frequently due to safe-light fog, which can be prevented by turning off the light during most of the development).

Figure 7.19
Three prints made on different contrast grades of paper. Each was printed for similar highlight values in the shoulder area of the woman leading the horse. Note the overall increase of tonal separation and how the change in contrast affects the mood of the picture.
a. Print on contrast grade 2.
b. Print on contrast grade 3.
c. Print on contrast grade 4.

## Manual Printing Controls

Parts of a print can be made darker by **burning-in,** or kept from darkening by **dodging.** Figure 7.20 illustrates two common methods of burning-in an area of a print, and figure 7.21 shows two popular methods for dodging part of a print that would otherwise become too dark.

Burning-in an area means using a mask to add image light only to selected areas of the print before or after an overall exposure. Burning-in requires an opaque mask with a hole through which the enlarger light may pass. The mask used for burning-in may be a sheet of red-colored plastic, a piece of cardboard, or simply your cupped hands, shaped to cast a protective shadow over the rest of the print while image light passes between thumb and fingers.

Dodging the print describes holding back light from a part of the picture for a portion of the overall print exposure. Your own hand is a wonderfully flexible dodging tool, capable of assuming very intricate shapes. A dodging tool may be as small as a dime or as large as the print itself. Dodging tools are often made of circular or oval pieces of cardboard taped or glued to handles of stiff wire. The handles should be long enough to easily reach the middle of the picture, otherwise the shadow of your hand holding the tool will appear at the edge.

Figure 7.20

**a.** *Burning-in* an area of the picture to make it darker by using a sheet of cardboard with a hole in it. The photographer literally paints in part of the picture with light. The cardboard cutout is moved constantly to avoid a sharp edge density.

**b.** Forming an aperture with your own hands, which can make complicated shapes. The closer the hands are to the lens the softer the edge of the illuminated area and the smoother the tonal transition.

Figure 7.21

**a.** *Dodging* holds back light in an area. A cardboard disk is taped to wire from a clothes hanger to form a shadow. The dodging tool is moved constantly to avoid a sharp edge density.

**b.** The photographer's hand makes a very supple tool, which can make a complicated shadow shape easily.

Dodging and burning-in can achieve subtle control of local values and avoid obvious changes in the print. Too much burning-in produces obvious gray tones, values that have nothing to do with the picture. Clumsy or excessive dodging will also be quite obvious. But dodging and burning-in can be used to produce major changes in the image (fig. 7.22).

## Variable-Contrast Paper Controls

Variable-contrast filters can be combined with dodging and burning to produce good prints from complex negatives. Choose a contrast grade filter to correctly expose the larger area of the picture, while light for the smaller area (which may need more or less contrast) is partially held back with a dodging tool. Without moving the enlarger in any way, change the contrast filter to meet the needs of the smaller area and burn in the smaller area, allowing little or no exposure elsewhere. The first printing problem is to meld the edges of the exposed areas so no obvious printing manipulation is revealed. The second problem is to balance the two exposures so there are no obvious differences in value.

a.

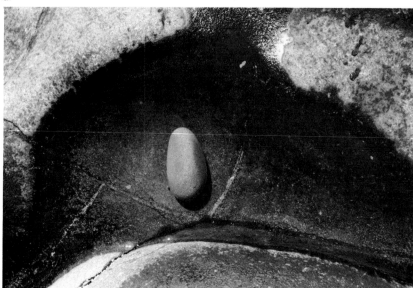

b.

c.

Figure 7.22
Bringing all the tools together to make a finished print. **a.** The test strip exposure was developed for 1 1/2 minutes and reveals that the third exposure strip is close to the desired densities.
**b.** A ''straight'' full-frame print at that exposure validates the test, but the center is too dark and the corners too light.
**c.** The overall exposure is increased about one-third, but the center is dodged to lighten it, then a second burning-in exposure equal to the first is given *only to the corners.*

## Combining and Collaging Prints

The single print, presented as a finished statement, is not the only way to make a photograph. The photograph is not necessarily a single statement of the photographer's reality, and there is no reason why the photographer cannot bring together two (or many) views to create a composite that suggests or describes complex visions. Figures 7.23 and 7.24 illustrate manipulations that can be used to create new visual realities from existing negatives.

Figure 7.23
**Untitled. Steven Spencer.** Sequential printing of two negatives onto a single piece of paper produces this mysterious combination of wood, woman, and gesture.
Courtesy of the photographer.

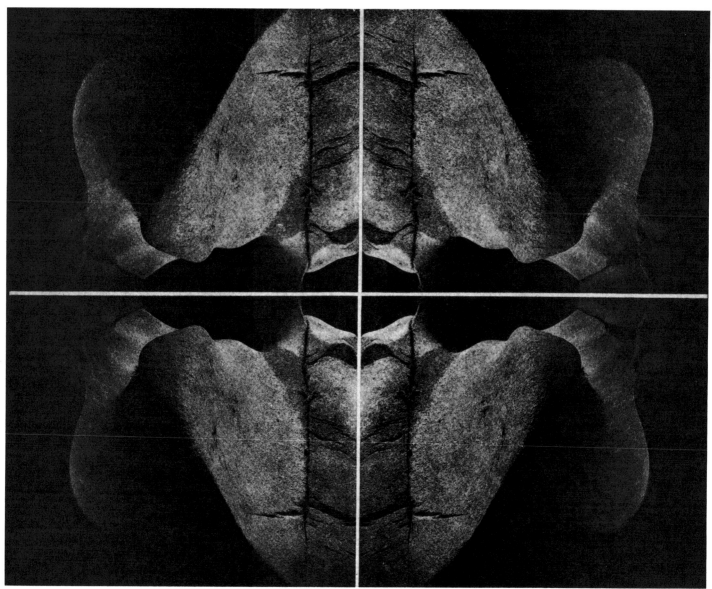

Figure 7.24
**No. 7, The Grottoes. Arnold Gassan.** The subject is granite cut by water and erosion. The same image is symmetrically printed four times to create a composite space.
Courtesy of the photographer.

## Permanence of Prints

Finished prints should be processed for permanence by fixing in two fixing baths (with the second being a fresh solution), using a print washing aid to help eliminate fixer, protecting the silver from atmospheric sulfur with mild selenium toning, and finishing with a careful final washing. Kodak publication no. F30, *Preservation of Photographs,* may be consulted for further information on causes of deterioration in prints and prevention of chemical damage.

Incomplete fixing leaves silver halides in the emulsion. These halides eventually "print out," and appear as color patches. Improper fixing will also leave silver or sulfide compounds in the emulsion. These are difficult to remove and will eventually cause the print to discolor or fade.

Two separate fixing solutions are needed to provide full removal of unused silver halides. An economical procedure is to prepare two gallons of paper-strength fixer (mixed without using the hardener solution provided) from the Kodak (or other) Rapid Fixer concentrate. Mark the bottles to indicate first and second fixer. The first gallon bottle is used for fifty 8″ × 10″ prints and then discarded. The second bath is used for the first fifty prints and *then moved to the first bottle;* fresh fixer is prepared for the second bottle. After the first cycle of use, every gallon of fixer is used for 100 prints in all, and the second bath is always the freshest—it remains an effective final fix.

Fix each print in the first fixer for one-half the total suggested fixing time, agitating constantly. Remove the print and place it in a tray of running water or store it in a tray of water, but change the water after every four or five prints. When you have finished printing for the day, cycle the prints through the second fixer for the second half of the total fixing time, rotating them constantly from bottom to top.

Prints cannot be rotated in fix or wash baths with print tongs without grave risk of damaging the prints, and this rotation needs to be done by hand. If your hands chap easily, wear rubber gloves. In any case, dry your hands between print-handling operations to prevent cumulative skin damage.

## Toning for Preservation

Selenium toner can ensure greater silver print permanence without color change if a 5–10% solution is used, as described in chapter 11. Sufficient selenium will be deposited in three to five minutes to form a protective barrier of silver selenide. Selenium toning should be done in a well-ventilated room to avoid inhalation of the toning procedure gases. The toning procedure outlined can follow the regular second fix bath, or a special third fixer bath, a simple thiosulfate solution (also described in chapter 11), can be used to reduce acid carryover into the toning solution.

Different papers and paper grades will tone at different speeds. Toning should be done under a good work light so that the change in density and color can be monitored. When toning for permanence or print intensification, place an untoned wet print beside the toning tray to use as a standard of comparison. After the desired tone is reached, a very thorough wash is required in water (not hotter than 70°F). The Automatic Tray Siphon is an adequate washing aid if no more than five to six prints are washed (and the tray is a size larger than the prints), and the prints are *constantly* rotated. Wash prints for five minutes, empty the tray and refill with fresh water, then wash another five minutes.

## Reexamine the Print

Study the finished print to discover what you have made and what might be changed. Ask yourself these questions:

- Do highlight areas have detail?
- Do shadows have detail and solidity?
- Is the contrast appropriate?
- What is too dark and should be dodged?
- What is too light and should be burned-in?
- What more could be cropped?
- Is this the picture I wanted?

The photographic cycle began when you saw a possible subject for a picture and is now complete. The photographic cycle also involved framing the subject in the viewfinder, choosing an exposure, developing the film, and making a print. It concludes with your assessment of what has been accomplished.

The type of camera used will also change a photograph, as will the film used and the way it is developed—with the resulting variations in contrast, grain, and tonal separations in shadows or highlights. Major changes can be caused by using different papers. Finally, the size of the print, toning, mounting, and presentation will all modify the meaning of the picture.

## Summary

Printing papers are made in a wide range of contrast grades (from 0–4, very soft to very hard). These permit the photographer to produce full-scale prints from negatives of different contrast, or density ranges. Variable-contrast filters should only be used with their own paper brands as they provide accurate contrast grades only for their own paper system. Print exposure and development controls will usually not modify the contrast grade of a print much more than half a contrast grade up or down. Major manipulations of the contrast are best accomplished on the negative. Other manipulations of the print (developer changes, intensification, toning, and reducing) are described in chapter 11.

## Discussion and Assignments

The photographic process uses silver compounds called halides (salts), which are changed by light and the change is usually made visible by the action of developing agents. But these salts are also affected by heat and other kinds of radiant energy, and this can be demonstrated, as in the following assignments.

The silver print can be a very beautiful object, but it is also easily damaged by rough handling and improper chemical treatment. What constitutes a "good" print is always a decision based on tradition and experience. Seek out galleries or museums in your area that display prints by master photographers and see how they solved problems of contrast and print color.

Although the text has discussed only a few print developers, there are a number of excellent commercial developers on the market. Other producers of both print and film chemicals should be investigated (see appendix 5 for addresses): Edwal, Sprint, Ethol. You may find others worth working with that are not listed here at your local camera store.

### Assignment 1

Take a piece of photographic printing paper and a strip of negatives. Place the negatives on the paper—emulsion to emulsion—under a piece of glass and in direct sunlight. Over a period of several hours, there will be a distinct color change; a low-contrast image from the negative will have formed on the paper. Examine the print you make. It is an example of **printing out,** where the light breaks down the bonds in the silver halide, producing a new chemical and a visible change. It is this change that is at the heart of photography, and it was first observed more than 200 years ago. Printing-out paper was the standard from 1851 until the late 1880s, when "gaslight" or **developing out** paper was introduced. Aside from sensitivity to light, the difference between the two kinds of printing is the use of a developing agent to make the process faster, and ultimately more economical. Printing-out paper had more silver in it than contemporary developing out papers have. Because it had more silver, it produced prints of greater density, and because it did not use chemical development, the prints were of a different color and greater tonal range.

## Assignment 2

Make a duplicate copy of your proof sheet. Cut out each frame and glue *all* those individual pictures on plain 3″ × 5″ file cards. Do this whether they look "good" or "bad." Spread the cards out on a table in an orderly way to discover the ways in which you *approached your subject* as compared to the way you *photographed the subject*:

- Look for repeated patterns in your pictures
- How many times the same scene was photographed
- Discover pictures you had not seen in the whole proof sheet
- Stack the cards in the order they were shot and study the sequence of pictures

## Assignment 3

Choose a negative of your own that you like and that has interesting detail in both the dark shadows and the bright, highlighted areas (such as white shirts, or light-colored hair in the sunlight). Carefully make the best 5″ × 7″ print you can on your normal contrast paper grade.

Make careful prints on the next higher and lower contrast grade paper, printing in both cases for good detail in the highlights (without letting the print get "dirty" or gray-looking). Dry these prints and examine them. Decide which you like best.

On the basis of the contrast test, buy or borrow some "warm tone" paper (Agfa Portriga Rapid, or Oriental Center, for example) of the correct paper grade. Print the same negative on this paper. Trim away the white edges and place all four prints together on a clean, neutral white mount board. In a comfortable light, examine the prints slowly and carefully and decide which you like best and why you like it best.

## Assignment 4

Perform the following exercise for an entire roll of film:

- See the picture you want to take, and expose the film.
- Immediately turn your back on the subject and make a simple outline sketch, indicating carefully the composition of the picture you *thought* you had made.
- Turn back to the subject and compare your sketch to the subject. You may find you wish to remake the picture to fit the sketch.

## Assignment 5

Photograph can be composed in camera or in printing. After you expose the first frame, make these pictures on the following frames of film:

- Rotate your camera 90° (from vertical to horizontal, or horizontal to vertical) and reexamine the same subject.
- Recompose the picture so the subject is no longer in the center, but is at one edge of the frame.
- Move closer to the subject so that it must be recomposed in the viewfinder.
- Move closer again and find three significant details from within the original picture.

## Assignment 6

Bring together five or six prints that interest you. (These can be your pictures or some made by friends.) Put them in line on a print rail or in some convenient place. Sit quietly and look at them. Discover how one relates to the next. Is there an implied narrative (a story line that develops as you look from one picture to the next)? Do shapes in one picture point toward or away from the next? Often one picture draws most attention to itself: find that one and move it to either end of the set and see how that changes meaning.

Write a brief outline of the relationships you have discovered. Shuffle and reorder them as though they were a deck of cards to create a new sequence of pictures; repeat the analysis. Discover how the apparent content of any one picture is changed by interaction with neighboring prints. Arrange them a third time so the pictures progress in different ways:

- "Active" to "quiet"
- By value from dark to light
- "Complicated" to "simple"

and in another way *these* pictures suggest to you.

# 8 Finishing, Protecting, and Storing

Figure 8.1
**Arline McCarthy as Mother Teresa. Elise Mitchell Sanford.** Photographs work well as art and as decoration.
Print courtesy of the photographer.

a.

Figure 8.2
The photographer searches out significant
form. **a.** The elegant, complex architectural
space was photographed using only
environmental light. **b.** Large pieces of
corrugated pipe create this complex wave
pattern.

**a.** Photo by Kate Keller. Print courtesy of the
photographer. **b.** Photo by Richard Albertine. Print
courtesy of the photographer.

b.

## The Damaged Print

Dust is the most common source of unwanted spots in the print. Dust often clings to the dry film because of electrostatic attraction. This dust can be brushed or blown off. Cleaning the film with a brush or compressed gas just before printing will not remove dirt or dust embedded in emulsion.

Water droplets that dry on the negative also create density variations and white marks on the print. Water spots on the support side can often be removed with film cleaner and the print remade. Water spots on the emulsion side are permanent, but if not too extensive, they may be spotted out on the print.

## Spotting Prints

Spotting colors are used to paint a correct value on the print. Small white or black spots can be retouched without remaking the print. Spotting makes a blemish inconspicuous, and it is sometimes possible to hide the blemish entirely. Repairs can usually be seen when the print is held at an angle and examined by reflected light. In many cases, repairing a print may require remaking it.

The equipment needed for spotting a print is shown in figure 8.3A. Start spotting the darker areas and continue with middle gray and consecutively lighter areas until you reach highlights. Work on a flattened print in a strong light that makes all defects visible. A protective cover sheet (a clean piece of typing paper or an old print) is used to avoid fingerprinting the emulsion (fig. 8.3B). A magnifier helps to see fine details. Clean, dry hands are a necessity, and cotton film-editing gloves will be needed if you have damp skin.

Figure 8.3
**a.** Spotting dyes and a very fine brush are needed to spot a photograph. Water may be used to thin the dyes, and a magnifier is useful when spotting fine detail.
**b.** Cotton gloves and a sheet of plain paper protect the surface of the print from skin oils.

**Photographs by Sarah Kracke**

Table 8.1    Spotting and Mounting Equipment

**Print Finishing**

Work table

Mat knife

Metal straightedge

24–36″ scale

Logan or Dexter mat cutter

Print mounting materials: spray cement, dry-mount tissue, or linen tape and mounting corners

Spotone print spotting dyes (available in three-color sets or by the bottle; #3 is a good match for most contemporary papers)

Spotoff (for removing black spots on prints)

Windsor & Newton tubes of white and black watercolors

Spotting brush: Windsor & Newton (#00 or #000) Sable

Xacto knife

Utility knife

Steel straightedge

Plastic triangle (10″, 45° or 30–60°)

Mounting materials: Seal Dry Mount Tissue (requires heated press), 3M Photo Mount Spray Cement, rubber cement and thinner

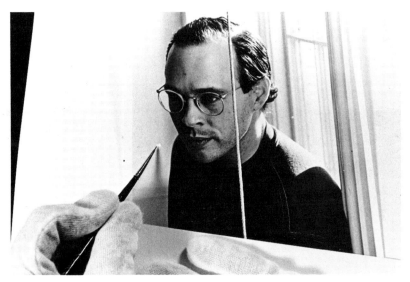

a.

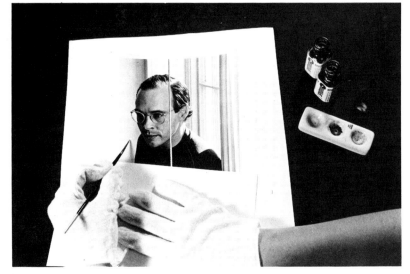

b.

a.

Figure 8.4
The informal, personal document remains
the most popular kind of photograph.
**a. Sloan Sisters, 1930s. Jean Thomas.**
Differences of posture and expression
vividly separate the personalities of three
sisters photographed on a Kentucky
hillside. **b. Untitled. Sarah Kracke.** A
contemporary portrait.

**a.** University of Louisville Photographic Archives.
**b.** Courtesy of the photographer.

b.

Before the introduction of print washing
aids, prints required washing for at least
one to two hours in an attempt to
remove the sodium thiosulfate, or
"hypo," that would inevitably cause the
silver image to fade away. The problem
of image stability was acknowledged in
the 1840s, in the first years of
photographic history. Kodak Hypo Clear,
Heico Perma Wash, and other
proprietary washing aids have
eliminated long wash times and
enhanced longevity of silver-image
negatives and prints. With the use of
these, wash times *can* be reduced to as
little as five minutes.

**Spotone** spotting dyes penetrate
the emulsion and are permanent. Test
the spotting solutions on the white
border of a throwaway print (of the
same type of paper) to match dye

value and color against the area to be
spotted. The dye will darken slightly as
it dries. Spotting a print is a kind of
painting and you will need to experiment until you gain a feel for the process. The spotting dyes can be used
either with a full brush and a bit of dye
placed carefully in the center of a dust
spot, or use an almost dry brush,
placing dye on the print in a cross-
hatch pattern.

The shape of the spot and its location affect both its visibility and the
technique needed to disguise it. If the
white spot on the print is a wriggly line
in a dark place, start repairs with a full
brush of undiluted dye. Draw a continuous line along the center of the spot,
holding the brush parallel to the line.
Do not try to fill the line completely—it
is easy to overspot and make a mark
even more obvious than the original

blemish. If the line is in a light gray
area, dilute the Spotone to match the
surrounding value and proceed as described. For small, irregular areas, use
less dye on the brush and stipple or
cross-stroke the area. With a difficult
spot, work a bit, wait until it dries, observe the results, and repeat if necessary.

Watercolor spotting pigments may
be used to paint out black spots; this
is more easily done than etching them
out, on either fiber-based or RC paper.
Black spots on fiber-based papers may
be chemically removed by using Spotoff, or by stroking the surface with an
**Xacto knife.** Shaving density requires
*a lot* of practice to be successful (i.e.,
to change density without visibly scar-
ring the print).

## Crop the Print

In chapter 7, it was suggested that initially the entire frame be enlarged. There are three reasons. First, to learn *what* it is you are actually seeing when you press the shutter. Second, viewfinders of most 35mm cameras do not show all of the scene being photographed. Only the most expensive professional cameras show you exactly what will be recorded on the film. Third, to reveal negative development agitation faults (which often appear at the edge of the frame).

Physical cropping is a way to change a picture and often make it more effective. Cropping the picture usually changes (and may intensify) meaning by removing unexpected edge events. Cropping also reveals alternative photographic compositions within the picture. Often pictures were seen momentarily at the scene and then overwhelmed (or lost) in the composition actually exposed on film.

Make two L-shaped pieces of cardboard at least three inches wide and with sides at least as long as the print. Lay them over the enlarged print to make a rectangle of varying proportions. Figure 8.5A shows a full-frame print, and figures 8.5B and 8.5C show other possible croppings.

When you have found an appropriate composition by using the cropping Ls, make a small mark just inside the corners of the Ls with a sharp felt-tip pen to show you where to cut. For a very neat edge, trim the print on a plastic cutting mat, or on a piece of thick cardboard. Physically crop the print with a sharp mat knife and a metal straightedge. (This makes a cleaner cut than most print cutters do through the paper and emulsion.) Never cut a print lying on an unprotected table.

a.

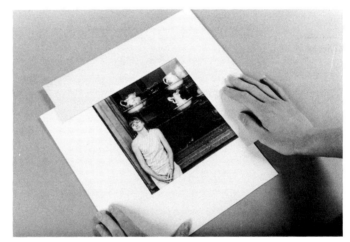
b.

c.

Figure 8.5
a. A full-frame print of the negative.
b. Different possible pictures can be discovered by using cropping Ls.
c. Extreme cropping reduces the picture to a portrait with a background of the window frame and a pitcher.

## Health Hazard

Scotch **Photo Mount** spray adhesive contains hexane, acetone, and alcohol; all are neurotoxins. The propellant is propane, a liquified gas commonly used as fuel in portable heaters. Pressurized containers must be used with care as both the contents and the packaging have dangers. When the contents are used up, the cans are still dangerous and must be disposed of carefully. Never puncture an empty spray can or put one in a fire. Avoid breathing vapor and overspray (the airborne adhesive mist). Spray only in well-ventilated spaces. Wash adhesives from skin with soap and water. If your eyes are exposed to the spray, wash thoroughly with water for ten minutes and see a physician.

## Justifying Mounting Prints

The unmounted photograph is easily damaged by normal handling. The paper cracks easily, the emulsion gets scratched, and fingerprints dim the surface of the protective gelatin or plastic. But many photographs need not be mounted, and for some uses mounting is undesirable. For example, prints intended for reproduction should be left unmounted (and often these pictures are not required to have great longevity). A significant investment is required to produce and protect a finished print, and this cost should be considered when choosing how to protect a photograph.

A print that has been firmly bonded to a smooth sheet of mount board is very attractive, especially if space has been left around the picture to isolate it from a cluttered environment. However, sometimes mounting the print does more harm than good. When the print is mounted permanently, it is difficult to salvage when the mount itself is damaged.

An alternative is to not mount the print directly to the supporting board. An unmounted but overmatted print will not be as smooth and flat as a mounted print, but the very slight curve is usually not objectionable. Unmounted prints can be made to lie flat by dry-mounting them back-to-back with another print (a test print that has been thoroughly washed is a possible source of a backing print). The double thickness of photo paper becomes rigid and smooth, and the assembly can be held in place with corner clips alone, framed behind a window mat without fear of the print curling.

Prints intended to be finished to the best standards and kept as long as possible are made with a wide (1

**Table 8.2  Dry-mounting and Matting Equipment**

Thermostatically controlled dry-mounting press
Tacking iron
Metal straightedge: 24–36″
12″, 30–60° triangle
Utility or mat knife and blades
Pencil
24″ ruler
Logan or Dexter Mat Cutter and replacement blades
Two- and four-ply acid-free mat board
Acid-free linen tape
Acid-free print corners
Print storage bags
Print storage boxes

inch) white border to protect the image area. This is a working space against inevitable damage to corner and edge, and it also allows for concealed corner mounts when the print is protected by a window mat.

A glossy print reflects light like a mirror. Reflections from a print weaken the shadow areas. Mounting a print holds it flat, and presenting it on a larger board isolates it and enhances its beauty. Dry-mounting the finished print is outlined in detail in table 8.2, but even trial prints need to be mounted flat in order to be seen correctly.

Print-mounting cardboard comes in many grades. The cheapest boards consist of pretty papers over highly acidic, coarse filler. The acid in the filler will quickly destroy both the board itself and the silver print image. The best papers are "pH buffered" or "acid-free" where the acidic residue from the paper-making process is smothered; the paper will not harm the print. These mounting boards are referred to as "rag" or "museum" mounting board. The cost difference is easily 1:10 from the least to most expensive. All materials used in protecting the final print should be acid-free, but cheaper materials are often used for trial prints.

There is no point in using expensive acid-free or pH-buffered boards for study prints. Use less expensive, student-grade precut boards. (For suppliers, see appendix 4.) When a full-frame 35mm is negative-printed onto a sheet of 8″ × 10″ paper, the final trimmed print is no larger than 6″ × 9″, and it will fit comfortably onto an 11″ × 14″ mount. Standard-size boards (8″ × 10″ and 11″ × 14″), in white, cream, gray, and black surfaces, are available at art or photo supply stores.

The color of the mat board is important. A neutral white board is the least distracting. Black boards are frequently used by photojournalists, because the black border was found to make contest prints "pop" when hundreds of photographs were being reviewed in professional competitions. A black board also generates a compositional edge for a picture with a featureless sky or other blank areas at the edge of the print.

There are several ways to mount prints, which include photo corners, cement, and dry mounting. Photo corners have been popular for more than a century; unfortunately, the cheap black paper corners used in scrapbooks retain acids that damage the photograph. Better quality corners are now available in black or white paper or clear plastic, and these are suitable both for permanent print presentations and study prints.

a.

b.

Figure 8.6
Accurate, unsentimental documentation of how life changes is the source of much photographic effort. **a.** Overview of the construction of the Union Railway station in Nashville, Tennessee, in 1895. Note the tiny figures of workers in the lower left.
**b.** Roadside gasoline service, hardware, general store, and antique pressed-metal siding are crisply described in this photograph of a three-generation family business.

**a.** H. C. Griswold Collection, University of Louisville Photographic Archives. **b.** Photo by Arnold Gassan.

Lay the trimmed print on the mat board and move it around to where you want it to be. When satisfied with the placement, make light pencil marks at corners of the print to help position it when mounting. Photo corners can be glued or taped in place and the finished, spotted print slipped into them.

Work prints—prints *with no lasting value*—may be cemented to mount boards with 3M **Positionable Mounting Adhesive** (which is convenient but not acceptable for long-term mounting, as it is very acidic, with a pH of 8.9) or Scotch brand Photo Mount, a spray adhesive. Neither of these adhesives are recommended for longevity, but both are convenient for finishing study prints. These adhesives are used frequently for temporary displays, where the work is not expected to last.

When using spray cement, place the mat comfortably near where you are spraying the print, but safe from adhesive overspray. Protect your work area with sheets of newspaper. Place the print to be mounted face down on the newspaper. Hold the spray can about 6 inches from the paper and spray across the print and past it (to avoid too much spray at the print edge). A single layer of adhesive is adequate for small prints; for a larger print or a heavier bond, spray a second coat at right angles to the first.

Once the print touches the mat it cannot be moved. A disadvantage of the spray cement is that the slip sheet, which works well with rubber cement, cannot be used because it will grab the slip sheet as firmly as the print. Place the print carefully on the mat and then put a sheet of clean, white paper over the print to protect it and apply pressure from the center out to the edges, using a rubber roller or the palm of your hand.

3M Positionable Mounting Adhesive is a mildly sticky sheet (sold only in a roll) that adheres to the back of the print. A protective sheet is removed from the mounting tissue just before the print is positioned on the mount board. A rubber roller is used to supply pressure, which bonds the print permanently to the mount.

The most permanent mounting is done with heat-sensitive tissue. Seal manufactures several **dry-mount tissues**, including a low-temperature material for use with RC prints (whose plastic can be damaged by mounting tissues, which melt at temperatures that are safe for fiber prints).

Dry-mounting a fiber-based print consists of pressing the tissue, the print, and the mount board together and heating them until the tissue surface melts. When the tissue coating melts, it penetrates fibers of both the print and the mount. Adhesion takes place as the tissue cools. The adhesion is permanent and even overall if there is no moisture present. In a damp climate, the mount board itself will hold moisture and you will want to preheat it with a mounting press or hand iron. Heating drives out excess moisture and helps guarantee a firm bond with the mounting tissue.

A cover sheet larger than the mount board is needed to protect the surface of the print from the heated iron or mounting press platen. The cover sheet will visibly emboss the mount board if it is smaller. It is necessary to use a cover sheet that is acid-free in order to avoid contaminating the print and mat board.

Always be aware of what the print will touch. For example, it is foolish to eliminate sulfur in the processing and then work the print on cheap cardboard or newsprint. Be certain your hands are clean; avoid fingerprinting the picture or the mat; wear cotton editing gloves.

A dry-mount press is desirable, although a household iron can be used for small prints, but prints larger than 5″ × 7″ should only be mounted with a mounting press. A mounting press consists of a thermostatically controlled, electrically heated platen, a support mechanism with controlled pressure of the platen, and a cushioned base on which to lay the print and mounting board. The thermostat should be set for the tissue being used.

Prints must be dry, smooth, and flat before being mounted. If they have not been stored flat, they may be flattened quickly in a hot press.

Place a dry print face down on a piece of acid-free board, and reach into the press with the board resting on the palm of your hand. Press the board up into the heated platen, closing the press and withdrawing your hand. Keep the press closed for five to seven seconds. Open it, remove the print, store it at once under a weight while it cools, and it will remain flat.

Follow this sequence to mount a print (fig. 8.7):

1. Turn on the press and allow it time to heat.

2. Place a flattened print face down on a clean working surface.

3. Lay mounting tissue on the print and adhere it with a stroke of a tacking iron near the center of the print.

4. Trim tissue and print together. Use a mat knife, triangle, and metal straightedge. Blade trimmers cut tissue badly and although rotary trimmers make a clean cut, some find it difficult to cut square prints, or to keep the tissue from being cut a bit larger than the print.

5. Place print face up on the mat board, lift a corner, and tack the mounting tissue. Check for correct position and then tack a second corner.

6. Protect the print with a cover sheet and place board and print in the press. Close it for twenty seconds. Remove the newly mounted picture, and immediately place it face down on a smooth, cool, dry surface. Apply moving pressure with the palm of your hand to the back of the mat until it cools. Set the thermostat control on the press for the temperature recommended by the tissue manufacturer. A hotter press will not speed the mounting and may damage the print, and a cool press will not melt the tissue adequately or evenly, resulting in poor adhesion.

Figure 8.7
**a.** Electrically heated, thermostatically controlled tacking iron melts dry mounting tissue into a print.

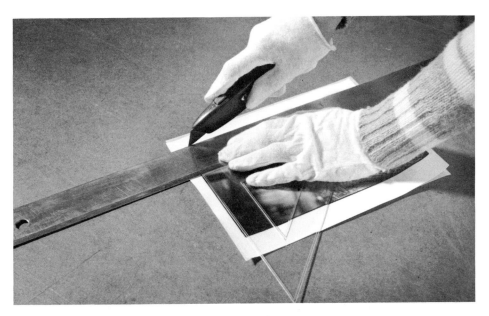

**b.** Print and mounting tissue are trimmed: a sharp mat knife and metal straightedge cut them together. Keep sides at right angles by using a large triangle.

**c.** Place print on mat board: fuse mount tissue by lifting one corner and pressing the tacking iron lightly into the tissue. Do not touch the mat with the iron. Keep tissue smooth and flat and fuse an adjacent corner. Cover the print with a large piece of acid-free paper and press mat, print, and protective cover in the heated mounting press.

## Window Mats

Window mats made of acid-free materials are the best primary protection for the print. Overmatting permits you to use an unmounted print. When using a window mat, the print is attached to the backing board only by corner pockets or tape hinges. The window mat can be replaced if it becomes soiled. The mat can be combined with interleaving and a protective bag.

Mat boards are made in various thicknesses. Two-ply is usually used for the backing, with the more expensive four-ply reserved for the window mat. The board can be purchased in precut sizes (8″ × 10″, 11″ × 14″, 16″ × 20″, etc.) or in full sheets (either 30″ × 40″ or 32″ × 40″), which are cut to size as needed. Examine the board to decide which surface will be seen (most matting materials have slightly different textures on each side), then cut the front and back pieces to the same size.

Mat a print by following this sequence (fig. 8.8):

1. Measure the size of the window (usually just smaller than the image area, though a white print border may show).

2. Place the mat face down on a clean working surface, and draw light pencil lines for the opening.

3. Use a **mat cutter** and a metal straightedge to cut the window. The knife cuts outward on a bevel. The cut begins 1 1/2 thicknesses of the mat board *outside* the opening. (If the cut line is shorter, the window will not separate and the mat will be ruined; if the cuts are too long they will be obvious from the front). Repeat for all four sides. The window should fall away when the mat board is lifted.

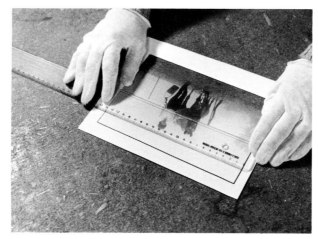

Figure 8.8
**a.** Measure the window mat opening carefully. The clear plastic scale in this figure is calibrated in centimeters.

**b.** Draw the window in pencil on the back side of the cover sheet.

**c.** A Logan mat cutter uses a single-edged razor blade and has marks to show where the beveled cut should begin and end. It is shown here being used to cut the window.

Note that the straightedge that guides the cutter is *outside* the window area, so that the mat edge will taper away from the print.

**d.** The window is hinged to the backing board with an adhesive linen tape. Pressure-sensitive paper tapes dry out, and the adhesives damage both print and mat.

**e.** Acid-free paper corner pockets are taped to the backing board with 2″ linen tape strips. The pockets hold the unmounted print in place and permit it to be removed easily if the mat is damaged.

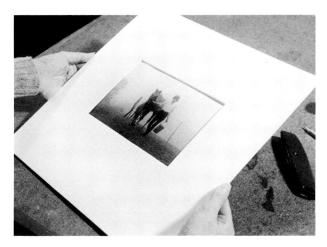

**f.** The finished window mat frames the print and protects it from damage.

The window mat and the backing board are usually joined, but need not be if the print is to be framed. Figure 8.8D shows gummed linen tape used as a hinge. Never use drafting tape or other common pressure-sensitive paper tapes. The paper tape itself is acidic, and the adhesive contains sulfur. The adhesives in most pressure-sensitive tapes fail with age.

*Helpful Hints*

- The sharp tip of the mat cutter blade must not drag: place two pieces of cardboard under the mat to form a channel for the blade so that it contacts only the mat.
- Mat boards vary in quality and some will tend to tear, rather than cut cleanly. Two knife passes may be needed: the first to score deeply, the second to open.
- Use the heaviest straightedge you can find to guide the cutter.

## Protective Storage

Safe storage is needed for negatives, proof sheets, work prints, and finished-but-unmounted prints (fig. 8.9). Print and negative storage temperatures and humidity must be moderate. Do not store photographs where temperatures are above 80°F or where humidity is high (e.g., in attics or basements).

Figure 8.9
A sturdy homemade worktable with wood print storage drawers. Because wood is acidic, prints must be kept in protective, nonacidic plastic bags.

Contemporary photographic paper consists of silver halide crystals in a gelatin emulsion, supported by the paper. Between the paper and the gelatin is either a thin layer of baryta (a special clay) or a layer of plastic (polyethylene). The baryta in fiber-based and the plastic in RC papers provide a reflective base color controlled by the manufacturer. The plastic surcoat prevents chemicals from penetrating the photographic paper.

The baryta or the plastic subcoat in contemporary papers usually contains a fluorescing agent that brightens the photograph by capturing ultraviolet light and transforming it into white light, so the visible light reflected is actually greater than that striking the print. The amount of the flourescing dye present can be seen by examining prints under an ultraviolet (UV) light source: most contemporary papers will "glow in the dark," whereas papers from a generation ago do not.

The silver in the print will be contaminated and eventually destroyed by acids found in all cheap paper. Prints should be stored flat and may be kept in archival plastic sleeves or interleaved with acid-free paper. The black plastic bags in which photographic paper is sold provide dry, economical storage for unmounted prints. More elegant storage for finished prints is provided by acid-free storage boxes, sold by several manufacturers (see appendix 4).

The mounted (but not overmatted) print is protected from corner damage, but not from abrasion. Prints that are stored without interleaving (sometimes called a cover sheet) are inevitably scratched by normal handling. Prints can safely be interleaved with a smooth, lightweight sheet (such as Hollinger Bond, an archival paper), which will shed dirt and also protect the print. Soft tissues are less than desirable for interleaving; though they will not scratch the print, they do hold dirt, which will scratch deeply. Prints can also be protected by individual clear polyethylene print storage bags, which keep both dirt and moisture away.

Figure 8.10
**1401 Larimer Street. Arnold Gassan.** This
is the first of a set of twenty-five
photographs documenting nine blocks of a
Denver street before it was destroyed by
urban renewal. The cultural information is
dense (advertising, signs, prices,
architectural details, quality of the light and
clarity of the sky before smog became
routine), but the meaning of the picture is
determined by the viewer.
Photo by the author.

## Summary

Silver prints are easily damaged and must be protected from physical as well as chemical damage. Mount them on acid-free board and provide additional protection from abrasion with window mats. Store mounted and un-mounted prints in acid-free sleeves, folders, or boxes.

## Discussion and Assignments

Meaning is affected both by context and arrangement of pictures. Finishing and presenting a print includes not only spotting and mounting, but arranging or sequencing a group of pictures so that interactions between them are accounted for. The print's surroundings also influence its perceived content.

### Assignment 1

Make three identical prints of a picture. Mount each one on a different color of mounting board: one a flat, hard white; one off-white, but neutral; one black. Place the prints in different parts of your house or apartment where you will see them casually. Over a period of several days, watch the pictures and discover how the one you liked first stands the test of time.

### Assignment 2

How the photograph is placed on the mat affects how it looks. Make two identical vertical pictures about 5″ × 7″ and then *center* mount one on an 11″ × 13″ piece of board. Mount the second on an 11″ × 14″ board with the top and side spacings equal. Place them where they can be viewed comfortably and see how the space at the bottom changes the effect of the mounting.

### Assignment 3

Estimate how many contact proof sheets, negative sleeves, and mounted, finished prints you make a month. Using catalog prices for the following list of items, calculate the cost of protecting and storing a five-year collection of your own photographs.

- File folders
- Ring binders
- Negative sleeves
- Linen tape
- Two- and four-ply mount board
- Protective print sleeves
- Print storage boxes

### Assignment 4

Make four identical full-frame prints of a complex, interesting photograph you have recently made. Neatly trim and mount one full-frame print. Use cropping Ls (see page 147 for details) to discover an interesting picture within the frame of a second print, then physically trim out and mount that version. Repeat for each of the other two prints, finding a different composition in each. Place all four prints in different places in your living space, where you will see only one at a time as you pass by. Watch how your response to them changes over several days. Often, one will appear to be "obviously" better than the rest at first; mark it on the back and then decide again at the end of a week if you feel the same.

# 9 Lighting Basics

Figure 9.1
**Ohio Landscape. Peter Bosco.** Light is all the photographer can capture on film. The photographer sensitively balances the delicate spring sunset which illuminates grasses in the foreground and the richly detailed light from the full moon.

## About Light

Beginning photographers often literally do not see light; it is just the stuff that they use. Light has powerful effects on us, and its "quality" is seen in every photograph. Each place has "characteristic" light, and discovering the magic of light (for that place, for each time of day) is part of the magic of photography. But when we speak of characteristics of light, we are actually describing different energy levels, different wavelengths, refraction and diffraction, and absorbtion in the atmosphere.

Light is a special form of electromagnetic energy. Blue light is a shorter wavelength than red light. Light travels in straight lines in a vacuum or in clear air and so we say it is *radiated*. Light is changed in direction when it is reflected, refracted, or diffracted; some of it is absorbed when it passes from one medium to another (e.g., from air to water or air to glass):

- **Reflection**: light meeting a dense, polished surface is reradiated in another direction with little loss of energy. The angle in which the light leaves is the angle of reflection, which is equal to the angle of incidence, the angle between the incoming light and the reflecting surface.
- **Refraction**: light slows down and changes directions, or is bent as it passes from one medium to another.
- **Diffraction**: light is scattered when it meets small reflecting surfaces (e.g., air with dust and moisture particles).
- **Absorption**: light is absorbed and turned to heat in all mediums (including air).

Light the eye sees is not the same light the camera sees: there are differences between sensitivity of the film and the eye, differences between camera lenses and the eye's lens, but the big difference is in how our mind interprets light. We ascribe meaning to the light itself, give it emotional and associational qualities that the camera cannot record.

Cameras only make a record of the light reflected from the subject. They cannot photograph actual people or places or things, and so the photographer always uses the quality of the light to ascribe meaning to what the camera can record.

## Qualities of Light

Terms describing light which are important to photography are

- Intensity
- Direction
- Specularity
- Source
- Color

*Intensity* describes the amount of light. This determines the shutter speed and aperture needed to make a picture. Intensity must be measured by meter or estimated by eye to determine accurate exposures. The problem with estimating is that the human eye adapts easily when we move our eye from one light intensity to another.

Although most cameras have meters built-in that are electronically coupled to both aperture and shutter, some cameras do not. A light meter is needed to accurately predict exposures. However, many common scenes (with outdoor sunlight) can be estimated accurately enough to make useful exposures.

*Direction* refers to the way the light falls on the subject, relative to the camera. Early camera instructions suggested that you expose pictures only when the sun was over your left shoulder as you held the camera. This guaranteed frontal lighting on the subject, illuminating important details and offering some modeling, or roundness, while assuring important subject areas adequate exposure.

Changing the direction at which light meets the subject significantly changes perception of relationships between near and far subjects, as illustrated in figure 9.2.

Specular light implies contrasty lighting because specular light is from a single source, often called a **point source**. Specular light makes very sharp-edged shadows. The sun is usually a specular light source (especially in the desert and high mountains when there is little atmospheric dust or moisture to diffuse sunlight). Another common specular source is a small electronic flash light.

Diffuse light is the opposite of specular light; it appears to come from many directions. Diffusion softens edges of shadows and lowers contrast. Diffuse lighting in nature is created by atmospheric moisture or dust that refract and reflect the light until it seems to have an undefined direction. Studio lights are diffused with screens or grids, which vary the direction of the light rays.

Figure 9.2
**a.** Diffuse early morning light illuminates
fence and barn wall equally, minimizing the
space.

**b.** Late-afternoon light dramatically isolates
the fence from the barn.

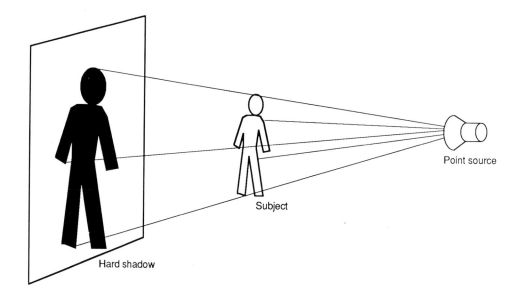

Figure 9.3
Environmental or artifical light may be specular or diffuse, and the quality of the light strongly affects the picture.
**a.** Specular light is harshly directional and creates sharp-edged shadows.

Point source

Subject

Hard shadow

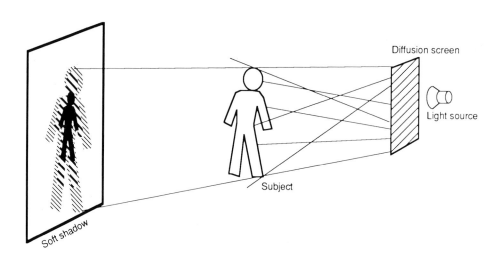

Diffusion screen

Light source

Subject

Soft shadow

**b.** Diffuse light makes soft-edged shadows.

Source light is ambient or supplemental: these are often called *natural* or **artificial light**. These terms suggest the physical origin of the light. Supplemental, or artificial, light often is a momentary light that exists for the eye or only for the camera. Figure 9.3A–9.3B is an example of ambient, or existing, environmental light.

Supplemental light is added to the photographic scene to modify ambient light and create a desired quality of light. Supplemental lighting may be **steady state** and predictable (sun, electric light, fire, candles, "hot" lights, be they quartz or tungsten lamps) or **momentary** and transient (electronic flash, lightning). The effect of steady state lights can usually be measured with conventional exposure meters and evaluated by eye. The precise effects of momentary light on the subject can usually only be guessed, though a Polaroid proof can be made. Professional studio flash units have **modeling lights,** which aid the photographer in anticipating overall effects.

The sun is the principal continuous light source for the photographer (fig. 9.3C–D). Sunlight may be modified by diffusion or reflection, and supplemented by steady-state or momentary

c. Direct sunlight is an example of ambient specular light, which creates a contrasty subject.

d. Diffuse sunlight creates a lower contrast scene.
Photo by Allison Petit.

lighting. Sunlight varies in quality from specular to diffuse, and in color from deep red to vivid blue-white.

Color refers to both the subjective descriptive terms we use to describe light as *cool,* meaning toward the blue, or *warm,* toward the red. When light color is described scientifically, a colder light is more red and a hotter light is more blue, just opposite from the emotional terms commonly used, where blue is *cold* and red is *hot.*

The scientific description of *light* is radiation from a black body at a certain temperature measured in degrees Kelvin. This is important to know only because all photographic light sources are measured by their **color temperature.** Visible light ranges from deep red (about 1,800°K) to blue-violet (about 6,800°K). The *hotter* a light source is, the *bluer* the light appears to the eye.

Color temperature of the light is important even in black-and-white photography because films are not equally sensitive to all colors of light, meters do not respond equally to different color temperatures of light, and our subjective responses to the subject are affected by the color of the light.

- Electric lights used in Paris by Gaspard-Félix Tournachon (neé Nadar) in the 1860s to make photographs in the catacombs.
- Color photography was outlined in theory by du Hauron in the 1860s, using James Clerk Maxwell's theory of light being divisible into primary red, green, and blue.
- Magnesium flares used to illuminate photographic scenes in England in 1864. The magnesium was later powdered and mixed with an oxidizer to produce **flash powder** to provide enough light to make pictures anywhere.
- **Flashbulbs** patented in 1925 and manufactured in 1929. These are the first portable "noiseless and smokeless" light-producing sources for photography.

## Modifying Existing Lighting

Modifying light to limit contrast is an important alternative to exposure/development contrast control. When shortened developing time is used to reduce contrast, shadow detail separations are always diminished, but when light is added to the scene the details are retained and contrast is diminished.

Photographers often choose to accept the light as it exists. Even when the existing light is accepted, the photographer can often choose how to use that light. Figure 9.4 describes the same subject from three different points of view. These are also examples of three different uses of the same light. Figure 9.4*A* is an example of the almost flat light suggested by George Eastman, made with the sun over the photographer's shoulder. Figure 9.4*B* shows **backlight,** and figure 9.4*C* shows strong side- or **cross-light.** All three of these pictures used the ambient, or environmental, light as it existed; the exposure of the film was adjusted to the light, and the contrast grade of the paper was chosen to fit the negative.

Figure 9.4
**a.** A "safe" lighting, suggested by George Eastman a century ago, with the sun over the photographer's shoulder.

**b.** The cactus from **a** up close and photographed at the same exposure, with the sun behind the cactus but no increase in exposure.

**c.** Eight feet to the left with the same exposure, the cactus is recorded descriptively rather than dramatically.

The most simple (and often dramatic) photographic light is a single source (usually sunlight), but more complex lighting is frequently used. Strong cross-lighting is often used in portraiture to accentuate details of skin and hair. Texture is reinforced when the light is more specular than diffuse. Window light and table and floor lamps work well for illuminating portrait subjects because they are combinations of strong directional sources that create semi-diffuse light.

Whether steady state or flash units are used, a **key light** establishes the direction of the light and the shadows, and the quality (contrast, overall diffusion and modeling power) of the light while the **fill light** softens shadows and controls contrast. Key and fill lights may be specular or diffuse, or be combined.

Key light is the principal light, and fill light is a secondary light that illuminates the shadows and reduces contrast. Placing the fill light *on axis,* (in line with the lens and the subject) is the simplest fill light, limiting contrast without making strong new shadows, which might call attention to the light itself. The fill light both controls the luminance range and illuminates deep shadows so that detail is preserved.

The portrait photographer often manipulates the light, adding a fill light to the existing key light. Figure 9.5 shows a portrait setting where a circular portable diffuse reflector is placed at the camera, where it creates an axis fill.

A reflector (which may be a piece of white paper or a white cloth) can reduce the luminance range of a contrasty scene and also significantly increase shadow details without creating noticeable new shadows in the picture or weakening the dramatic impact of the key light. A reflector also permits you to keep the sense of the light (direction and overall feeling of specular or diffuse light) and illuminate shadows to reduce contrast and permit *normal* negative development.

a.

Figure 9.5
**a.** David Vestal (being photographed in the shadow of the worn rocks of coastal Maine), Bärbell, the photographer and her camera, and a folding reflector, which is used to fill shadows and limit contrast.
**b. Portrait of David Vestal. Bärbell.** David Vestal's eyes would have disappeared in deep shadow without the reflected light.
Courtesy of the photographer.

b.

## Lighting Ratios

Lighting ratios are used to measure and describe key and fill lights. The lighting is often described as the ratio between the light and dark side of the subject. If both sides of a portrait subject are the same, the lighting ratio is 1:1; if they differ by one stop, the ratio is 1:2; if there is a two-stop difference, the ratio is 1:4, etc. Rather bland effects are produced by lighting ratios of 1:2, or less. Stronger ratios (1:3 to 1:8) are frequently used for dramatic effect.

Strong lighting ratios can also be achieved by placing a single light source very close to the subject (see fig. 9.13). Figures 9.6 through 9.13 illustrate basic key and fill light relationships. Small studio flash units—with and without diffusion—were used to create these illustrations, as indicated in the illustrative sketches. The flash lights were of equal size and power. This permits easy calculation of lighting ratios.

Figure 9.6
**a.** Basic lighting consists of a single *key* light: here it is placed high to one side. Specular highlights in the hair and sharp shadows reveal the small size of the flash used.

Figure 9.7
**a.** Contrast control is achieved by adding *fill* light on axis (directly behind and slightly above the camera). The lighting ratio is about 1:9: the key light is 5 feet from the woman's face, and the fill light 15 feet away.

**b.** Sketch of the lighting used in **a.**

5 feet

15 feet

**b.** Sketch of the lighting used in **a.**

Figure 9.8

**a.** A lighting ratio of about 1:3 created by moving the fill light closer, until it is 9 feet away. The key light *has not* been moved and the softer image is strictly a result of the lighting ratio.

Figure 9.9

**a.** Basic lighting consists of a single *diffused key*. A plain shower curtain is used as the diffuser. Notice how the contrast in this picture is similar to that in figure 9.6, and the quality of the shadow edge has changed. The diffusing panel now appears to be the light source and its size and shape control the shadow edge. Moving the diffuser closer would soften the shadow line even more.

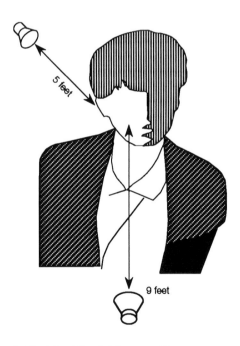

**b.** Sketch of the lighting used in **a.**

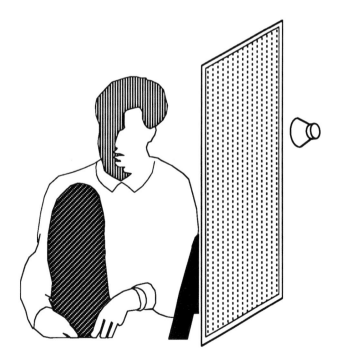

**b.** Sketch of the lighting used in **a.**

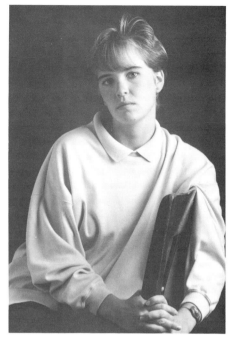

Figure 9.10

**a.** Basic diffused key lighting supplemented by a reflector card at left. The reflector was a hand-held 3' × 4' sheet of white foam-core board. Diffuse reflected fill lowers contrast and further softens shadow edges.

**b.** Sketch of the lighting used in **a.**

Figure 9.11

**a.** Diffuse fill light approximately on axis. The stretched shower curtain is about twice the distance of the diffused key light to create a lighting ratio of about 1:4. The size of the diffuser made it difficult to place "on axis," and subtle secondary shadows have been created.

**b.** Sketch of the lighting used in **a.**

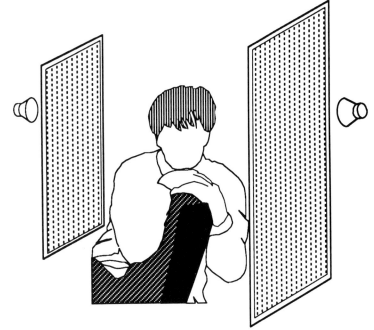

Figure 9.12

**a.** Diffused lights placed on both sides of the model, the right hand light slightly closer. Diffused *cross light* almost destroys hard shadows. Placement of lights is always critical and these are far enough back to create shadows between cheek and nose.

**b.** Sketch showing placement of balanced diffuse lights.

Figure 9.13

**a.** Dramatic light is produced by flash used very close to the model. The flash itself is only a few inches away from the model but points away from her into a silver umbrella reflector. The slight diffusion can be compared in the shadow at the nose and the softer shadow line at the throat. The curvature of the head itself and the inverse square law cause dramatic changes in value.

**b.** Sketch of the lighting for a single-flash portrait.

## Synchronization

Electronic flash lights must be **synchronized** to fire when the shutter is open. Synchronization is done by switches attached to the shutter. The light source is electrically connected to the shutter through a **PC connecter** on the side of the camera body, or a sliding contact on top, called a **hot shoe**. Older cameras may have two PC body connectors, one for **M** (flashbulb) and the other for **X** (electronic flash) synchronization, but later cameras use a single contact and have an internal synchronization switch, usually located on the shutter speed adjusting ring. The correct switch position is indicated by jagged lightning (for electronic flash).

Focal-plane shutters can be synchronized only at slower speeds when both curtains are open and the entire image frame is exposed. Pictures made at higher speeds will have flash light on only a part of the frame. The highest synchronization speed is usually indicated by a colored number on the speed adjusting ring. Most shutters are limited to 1/60 as the highest speed, though some professional 35mm cameras shutters with vertical focal-plane will synchronize at 1/250 of a second.

The length of the electronic flash exposure is controlled by the flash unit's internal circuit. The modern electronic flash has its own light meter that is sensitive to the flash light itself and measures how much flash light is reflected back from nearby subjects. When the "right" amount reflects back toward the camera, the electronic flash shuts itself off.

Flash powder was invented in the 1860s to provide a portable light for photography. It was a mixture of an explosive and powdered magnesium. Thin magnesium ribbon replaced flash powder. The flashbulb sealed magnesium strips that were electrically ignited into ordinary household lightbulbs. These bulbs sometimes exploded (under the pressure of the gases from the burning magnesium), but were generally safe, consistent in light output, and portable (although not cheap). Flashbulbs were the best choice for portable lighting from 1930 until late in the 1950s, when electronic flash became available.

Electronic flash dates from the 1930s. Dr. Harold Edgerton perfected the use of a high-voltage electrical discharge through a rare-earth gas in a glass tube, which produced an intense white light that lasts a very short time (1/1000 to less than 1/1,000,000 of a second). These lights could be fired many times a second, at regular intervals, and were called **strobe lights**. Electronic flash is often erroneously referred to as strobe light. Early flash units were bulky laboratory equipment. Portable and powerful hand-held units needed the development of solid-state electronic circuits and powerful small batteries, which were not available until the 1960s.

Automatic control of flash exposure is convenient but may cause new problems. First, the flash has no way of knowing what is the actual subject of the picture and reflective areas nearer to the light than the intended subject may confuse the meter and cause underexposure. Second, it is possible to achieve *very short* exposures.

Figure 9.14

**Untitled. Edward Pieratt.** Electronic flash used to "freeze" action; this is most easily done when there is little or no ambient light. Courtesy of the photographer.

Full-exposure burn times for automatic electronic flash lights in small cameras are about 1/600 of a second. The flash control circuits cannot change the intensity of the light, only turn it off before the full energy can be discharged, which means that the minimum exposure time can be as short as 1/50,000 of a second. The shorter speeds are a result of the automatic exposure controls shutting down the flash tube, and these very short times produce reciprocity effect exposure errors.

The closer the light unit (with its exposure-sensing device) is to the subject, the shorter the exposure time will be. The effect of these very short exposures are a loss of density and less contrast. T–Max films are less sensitive to short-exposure reciprocity, but most other films will produce better contrast if developed 10% longer than normal when flash is the principal light.

Figure 9.15
**a. Dharan, Al Hasa, Saudi Arabia, 1947.**
**Harold Corsini.** Flash-on-camera illumination "makes" the picture, a culturally significant detail of bare feet and western dress in an Arabic setting. The specular light maximizes the reflective quality of the dress.

Figure 9.15 continued
b. **Woman Carving Portrait Pumpkin.** The fluorescent backlight has been balanced and filled by flash light at the camera. Notice the highlight in the center of the pumpkin and the "catch lights" in the eyes of the woman.

c. **Appalachian Child and Her Dolls.**
**Christine Keith.** Bounce flash produces vigorous, diffused downward directed light.

Figure 9.15 continued
**d. Untitled. Barbara Rascher.** Harsh room light is overcome by using a 3″ × 5″ "kicker" card held at the flash to reflect some diffused light directly onto the subject when flash is bounced.
**a.** Photo courtesy of University of Louisville Photographic Archives. **b.** Photo by the author. **c.** Courtesy of the photographer. **d.** Courtesy of the photographer.

## Computing Flash Exposure

Momentary light sources also impose other exposure variables on the photographer. One is determining what aesthetic effect the new light will have, and the other is estimating the exact exposure required to bring the momentary light and the steady-state environmental light into a suitable balance. Balancing two light sources (existing, or ambient, light and a flash) requires the photographer to predict accurately the exposure for each.

Because electronic flash duration is much shorter than any standard shutter speed, only an f–number need be calculated when estimating flash exposures *if the flash is the only source of light.* Then the shutter is irrelevant (unless the shutter is open long enough to make a significant exposure by itself).

The exposure needed for electronic flash lights can be determined by using a **guide number (GN)** or a **flash meter**. The flash meter is the more accurate method, but it involves purchasing a meter, which may be as expensive as the camera itself.

A flash meter is an electronic device to measure the intensity of one or several flash lights. You set it for a shutter speed, then use the meter as a switch to trigger the flash. The meter measures and integrates both ambient and flash light and calculates an f–number. Remember, *Exposure equals Intensity times Time,* and light intensity at the film is limited by the total quantity of light available and controlled by the aperture (f–number). Variations in metering method affect suggested exposure and the resulting negative densities. Flash meters should never be used without testing: expose a test role and develop it before making the important pictures.

Exposures can be made by simply turning control over to the flash itself and using its automatic exposure control circuits, or you can predict exposure by using the guide number (GN). All flash units have a GN, which can be used to predict the exposure. The GN calculation incorporates both film speed and certain environmental assumptions.

American small flash units have a built-in GN assumption: the photographic subject is being photographed in a small room with an 8–foot white ceiling, beige walls, and moderately light furniture. In real life, when the ceiling is higher and the room is larger or darker, the GN is wrong.

If the flash is the only light source to be considered, calculate the exposure f–number needed by dividing the GN by the distance from the flash unit to the subject (measured in feet):

$$f = \frac{distance}{GN}$$

For example, if the GN is 220 and the distance from the flash to the person being photographed is 10 feet, then the aperture would be set at f–22.

## Inverse Square Law

Flash light is difficult to use because its brightness in the picture changes rapidly as subjects move relative to the camera. It is intuitively obvious that the closer the subject is to the light, the lighter it will appear on the print. But what a beginner finds hard to predict is that seemingly small changes in distance from the light source to the subject create big differences in exposure of the two subjects.

The amount of change is predicted by the **inverse square law**. The easiest example to show and to remember is that intensity of the light on the subject is reduced by 1/4 each time the distance from the light to the subject is doubled, as shown in figure 9.16A. This basic law of illumination proves that as the distance from the light is increased, the intensity is reduced by distance times itself (i.e., is squared).

The photographic impact is shown in figure 9.16B: the two women are placed in just the same relationship to camera and flash as the rectangular areas in figure 9.16A. The distance from the camera to the near person equals the distance between them, and the darkness of the more distant person shows a 2–stop inverse square law change in brightness.

The mathematics of this is:

$$\text{Intensity Range} = \frac{(\text{Near distance})^2}{(\text{Far distance})^2}$$

The inverse square law applies to all light sources. In everyday lighting, it often is not noticed because there are many sources of light and each tends to fill shadows caused by another.

When making pictures by direct flash (when the flash light is pointed directly at the subject) and there are a number of subjects in the scene being photographed, the inverse square law limits the usefulness of automatic exposure controls. The light measured by the photocell controlling the flash is always the light from closer subjects, which may not be the photographer's principal subjects.

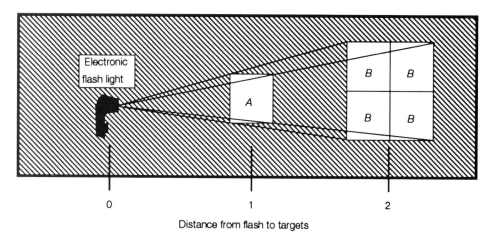

a.

Distance from flash to targets

b.

Figure 9.16
a. Inverse square law: light disperses as it leaves the lens of the flash. The intensity of light on area A 1 meter from the flash is spread over four times that area at 2 meters; at 4 meters the same light would be spread over sixteen times the area.
b. Inverse square law demonstrated: the closest woman is 4 feet from the flash; the farther woman is 8 feet from the flash. The lighting ratio is the same as drawn in a.

## Bounce Light

A way to minimize inverse square law brightness changes is bouncing the light as shown in figure 9.17. **Bounce light** looks different than direct flash. A small flash unit looks like a point source and produces specular light with hard-edged shadows. When specular light is mixed with environmental light, the shadows from the specular source are usually more obvious. Specular lights can be transformed into diffuse lights by being reflected (or bounced). The reflector commonly used is the ceiling or a wall.

Specular light is scattered when light is bounced. The *apparent size* of the light source is the circle of light on the ceiling. The point source of the flash disappears. Pointing the flash at an 8–foot ceiling produces a patch of light on the ceiling about 1′ × 3′, which becomes the apparent source, instead of the flash itself. The ceiling light is a broad diffused source compared to the 1″ × 2″ lens on the flash.

Walls and ceilings are sometimes replaced by a 3″ × 5″ file card held just above the flash unit. Called a **kicker card**, the smooth white card both diffuses and reflects light toward the subject and makes a significant difference in the quality of the light (see fig. 9.15*D*).

The inherent inefficiency of bounce light sharply reduces the effective GN. Bouncing the light is only practical when the flash is strong, because much of the flash is absorbed by the reflecting surface (or not usefully reflected toward the subject).

The loss of light is apparent if you examine figure 9.17 and see how both the light-to-subject distance and overall usefulness of the light change with bounce. If the direct distance between subject and light (at the camera) is 5 feet, the bounce distance (with an 8–foot ceiling) will be at least 8 feet, and though the light is less specular and more diffuse, much of it will be absorbed by the ceiling itself.

Loss with bounce is intuitively obvious, but it can also be predicted by modifying the GN formula (in this example a GN of 100 is assumed just to make the math simple):

$$\frac{100}{5} = \text{f–20; round off to f–16}$$

$$\frac{100}{8} = \text{f–12.5; round off to larger}$$

aperture of f–11

Calculated exposure correction is about a full stop. Now add absorption loss from the ceiling. If the ceiling were glossy enamel and white, there would be a half-stop loss due to absorption (and more if it is cream or beige). A full-stop loss is expected from flat white paint. A practical exposure would then be f–8.

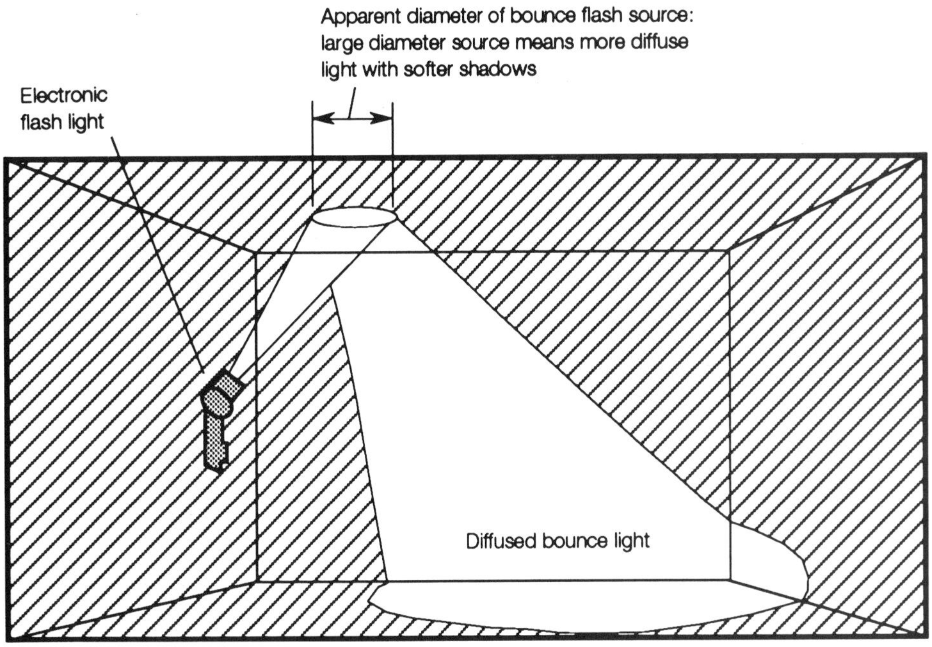

Figure 9.17
Flash will produce a softer quality of light if it is bounced from the ceiling and walls. Bounce light loses intensity by dispersion and absorption, while contrast is lowered as the light becomes less specular and more diffuse.

One rarely has time to make this kind of mathematical calculation and photographers make up "rules of thumb." When the flash is being considered as the *only* source of light, these usefully predict bounce light exposures. When there are other intense lights in the scene, the computation becomes more complicated and the practical solution is to take as many pictures as possible, using a variety of shutter–aperture combinations.

- Small room, white ceiling bounce: open up 1–2 stops from GN prediction (depending on light-subject distance)
- Kicker card or high ceiling: open up 3 stops over predicted GN exposure.

## Mixing Flash and Ambient Light

Flash light exposures can be calculated two ways. First, as though flash is the only light; second, when flash is more or less balanced with ambient light. The flash can be used to lighten (i.e., "fill") shadows and to control contrast.

Calculation using GN produces an f–number exposure, making the flash into the key light, as though it is the only source. When flash light is intended to fill, and the key light is the sun or any other steady-state light source, the exposure should be calculated twice, once for the ambient light and once for the flash.

The TTL meter can easily measure the ambient light exposure, whether it is the key light or not. In the following example, sunlight is the key light but is too harsh. The first exposure calculation is made *as though no flash were being used.*

- Direct sunlight
- Ilford FP4, EI = 100
- GN = 180
- Subject distance = 8 feet
- Incident meter exposure = 1/125 at f–8

A variety of fill levels may be chosen, depending on aesthetic and professional needs. You may allow the flash to dominate or let it be almost invisible (as a contrast control and to create "catch lights" in the darkly shadowed eyes of the subject).

## Flash Dominant

When you want the flash to dominate the lighting, first calculate the exposure using the GN. In this example, the GN is again assumed at 180:

$$f = \frac{GN}{d} = \frac{180}{8} = 22.5.$$

The aperture would be rounded up to f/22. With black-and-white photography, round off the exposure to the next larger f-number.

Note that there is no shutter speed in this exposure because the flash lasts such a short time. Unless the ambient light is very strong, you might as well use your camera's standard synch speed (1/60 or 1/125 of a second). Next, meter the ambient light and compare its exposure to the flash exposure.

In this example, the sync speed is 1/125:

Flash-only exposure $= \dfrac{1}{125}$ at f-22

Metered ambient light exposure $= \dfrac{1}{125}$ at f-8

*Difference* between flash and metered aperture $= -3$ stops.

This example indicates that the flash exposure of f/22 or an ambient at f/8 would each make the same exposure. From f/8 to f/22 is 3 stops. At f/22 (for correct flash lighting) the areas *not lighted* by the flash would be *underexposed* 3 stops: middle gray objects would be almost black in a print and white shirts or walls would appear middle gray.

Dominant flash calls attention to itself and isolates the subject. This kind of lighting was commonly used in photojournalism before high-speed, fine-grain films became available. Like any other photographic tool, this lighting can be used to achieve special effects.

*Flash Balance*   Flash can be balanced with ambient light to limit and control contrast and not be obvious. When the flash is in balance with ambient lighting, low contrast results; the film may be overdeveloped to produce crisp separation of middle values.

Balance between flash and ambient light exposure requires finding two exposures that use the *same* f-number. Reusing the same example, the flash exposure could be adjusted (by changing power settings, using bounce flash, masking the flash with tissues) to an estimated f-8 exposure. Or the ambient TTL exposure could be changed by using a slower shutter speed (1/15 second at f/22).

Many flash units have half- and quarter-power settings. Most popular amateur flash lights have an automatic exposure control dial that can be set to a specific f-number; this dial adjusts the unit's computer to turn off the light when light for that f-number exposure has been generated.

Units without control circuits can be physically manipulated to provide less light. A diffusion screen may be clipped onto the light. These spread the light and absorb about 50% (and require a full f-stop increase in exposure at the same distance). Diffusers can be made by placing one or two pieces of white facial tissue over the light. A *half thickness* tissue absorbs about a full stop. Two complete thicknesses of tissue equals about 4 stops. Bounce light from ceiling or a kicker card will decrease direct light by 2 to 4 stops.

*Flash Fill*   Flash fill limits contrast (fig. 9.18). Using flash this way permits photographing scenes of high- and low-contrast on the same roll and yet produces negatives of only one contrast range. The photographer juggles exposures, revising ambient light exposures and flash distance, diffusion, or power settings to achieve a controlled *difference of indicated f-numbers* between the two exposures.

Figure 9.18
**a.** Late-afternoon sunlight with no fill light.

Calculate contrast by metering highlights and shadows (see chapter 5).

- If the scene is very contrasty, calculate an f–number for the flash that is 3 stops larger than the f–number for the ambient exposure.
- If the scene is contrasty, calculate an f–number for the flash that is 4 stops larger than the f–number for the ambient exposure.

The flash merely adds light to the shadows when the calculated exposure for the flash indicates a *larger* f–number is needed and a smaller f–number is actually used. The flash portion of the *total* exposure is underexposed and the flash merely adds detail to shadows.

The ideal flash fill provides *just enough light to change the shadows* but not enough to obviously affect the middle values. The result is the existing, or ambient, light dominates and the flash merely fills. The combination is sufficient to produce well-lighted shadows. The ambient, environmental light remains the key light.

b. Flash fill softened the contrast.

c. Flash calculated to equal the sunlight exposure produced this "over-filled" picture.

Figure 9.19
Examples of existing and modified lighting.
**a.** The delicate white-on-white room was recorded on 35mm film by carefully ''overexposing'' two full stops and developing the Tri–X negative for only 60% manufacturer's recommended developing time.

**a.** Photo by Charles Saus, courtesy of the photographer.

**b.** Architectural interior photographed as a
class project. Existing window light was
balanced and contrast limited by lights
placed in the kitchen, to the right and left
of the camera, on axis above and behind
the camera, and in the hall.

## Summary

The quality of light is determined by whether it is specular or diffuse. Environmental light can be modified by using steady-state or momentary supplementary lighting. The secondary lighting can reinforce or change the ambient light quality, as well as modify luminance range or contrast.

Electronic flash is the most popular supplemental light source and the exposure can be predicted by using a guide number (GN). The flash must be synchronized to the shutter, and the upper shutter speed limit is determined by the design of the focal-plane shutter. Exposure calculations are determined by the inverse square law and by the GN. Bounce light requires larger aperture settings both because of the increased distance and the absorption from reflecting surfaces. Flash can be used either as key or fill lighting.

## Discussion and Assignments

The work of great photographers constantly demonstrates the power of light to modify and control meaning in the photograph.

### Assignment 1

Choose three photographs each by W. Eugene Smith, Mary Ellen Mark, Mark Cohen, and three from the work of another photographer you admire. Analyze how Smith used supplementary artificial light, how Mark uses environmental light, how Cohen balances daylight and flash, and how your photographer uses light. Try to see (by examining catch-lights in eyes, reflections in polished surfaces, and discovering where the shadows are) what the light sources were for each picture.

### Assignment 2

Find a subject and photograph it under at least three of these different lighting conditions:

- Back lighting
- Front lighting
- Side lighting
- Natural diffuse light
- Natural harsh light
- Mixed: ambient and flash dominant
- Mixed: flash and ambient dominant
- Flash lighting only

### Assignment 3

Borrow an electronic flash light without learning anything about it (GN or BCPS rating) and experimentally determine a GN (for flash dominant lighting) for use in a typical living room or outdoors at night then validate the GN by making exposures depending on it.

### Assignment 4

Make a series of photographs in low-light level (at twilight, or indoors) using a correct exposure for the ambient light (with exposures of 1/4 second or longer) and flash lighting. The flash will illuminate and "freeze" the foreground action, while the rest of the scene will be recorded with some blur because of camera movement.

# 10 Filters and Films

Figure 10.1
*T–Max 400 Silver Halide Crystals Magnified 3000✕.* An array of new photosensitive silver emulsion salts in "tabular" form. The thin crystals and the even pattern combine to make an enlarged photograph with very little grain. Compare this to the irregularities of figure 10.2.
Photo courtesy Eastman Kodak Company.

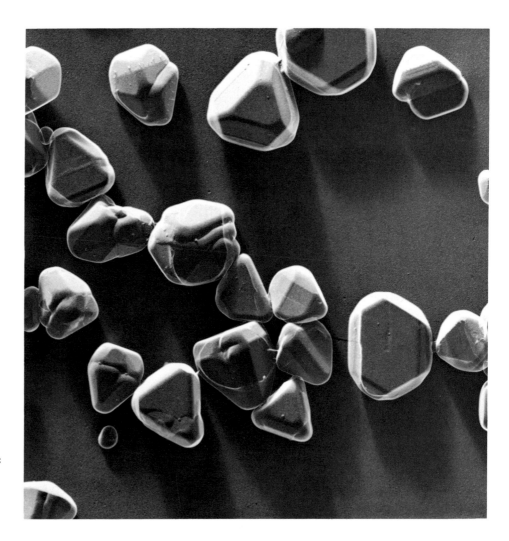

Figure 10.2
Tri–X Pan silver halide crystals magnified
3000×. The silver photosensitive crystals
shown here are typical of how photographic
emulsions have been structured for 150
years. The silver crystals are of varying
thickness and size, irregularly dispersed,
producing an enlarged "grain" image.

## Colors and Light

Our eyes see only a tiny portion of the
electromagnetic radiation that constantly surrounds us, and we call that
visible portion *light*. Because of the
ways our eyes are made, we are sensitive to three parts of this radiation,
which we call **primary** colors: red,
green, and blue.

When the primaries are present in
equal measure, we see white light.
From these primaries, all other colors
we see can be compounded. Our perception of color is a physiological response to how the eye is made. The
lens at the front of the eye focuses
light on the retina at the back of the
eye, where there are sensors that send
signals to the brain.

The exact physics of light or the
eye need not be understood to work
with light, and all these numbers may
seem extraneous to your photography,
but some key numbers and relationships need to be learned.

Light is described in many ways,
some poetic, some more exact. Light
can be defined by temperature (°K).
Light is radiating energy from heated
bodies. Burning wax in a candle produces a red-white light (about
1,800°K). Photographic daylight (or
white light) is defined as having a color
temperature of 5,500°K. This is a nominal value, and the actual color temperature of daylight will vary from about
2,500°K to as high as 8,000°K (in the
high mountains on a clear day when
there is a lot of ultraviolet).

There are two ways of describing
the primary colors we are all familiar
with. Paints and pigments are described by **subtractive primaries,**
which describe reflected light; these
are also called **secondary** or **complementary** colors. The subtractive primaries have professional names of
cyan, magenta, and yellow, which look
to most people like dark red, dark blue,
and yellow, but in fact *cyan = blue +
green* and *magenta = red + blue.*

These colors are used in dyes and
pigments, and subtractive primaries
are described by the colors they
*absorb.* Colored objects illuminated by
white light absorb part of that light. A
red surface absorbs the green and
blue light, reflecting red wavelengths.
A yellow surface actually absorbs blue
and reflects red and green light.

Photography is concerned both
with subtractive and **additive primaries**
(fig. 10.3). When working with light,
one must remember that red, green,
and blue light are the additive primaries. When these are added in equal
parts, the result is white light. This additive theory of light was created and
demonstrated by James Clerk Maxwell
in the 1860s. *Transmitted light* means
that an additive color filter *transmits*
the color our eyes see, absorbing light
from the rest of the spectrum. A *red*
filter passes red light and absorbs
green and blue. A *blue* filter transmits
blue light most and absorbs red and
green.

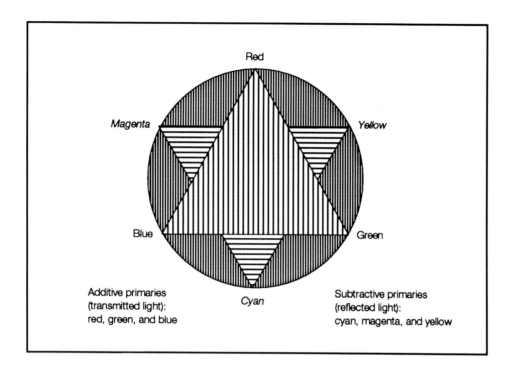

Figure 10.3
Color wheel schematic showing relationship between primary *additive* colors of transmitted light and the *complementary subtractive* primaries of reflected light from pigments.

Additive primaries (transmitted light): red, green, and blue

Subtractive primaries (reflected light): cyan, magenta, and yellow

## Films and Color

Early photographic films were only sensitive to the blue (or "actinic") portion of the visible spectrum, thus the term *actinometer* for early meters. Since the beginning of this century, most manufactured films are somewhat sensitive to most of the entire electromagnetic spectrum. All are also sensitive to ultraviolet and infrared to varying degrees. Table 10.1 lists the 35mm films that are available.

Films are not equally sensitive to all colors. Most contemporary films are **panchromatic,** meaning they respond to all colors of visible light, but panchromatic films *do not respond equally to all colors.* Most films have a lower EI under tungsten light than in daylight because of reduced red sensitivity—Tri–X is only half as sensitive under tungsten light. This means the film requires almost a stop more exposure under the same intensity of tungsten light and daylight. It also means that red objects will print darker than they look to the eye. T–Max films are more sensitive to red than other colors; they may be slightly more sensitive under tungsten than daylight and a red object will print as a lighter gray when photographed with T–Max than with Tri–X.

Table 10.1    Available 35mm Films (panchromatic unless indicated by *)

| Agfa-Gevaert | | |
| --- | --- | --- |
| Agfa Professional | ISO 25 | Very fine grain |
| | ISO 100 | Fine grain |
| | ISO 400 | Fast, moderate grain |
| **Eastman Kodak Company** | | |
| Technical Pan 2415 | ISO 25 | Extremely fine grain |
| Plus–X | ISO 125 | Fine grain |
| Plus–X Pan Prof 2147 | ISO 125 | Enhanced highlight contrast |
| T–Max 100 | ISO 100 | Tabular silver, long toe |
| Tri–X Pan | ISO 400 | Fast, moderate grain |
| T–Max 400 | ISO 400 | Tabular silver, medium fine |
| T–Max P3200 | ISO 3200+ | Tabular silver, moderate grain |
| High-speed Infrared 2481* | unrated | Infrared sensitive |
| Recording Film 2475 | ISO 1000+ | Grainy, very high-speed |
| Type 3 Orthochromatic* | ISO 8–25 | Orthochromatic, high contrast |
| Ektagraphic HC Film* | ISO 8–25 | Same as Ortho Type 3 |
| **Ilford Inc.** | | |
| Pan F | ISO 50 | Very fine grain |
| FP4 | ISO 125 | Very fine grain |
| HP5 | ISO 400 | Medium fine grain |
| **Fuji Film** | | |
| Neopan 400 Prof | ISO 400 | Medium fine grain |

Most films listed are sold in 24- and 36-frame cassettes and in 100-foot rolls.

a.

b.

c.

Figure 10.4
Primary red, green, and blue filters on panchromatic film produce very strong separations of value depending on the color of the original subject.
**a.** Red filter (Wratten 29): Neutral highlights (on mature green corn and grasses) are easily transmitted by the red filter, but blue shadows are absorbed, producing the most contrast. The sky has some color despite the summer haze and is darkened a little by red filter absorption of blue.
**b.** Green filter (Wratten 61): Separates grass in the foreground (which is somewhat lighter in tone) from the deeper green of the corn field.
**c.** Blue filter (Wratten 47B): Transmits light from blue flowers, and absorbs green and red light from the corn and tree. This is the color sensitivity of all nineteenth century films.

## Filters and Factors

A strongly colored object lighted by white light but photographed through a colored filter will create a different value in the negative, as compared to the same object photographed without the filter (fig. 10.4). Strongly colored objects photographed in colored light will have different print values than the same objects photographed in white light, as the light itself acts like a filter.

Colored filters absorb parts of the spectrum and make it possible to make one object lighter or darker than another in black-and-white photographs. When the object being photographed is white or gray, a colored filter will have little or no visible effect. Even a strongly colored filter will cause little change to an overcast sky.

The effect of a filter is to *lighten its own color and darken its complement*. A yellow filter, for example, will darken a blue sky, make a yellow street warning sign lighter, and brighten white clouds in a print. The yellow filter absorbs blue light, producing less density in the negative for sky areas, but it will also lower the density for most other colors because the colors contain some diffused blue sky light.

Photographic filters are thin pieces of hardened gelatin or optically flat glass, which have been carefully colored with dyes that transmit limited

portions of the photographic spectrum. Gelatin filters are excellent, low-cost solutions for the photographer. They are sturdy and lightweight. They easily pick up hairline scratches through normal handling, but they are so thin that these scratches have no effect on image sharpness. Cheap glass filters are actually a gelatin filter sandwiched between pieces of thin glass; more expensive filters are vat-dyed glass.

All colored materials absorb some light. The amount of light absorbed is determined by the dye density. A dark red filter will have more effect on a scene than a pale red filter, and will also require a greater exposure correction.

Photographic filters were given different names by each manufacturer for many years, but now have been assigned Wratten numerical names that define their color and specific absorption spectrum. These numbers replace an alphabetical notation (A, B, . . . X1, X2), used before the 1960s (but still encountered occasionally). A useful source for discovering how any standard filter affects white light is the *Kodak Filters for Scientific and Technical Uses, B–3*. It lists all Wratten filters, color conversion filters, light-balancing filters, safelight filters, and neutral density filters sold by Eastman Kodak Company.

Figure 10.5
**United Nations, 1951. Charles Sheeler.**
Dark red filter used to dramatize the United Nations building. The filter absorbs blue light from the sky, and also accentuates small variations in color of the surface tiles. **Library of Congress.**

## Table 10.2  Filter Factors and Corrections

| Wratten Filter | Filter Color | Daylight | Tungsten | Common Use |
|---|---|---|---|---|
| 2B | Clear | 1 | 1 | UV absorption |
| 8 | Yellow | 2 | 1.5 | Mild sky darkening |
| 15 | Deep yellow | 3 | 2 | Progressively more dramatic darkening through this red |
| 11 | Yellow-green | 4 | 4 | |
| 13 | Yellow-green | 5 | 4 | |
| 23A* | Light red | 5/6 | 2/3 | |
| 25* | Red | 6/8 | 4/5 | Full infrared filtration |
| 29* | Deep blue | 16/20 | 8/10 | Color-blind film |
| 47B | Deep blue | 8 | 16 | |
| Polarizing | Tan | 3 | 3 | Remove reflections |
| 96 | Gray | Variable | Variable | Absorb light |

### Comments

All filter factors are for "normal" sunlight conditions, and will change if the color temperature of the light rises or falls (goes blue or red), depending on the filter used. The factors for red and yellow filters should be doubled when photographing above 6,000 feet (to compensate for atmospheric blue shift). Filters should not be combined: the strongest will dominate and the combined effect is of neutral density plus the stronger color. Nothing is gained and sharpness is lost. Wratten 90 N.D. filters absorb all colors equally; see text for uses.

### Suggested Uses for These Filters

Wratten 2B absorbs ultraviolet and blue radiation scattered by atmospheric haze (commonly replaced by so-called **skylight filter**). Wratten 8 yellow (K2) and Wratten 15 deep yellow (G) are used to absorb blue light and darken skies; panchromatic film and the 8 filter combine to produce sky values similar to what the eye sees. Wratten 11 and Wratten 13 yellow-green filters darken skies and render foliage lighter in value. Wratten 23A, 25, and 29 are increasingly dark red filters. The first two are used to dramatically darken blue skies, and Wratten 29 is also used with infrared film, with which it has a filter factor of 1 (i.e., *no change in exposure*). However, Wratten 15 and either of the two red filters listed can be used with infrared film, producing increasingly vivid infrared effects as the color darkens and absorption of white light increases. Wratten 47B deep blue makes panchromatic film look like the color-blind film of the last century, producing white skies and very dark foliage.

*Use the smaller factors for T-Max films.

The increase in exposure required to compensate for the absorption is called the **filter factor** (table 10.2). The filter factor is an *arithmetic multiplier*. Filter factor exposure correction is calculated by multiplying the indicated exposure time (not the f–number) by the filter factor. For example:

- Yellow filter with a factor of 1.5
- Metered exposure = 1/125 sec. at f–11
- Filter factor = 1.5
- New exposure = meter exposure × factor
- = 1/125 × 1.5
- = 1/80 second
- Round off to 1/60 sec. at f–11
- Alternate: 1/125 second at halfway between f–11 and f–8.

An exposure with a filter *cannot* safely be calculated with TTL metering by putting the filter in front of the lens. This is because the meter rarely has the same spectral sensitivity as the film. Meters also have different sensitivities to visible and infrared radiation, which may cause errors in predicting exposures.

## Filter Colors to Use

Yellow-green filters are the least well-known filters but are effective for darkening skies, while creating greater definition in foliage. Trees and shrubs do not become much lighter (as might be expected) because the green foliage is saturated with blue, which is both integral to the leaf pigment and is present in all the shadows because of the diffuse blue sky light that illuminates the landscape.

There will be a sharp loss of shadow detail when the stronger yellow and red filters (Wratten 15, 23A, 29) are used with landscapes to darken skies because shadows outdoors are mostly illuminated by reflected blue skylight (fig. 10.6). This loss of detail is only partially compensated by the filter factor. When shadow detail is very important, additional exposure should be given and development reduced about 10%.

A deep blue filter (Wratten 47B) can be used to simulate the effect of the color-blind films of the last century, lightening skies and minimizing cloud formations. The blue filter will also increase atmospheric effects of haze when that is desired.

## Infrared Film Filters and Exposure

Infrared can be considered a special kind of light: radiation with a very long wavelength. Since the lenses on most cameras are not calculated for this wavelength, using infrared requires a slight focusing adjustment. On most cameras, there is a dot next to the focusing mark on the lens barrel (sometimes marked **IR**), which indicates how much further the lens should be *advanced* from the nominal point of focus when infrared film is used.

Infrared poses special exposure control problems: the light being photographed cannot easily be metered. The film itself is about equally sensitive to blue and infrared light; if no filter was used, the picture would look ordinary because the actinic sensitivity would dominate the infrared. When visible and ultraviolet light is filtered out, the unique world of infrared appears. Since infrared film records both heat from the body and reflected light, portraits and nude photographs often reveal the dark tracery of veins just below the skin, tree leaves appear white, skies and water seem black.

A range of effects on infrared can be produced by using dark yellow to deep red filters (Wratten 15 to 29), and the choice of filter color creates a mix of "normal" and infrared vision.

Infrared film does not have a standard ISO number. Part of the reason for this absence can be seen in landscape photographs, which vary as the camera is pointed toward or away from

a.

b.

c.

Figure 10.6
Medium red and yellow filters are most popular for landscape photography.
a. No filter: The sky has little or no detail.
b. Yellow filter: Sky detail is presented in the print about the same way the eye sees it.
c. Red filter: Clouds are dramatically presented and river values are separated from sky.
a. Photo by Sean Dupré.

the sun. Toward the sun, the film reveals a white sky (as it records the heat), away from the sun is a record of an intense black sky (with little infrared) and gray-white trees (because leaves release heat as they cool the plant).

The manufacturer's daylight exposure suggestion is misleading, and experience indicates the Kodak exposure should be *doubled.* The film is also very sensitive to development controls.

Reduce the suggested Kodak developing time by 50% to produce much smaller grain and more delicate tones, if those are desired.

The range of apparent grain size is suggested by comparing the white fence in figure 10.7A, in which a very fine grain results from minimum exposure and development, with figure 10.7B, in which a coarse grain structure and maximum "flare" has been achieved by gross overexposure and

overdevelopment. Figures 10.7C and 10.7D are typical of the medium grain and strong contrast usually produced with infrared film.

As an alternative to placing the filter over the lens, the light may be filtered. Electronic flash can easily be filtered for infrared, and unobtrusive photographs can be made in darkness by red-filtered flash. Again, there is no dependable metering, and initial exposures must be done by trial and error.

a.

Figure 10.7
Infrared film is sensitive to exposure-development controls and the image describes how heat is reflected from the subject. **a.** White fence seems to glow as the edges reflect heat in this overexposed and underdeveloped (relative to Kodak data sheet) picture. **b.** Skin glows and a granular flare is produced as infrared film is overexposed *and* overdeveloped to exaggerate the "infrared" look. **c.** White trees are produced as heat is radiated from leaves and the lighting is "over the shoulder." **d.** Dark leaves are photographed when the camera is turned 90° from the sun as most heat is reradiated directly back toward the sun. The clear sky is nearly black in both this illustration and the previous one as little heat is reflected toward the camera.

**a.** Photo by Nancy Roberts, courtesy of the photographer. **b.** Photo by Liz Cole, courtesy of the photographer. **c. and d.** Photos by Arnold Gassan.

b.

c.

d.

## Polarized Light and Filters

Light has been described as energy waves. In the wave model, light from the sun is random and vibrates in all directions. But light reflected from a polished surface (glass, water, smooth wet rocks) is strongly **polarized** (i.e., vibrates in one plane only). The polarization of light permits the photographer some control of reflected light by using a polarizing filter (fig. 10.8).

A polarizing filter consists of a thin layer of crystals oriented in the same direction. The filter can be visualized as a picket fence: particles moving up and down can slip through easily but those moving left and right are mostly blocked.

The polarizing filter can be used to remove unwanted reflections, whether they are entire scenes or simply reflected light sources (highlights in chrome trim, car fenders, reflections from water). The filter itself absorbs about 75% of the light, and so the polarizing filter has a factor of 3. The filter factor is constant, regardless of the direction of the polarization; all that changes is the presence of the reflected polarized light.

When you view reflections from a window or water through a polarizing filter, you see how the orientation of the filter affects the polarized light. When the polarized light and the filter are parallel, the reflection is not changed. Turn the filter 90° and almost none of the polarized light will pass, and the reflected light disappears.

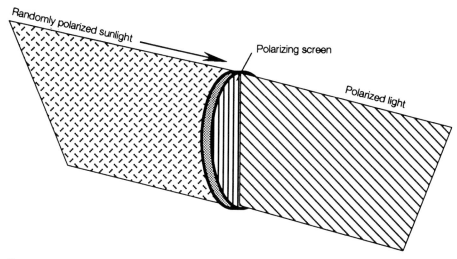

a.

Figure 10.8
**a.** Only light vibrating in a single plane passes through the ordered crystalline layer of a polarizing filter. More than 90% of the light vibrating at right angles to the filter is blocked, and about 60% of *all* the light is absorbed by the filter. **b.** Reflections from the glass consist largely of polarized light. **c.** Polarizing light filter blocks reflected polarized light and pass most other (randomly oriented) light, permitting a photograph of the window space behind the glass.

b.

## Neutral Density Filters

Wratten #96 **neutral density** filters are physically identical to colored filters but neutral gray, and therefore absorb all colors equally. Neutral density can be used to

- Expose contemporary films at large apertures (to reduce depth of field)
- Use very fast films in intense light
- Make very slow exposures in daylight (for blurred motion photographs)
- Create identical exposure conditions for dissimilar films (so that black-and-white and color films or Polaroid proof and production shots may be exposed with the same lighting and at the same aperture and shutter time)

Wratten #96 neutral density (N.D.) filters are sold in density increments of 0.1 and 1 to 3. As described in chapter 6, a density increase of 0.3 is equal to a one-stop loss of exposure. Knowing this, you can combine filters to create almost any desired density. An N.D. 30 filter has a transmittance of 50%, so N.D. 30 placed before the lens would be the same as closing down a full stop. N.D. 0.90 would be equivalent to closing down 3 stops, and N.D. 3.00 would be equivalent to closing down 10 stops!

These filters have very practical uses. Imagine planning a studio portrait that must be photographed in color using electronic flash to light the subject. Without a flash meter, exposure and lighting details can be immediately and accurately visualized by exposing Polaroid color film with an ISO of 100. Suppose the client wants both black-and-white and color transparencies. The color film has the same ISO as the Polaroid, but the black-and-white film is ISO 400. Use an N.D. 0.60 filter while exposing the black-and-white and absorb two stops of light. This effectively changes the ISO 400 film into an ISO 100 film. Remove the filter for the color. The aperture and shutter settings for both films remain identical.

c.

Figure 10.9
Both of these portraits were made with "color blind" blue-sensitive film, which subtly enhances tonal separations in caucasian skin (e.g., variations in red-yellow pigment). **a. Walt Whitman, 1864. Mathew Brady.** Portraits made with early wet-plate process required careful poses, which must be held for several seconds. Note how the photographer has focused on the eyes and used a large aperture (which shortens exposure time and also concentrates attention on sharp details, as in the eyes).

b. **Portrait of Clarence H. White, ca. 1905. Gertrude Kasebier.** One of the many portraits of photographers by photographers: Kasebier was a professional photographer and a member of the Photo Secession. Clarence H. White was initially an art photographer who began the Clarence White School of Photography in New York. Note how depth of field is used to concentrate attention on face and hands. White is carefully posed to permit using a smaller aperture (and longer exposure); popular dry plates in 1905 were not much more sensitive to light than the wet-plate process used for the Whitman portrait.

**a.** National Archives. **b.** Library of Congress.

## Summary

White light is partly absorbed by strong colored objects. Most contemporary films are panchromatic (i.e., they respond well to all colors of light). Films are available with special sensitivity (orthochromatic and infrared), and with a range of ISO speeds from 25 to 3000 or more. By using filters, controlled value changes of colored objects can be created in the black-and-white print. Photographic filters have standard Wratten number names that indicate color and chromatic selectivity. Exposures through these filters are specific to the film used and are calculated by using filter factors (rather than metering through the filter). The factors are arithmetic multipliers of exposure time. Infrared film is sensitive to blue as well as red light and is exposed with a dark red filter to remove actinic light.

Sunlight is polarized by reflection. Light may also be polarized by passing through a screen of crystals, called a polarizing filter. Such a filter can be used to eliminate or minimize reflected light. Neutral density filters absorb all colors.

## Discussion and Assignments

Filters are the only way for the photographer to manipulate the values colored subjects make without changing the lighting or physically manipulating the subject.

### Assignment 1

Photographic filters are expensive, but they can be approximated much more cheaply with colored acetate, available at any art supply store. (Because they may be less even in thickness, cheap acetate filters may cause some loss of sharpness. Most of the time the loss is negligible.) Purchase small sheets of three colors (perhaps one primary and two mixed colors) and experimentally determine the following:

- What is the filter factor for each?
- What effect does each have on the gray values created when photographing an array of oranges and bananas in a green bowl?

### Assignment 2

Investigate the following for yourself for several different colors of filters:

1. Make a TTL meter reading of a sunlit scene with a filter over the lens, and expose.

2. Make a TTL meter reading of the same scene without the filter, and use the filter factor to calculate the exposure. Expose.

3. Compare the indicated exposures and the resulting negatives.

### Assignment 3

Combine a medium filter (Wratten 8 or 15) with a polarizing filter, with the idea of darkening blues and removing reflections all at the same time. What is the new filter factor? Make a hypothesis and calculate an exposure; make a test and analyze the result. Were your test negatives under- or overexposed? What conclusions can you reach about combining densities and the resultant filter factors?

# **11** Photo Chemistry and Advanced Printing

Figure 11.1

**Corner of the Summer Kitchen.** Negative prints are easily made by exposing, developing, and washing a slightly overexposed and *very* flat print on RC paper. The RC print can be used as a *paper negative.* Unlike a film negative, it is hard to keep a paper negative in tight contact with the printing paper, but when both are wet it is easy. Working in safelight, wet the printing paper in clean water and squeegee it to the wet paper negative. Lay them on the enlarger baseboard and use the enlarger to expose the print through the RC paper negative.

Photo by Arnold Gassan.

**Table 11.1   Photo Chemical Equipment**

Measuring spoons (plastic or stainless steel)

Gram scale (optional)

Stirring rod

Mixing container (1/2 or 1 gallon size)

Graduates (25ml, 100ml, 500ml, and 1–2 liters are useful sizes)

Plastic storage bottles (1 quart and 1 gallon)

Large plastic funnel (cheapest available at an auto supply store)

Rubber gloves and safety goggles

Apron (or darkroom clothes)

Note: Photo chemicals should be mixed in glass, plastic, or stainless steel, and stored in glass or plastic. Avoid aluminum or zinc pans.

## Introduction

It is not necessary to mix your own photographic solutions, but making them will quickly teach you how each component works (table 11.1). Home-made developers are also less expensive, and often more responsive to your film developing or printing needs than packaged developers. There is a significant initial investment in chemicals (Elon and **hydroquinone,** for example, are sold only in 1-pound units by Kodak), but this investment will pay off in understanding the photographic silver process, and provide extended personal control of the medium.

Experiment with common formulas first. After the limits of these are reached, you may wish to try less commonplace formulas and chemicals. Differences between one developer and another are often very subtle, and extensive experience is needed to appreciate the differences.

Mixing a photographic formula poses no health risk as long as you avoid breathing chemical dusts and making skin contact with chemicals. As noted earlier, wash your hands before touching contact lenses after handling any photographic chemicals.

## Replenishment and Single-shot

**Replenishment** of a developer was standard procedure until the 1950s. Replenishment adds new chemicals to replace what has been used, and buffers the solution against the waste products that have been created by

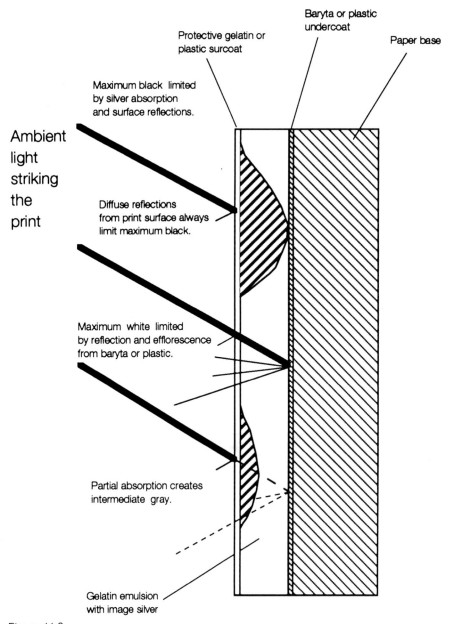

**Figure 11.2**
Drawing of the cross section of a typical print: intermediate values are created as light passes twice through silver in the emulsion and is both absorbed and reflected by the *baryta* undercoat.

processing. Replenishment is common for machine processing, but has been out of fashion with popular chemistry. It was reintroduced by Kodak for use with T–Max developers.

**Single-shot** (one-use) solutions minimize processing variations. Most popular photographic developers are dumped after being used once. This method is more expensive than replenishment. There is less oxidation of

**reducing agents,** and the developer is a known mixture each time it is used. Single-shot processing is best if you work at irregular intervals over a period of weeks. Even more dependability and repeatability comes from using premeasured foil-packed liquid concentrates that are diluted to create standard processing units for film or print developing.

Figure 11.3
**Appletree, Monhegan Island, Maine.**
**Frederick M. Schreiber.** Finding the
subject in dramatic diffuse lighting, using
central placement, great depth of field
(achieved by using a very small aperture
and focusing on the 1/3 point from near to
far), and exposure/development planning,
which retained shadow and highlight
details, are combined with subtle dodging
of the light coming through the trees and
foreground with burning-in the perimeter of
the picture to create the effect of simple
discovery.

## Table 11.2 Common Measures for Photo Chemicals

| Chemical | Volume / Gram | | |
|---|---:|:---:|---|
| Borax | 1 t | = | 5 grams |
| Hydroquinone | 1 t | = | 3 grams |
| Metol | 1 t | = | 3.5 grams |
| Phenidone | 1 t | = | 2 grams |
| Potassium bromide | 1/8 t | = | 0.8 gram |
| Potassium ferricyanide | 1 t | = | 5.5 grams |
| Sodium carbonate | 1 t | = | 6 grams |
| Sodium sulfite | 1 T | = | 23 grams |
| Sodium thiosulfate | 1 T | = | 18 grams |

t = teaspoon; T = tablespoon

## Table 11.3 Common Developing Agents

| Elon (Metol) | Hydroquinone | Phenidone-A (Kodak BD–84) |
|---|---|---|
| Neutral gray image appears quickly but density and contrast increase slowly; energetic developer with long storage life. | High contrast, brownish image but weak by itself and requires very long development if used alone; synergetic with Elon; becomes ineffective below 60°F; has short storage life. | Resembles Elon but works well in weaker concentration; acts as superadditive agent in conjunction with other developers; has long storage life. |

There are many other developing agents besides those listed above, but almost any print or negative desired can be produced with these three.
Note: See appendix 5 for sources of these and other chemicals.

## Measuring, Mixing, and Storing Solutions

You do not have to have a laboratory scale to mix your own photo chemicals (table 11.2). Formulas in this text are presented in simple common measures of tablespoons and teaspoons (and in metric units). The common measurements are not as accurate, but they are adequate for photographic print-making. Measure dry chemicals by spooning or scooping them out of the bulk container. All measurements are *level* teaspoon or tablespoons: fill the spoon and draw a straightedge across it to strike off the excess. Chemicals that tend to clump together must be broken up before being measured.

Where common measures are not available, use a balance scale. Treat any scale gently and protect the platforms: weigh chemicals onto half-sheets of clean typing paper (or use paper cups for large quantities). Place the scale on a firm, level surface. Scales can be "zero balanced" to cancel the weight of the paper or cup, or subtract the weight of paper or cup from the gross chemical weight. Never use a piece of paper for more than one chemical.

Mix dry chemicals by pouring them into the water in a smooth stream. Stir constantly. Avoid adding chemicals faster than they will dissolve. Never use a thermometer to stir chemicals. Use a plastic stirring paddle to speed mixing. A stirring paddle moves chemicals around effectively while adding very little air, which weakens solutions.

Solutions should be stored between 55°F and 80°F, and most should be stored in the dark. Chemicals are easiest to use when they remain at or near 68°F, the temperature at which most black-and-white chemistry is used. Partially filled bottles of print or paper developer will weaken when temperatures exceed 70°F. Store concentrated stock in full bottles.

**Developers** usually indicate age by changing color, though some (FG7 and Selectol-Soft, for example) always have a tan color, even when fresh. Hydroquinone changes color as it breaks down to a reddish-brown in solution, which smells of rotting leaves. A developer that has decayed may make prints, but they will be weak and gray compared to those developed in a fresh solution. Table 11.3 identifies the common developing agents.

Fixers are damaged by heat; if stored for twenty-four hours at temperatures above 80°F, a fresh rapid fixer will lose about half its strength. There is no obvious change of color to indicate loss of effectiveness. Weak film fixer will be obvious because the clearing time will increase markedly (and film fixed in exhausted fixer often has a cloudy streak down the middle). There is no obvious warning when using weak fixer with paper until much too late, when the print begins to discolor. Edwal Hypo Chek should be used (following directions on the bottle) to evaluate fixer strength.

### Health Hazard

#### Developing Agents
Hydroquinone is highly toxic by ingestion, produces contact dermatitis and is an eye irritant. **Elon** (Metol) is moderately toxic and an irreversible allergenic trigger. **Phenidone** is capable of triggering allergenic reactions.

#### Preservatives
*Sodium sulfite* is moderately toxic by inhalation or ingestion; some people are sensitive to sulfite, and respond to it with respiratory distress.

#### Accelerators
*Sodium carbonate* is moderately toxic and an irritant to mucous membranes and eyes.

#### Inhibitors
Inhalation or ingestion of **potassium bromide** can cause mental confusion or depression.

NOTE: None of these chemicals should be a source of danger if they are handled carefully and if the solutions are mixed in well-ventilated rooms. Never breathe chemical dusts, and avoid all unnecessary bare-skin contact with solutions.

Figure 11.4
**Untitled. Ben Brink.** Early morning light and heavy mist are enhanced by vigorous development and careful ferricyanide bleaching.

Photo courtesy of the photographer.

## Developer Components

All silver process developers are similar, and most contemporary developers for film or paper contain the following:

- Two developing (or reducing) agents
- Preservative
- Accelerator (or activator)
- **Restrainer** (or inhibitor)

All use water as a solvent. The chemicals used for the four functions outlined are

- *Developer:* Elon or Metol (low contrast, gray image); phenidone (low contrast, gray image); hydroquinone (high contrast, brown image)
- *Preservative:* sodium sulfite (absorbs free oxygen)
- *Accelerator:* sodium carbonate (for prints and film); sodium hydroxide (high-energy/contrast film)
- *Restrainer:* potassium bromide; benzotriazole

The significant difference between a film developer and a paper developer is pH: a paper developer usually is much more alkaline. It does not necessarily have more developing agent. For example, D–76 film developer and Dektol have about the same amount of Elon. D–76 will develop a print, but the print will be weak and lack contrast because the pH is much lower.

Only one developing agent is necessary to make the visible image and yet few developers use only one. The second developing agent modifies contrast in the negative and print, and modifies image color in the print.

a.

b.

Figure 11.5
Demonstration of contrast control using Selectol Soft. **a.** Technical Pan 35mm negative (inherently contrasty) printed on Kodak *Elite* contrast grade 2 paper and developed for three minutes in 2 liters of working-strength Kodak Selectol Soft to produce a fully detailed, but gray, print. **b.** Selectol Soft energized with 30ml of Kodak Hobby-Pac print developer (or another standard print developer) concentrate produces full development.

---

**Table 11.4   Beutler Developer (Economical, fine grain, high acutance developer)**

**For Maximum Storage Life**

Bring to a boil in an enamel or glass pan the quantity of liquid noted. Let the water cool to about 125°F. Stir in chemicals in order listed, pour into bottles, and let cool. Cap them when at room temperature. Because most free oxygen has been removed by boiling, the storage life is excellent. The chemicals are listed in common measure: **t** = teaspoon and **T** = tablespoon.

**Solution A**

| | |
|---|---|
| Elon | 3 t |
| Sodium sulfite | 2 T |
| Water | 1 liter |

**Solution B**

| | |
|---|---|
| Sodium carbonate | 8 T + 2 t |
| Water | 1 liter |

**To Use**

At 68°F, add A and B stock and water to complete 500 ml of solution. The following dilutions are for normal contrast. The range of A is 25–45 ml. The range for B is from 20–50 ml, depending on the film and the contrast desired; increasing either developing agent or alkali increases contrast.

Use standard agitation: developing times are five minutes at 68°F.

| Film | A | B |
|---|---|---|
| Pan F | 45ml | 20ml |
| FP 4 | 45ml | 25ml |
| T–Max | 45ml | 35ml |

Add water to make 500ml. Use mixed solutions immediately but only once.

---

## Water

Water is perhaps the most important chemical in a developer. The water must be free of rust and organic matter, and should be approximately neutral on the pH scale. It may be necessary to filter water for darkroom film washing to avoid dirt, and distilled water is often used for a final film rinse to eliminate any need to squeegee the film.

**Hardness** is a term that describes the amount of calcium, magnesium, or iron salts in water. Very hard water can cause nonsoluble precipitates to form as scum on negatives. Water softeners are used to sequester minerals, but the softening process may produce water that is not good for washing film or paper emulsions. Some water is more alkaline and has a pH greater than 7, and is called *hard*. Hard water requires that film developing times will need to be shortened. If your local water is heavily mineralized, you may wish to purchase bottled distilled water from a grocery store for mixing developers as well as for the final film rinse water. The ideal water is near pH 7 and has from 150–250 ppm (parts per million) of calcium carbonate. When the amount of calcium carbonate falls below this, print emulsion fixed in non-hardening fixers may scratch easily.

Most chemicals dissolve better in warm water. Sodium sulfite, for example, appears to dissolve easily at room temperature but actually dissolves only partially in water below 85°F, then floats as nearly invisible particles for many hours before completely entering solution. Although developing agents are weakened by very hot water, a mixing temperature of 125°F is not harmful.

Tap water is heavily oxygenated when the tap has an aerating filter (a small screen screwed on the end of the tap, common to almost all kitchen and bathroom faucets). Usually the filter can be removed to supply less aerated water. The filter adds air to the water, improving its taste, but the extra oxygen is not good for your photo processing chemicals.

## Characteristics of Photo Chemicals

Dry chemicals already contain different amounts of water.

- *Crystalline:* contains much water
- *Monohydrated:* crystalline form of the chemical, containing one part water
- *Anhydrous:* without water
- *Desiccated:* equivalent to anhydrous, meaning most water has been removed

Anhydrous is the most concentrated version of the chemical (by weight); monohydrated is the weakest. The change is significant, as monohydrated sodium carbonate is about 1/3 as effective as anhydrous. Be sure the specifications of the published formula are met.

Purity is usually not an issue, but it is safer to use *photo* than technical or commercial grade chemicals. The *analytical* or *reagent* grades are more highly refined, but their extra expense is not justified.

## Two-tray Developer Demonstration

The following demonstration shows how developer components work. The results are easy to see on a print, but what happens there also happens in the negative. (Note: Fiber-base paper must be used for this experiment. Many RC papers have developing agents in the emulsion, which will be discussed later in the chapter.)

Choose a negative with full detail in shadows and highlights that print easily on normal contrast grade paper. Carefully expose an 8 × 10 normal contrast grade test print and develop it in your usual developer. When you have a good print, expose five identical sheets (but do not develop them yet).

Mark the sheets on the back with a pencil before cutting four of them in half (making 5 1/2″ × 8″ pieces). Store all the sheets in a lighttight place while you prepare the darkroom. You

may wish to save your print developer for use again later by covering it against oxidation.

Use two clean trays for the experiment in table 11.5. Stir in the chemicals in the order noted, using a stirring paddle until they are dissolved.

## Two-tray Results Described

In table 11.5, step 1 contains only **sodium sulfite**, a preservative, and common developing agents. Sulfite acts as a weak alkali, establishing a pH basic enough for Elon, a very active reducing agent. Print 1–A should be a fairly complete, but gray picture, one that lacks solid blacks and is also gray in the highlights. Print 1–B will probably have little or no image (because the hydroquinone does not yet have a correct pH). There may be image in the darkest shadows, and that will be pale reddish-brown.

### Table 11.5  Two-tray Experiment

**Step 1**

| Tray A | Tray B |
| --- | --- |
| 1 quart hot water | 1 quart hot water |
| 2 teaspoons Elon | 1 tablespoon sodium sulfite |
| 1 tablespoon sodium sulfite | 2 tablespoons hydroquinone |
| 1 quart cold water | 1 quart cold water |

Mark the two halves of a print 1–A and 1–B with pencil on the back. Develop 1–A in tray A and 1–B in tray B (be sure each print is in its correct tray). Agitate frequently as you develop both prints for two minutes. Stop and fix both prints. Place them in a tray of plain water until all prints are made. Go on to step 2.

**Step 2**

| Tray A | Tray B |
| --- | --- |
| 1 tablespoon sodium carbonate | 2 tablespoons sodium carbonate |

Mark the two halves of a print 2–A and 2–B. Develop the prints for two minutes in their respective trays with frequent agitation. Stop and fix the prints. Go on to step 3.

**Step 3**

| Tray A | Tray B |
| --- | --- |
| 1/4 teaspoon potassium bromide | 1/4 teaspoon potassium bromide |

Mark the two halves of a print 3–A and 3–B. Develop these prints in their respective trays. Stop, fix, and store in the water storage tray. Go on to step 4.

**Step 4**

| Tray A | Tray B |
| --- | --- |
| 1 tablespoon sodium carbonate | 1/4 teaspoon Elon |
| | 1 tablespoon sodium carbonate |

Mark the two halves of a print 4–A and 4–B. Develop prints 4–A and 4–B for three to five minutes.

Finally, pour *half* of tray A and *half* of tray B into a common tray. Develop the last print (a full sheet) for two to three minutes in this mixture. Fix, wash, and dry all the prints. Compare them in a good light, and study the differences in contrast and color.

Step 2 adds alkali (**sodium carbonate**), which raises the pH to about 12.5 and energizes both developing (reducing) agents. Print 2–A, from the Elon tray, will be stronger but will lack strong blacks. The highlights will probably be gray. Because Elon is a strong developing agent, there may also be gray in the unexposed white borders.

Print 2–B will make a weak, high-contrast print with detailed shadows, but it usually lacks highlights. You may wish to expose another sheet of paper and develop it in the B tray for a much longer time, to discover how the hydroquinone will *eventually* produce a complete image.

Step 3 introduces restrainer: potassium bromide. This inhibits development of the latent image into a visible image. Print 3–A should have clear highlights (and no fog in the borders), more contrast than the earlier prints, and may have less shadow density. Print 3–B will show a great loss of density because the inhibitor has more effect on the hydroquinone, a weak developing agent. Deep shadows often appear brown. The addition of the restrainer may leave little image at all with some papers.

Step 4 illustrates the synergetic action of Elon and hydroquinone. Similar interaction takes place when **phenidone,** another popular and very

active developing agent, is added to a hydroquinone solution. Both trays have alkali, increasing the effectiveness of all the common developing agents. Print 4–A should be similar to 3–A, but have more density overall. Print 4–B should be a strong print with good contrast and shadow detail. The amount of highlight detail will vary, depending on the paper used.

The solution you have produced by mixing the two trays produces a "cold tone" print developer, and the color change is best seen when compared to a "warm tone" print resulting from development in D–72 (equivalent to Dektol). The color change is slight and affects depth in the shadows.

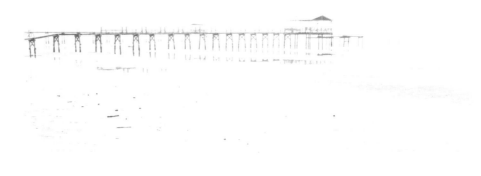

Figure 11.6
**a.** RC paper in water with only sodium sulfite and sodium carbonate. The faint image resulted from developing agents incorporated in the emulsion being activated by the alkaline solution.

**b.** A pinch of Elon added to the alkaline solution acts synergically with the incorporated developer. The resulting image is gray because there is no restrainer to control highlights.

If you compared the chemistry of Dektol (D–72) and this tray of developer, you would find that D–72 is similar but has about twelve times as much bromide as the developer you have created.

## RC Paper Experiment

Many RC papers incorporate developing agents in the emulsion to enhance print quality with rapid machine processing. Knowing whether the RC paper you use has built-in reducing agents is useful because such paper has very limited developing controls.

Begin by correctly exposing two pieces of RC paper, using the appropriate contrast grade filter. Store these sheets away from the light while you prepare the darkroom.

Add 3 tablespoons of sodium sulfite and 3 teaspoons of sodium carbonate to 1 liter of water at about 75°F; stir until they appear to be dissolved. The sulfite and carbonate create a chemical environment in which *any* developing agent in the emulsion can function. An image should result on an exposed sheet of photo paper if there is a developer present in the emulsion.

In normal safelight conditions, immerse one exposed print in this solution and develop for three to four minutes. If there is developer in the emulsion, there may be a faint developed image. The overall paper color resembles a light gray (fig. 11.6A). Stop, fix, and wash the first print.

Add a *pinch* of Elon to the tray (this is a fairly precise measure of about 1/10th of a gram), and stir until it dissolves. Develop the second exposed RC print in this weak developing solution for three minutes. If there is developer already in the RC emulsion, the Elon will act synergically and quickly produce a low-contrast gray image overall (fig. 11.6B).

Finally, you may wish to expose a piece of fiber-based paper with the same negative and develop it in the weak Elon solution for three minutes.

c. Adding potassium bromide to the homemade developer restrains highlights.

d. Developing the same picture in a standard developer reveals how the balanced developer interacts with the developing agents in the emulsion to produce a complete image.

Photo by Bobby Thompson, prints courtesy of the photographer.

Only a weak, gray image should result (fig. 11.6C). This demonstrates by comparison how effective the developer incorporated in the RC emulsion is, and also shows the absolute power of Elon as a reducing agent.

Expose a final RC print from the negative and develop it in a regular, fully balanced developer for only one minute with constant agitation to see how the developing agent incorporated in the emulsion interacts with the balanced developer to produce a rich print in a short time (fig. 11.6D).

## Modifying Developers

Developers are most often used as they come from the package or bottle, but they can be modified to meet your printing needs. The two-tray experiment in table 11.5 illustrated how each developer component functions.

Developers affect how the silver image reflects and refracts the light, causing it sometimes to appear more brown-black (warm tone) or more blue-black (cold tone). Color changes are subtle and require good working light and some printing experience to evaluate. Though the change is slight, it is often aesthetically significant. Changing the amount of carbonate, hydroquinone, and bromide will change the print color as well as contrast.

You can change any developer:

- Use Elon, sodium sulfite, and sodium carbonate to make a complete, low-contrast developer
- Add hydroquinone and sodium carbonate to increase contrast
- Add potassium bromide to increase contrast, or to make a warm tone print
- Add potassium bromide to keep paper whites clear of fog

Standard developer formulas are buffered to produce constant pH over a working life of several hours. Adding extra accelerator or developing agent is always permissible and will shorten the working life of a solution.

## Printing Paper Colors

All papers are pigmented to provide a base color. Agfa Portriga Rapid and Oriental Center, for example, have a pale tan color; Kodak Elite is neutral to cool white; Ilford Gallerie is very slightly green; Ilford Multigrade and Oriental Seagull are slightly creamy; and Mitsubishi Gekko is a brilliant white. The differences are both significant and obvious, and affect the aesthetic impact of the photograph.

Besides differences in print color, each brand of paper has slightly different ways of reproducing the photographic gray scale. Both Portriga Rapid and Oriental Center tend to exaggerate high value separations and produce bold, though less detailed, dark values.

Photographic papers are redesigned frequently to reflect changes in photographic technology and fashions in photographic printmaking. Japanese papers are significant members of the marketplace that was once dominated by Kodak, Ilford, and Agfa-Gevaert. The resulting competition has produced a greater range of print color and quality.

## Chemical Print Contrast Controls

Incremental changes of contrast between paper grades can be achieved for fiber-based papers by modifying the developing process. There are four ways of doing this:

- Two-tray development
- Mixing high-and-low energy developers
- Witch's brew
- Water bath

Two-tray development separates high-energy, Elon-based, and low-energy hydroquinone-based developers. Partial development takes place in one solution and is completed in the second. First development is usually in a developer containing only Elon (either Beers A, Kodak Selectol Soft, or some other paper formula without hydroquinone). See Appendix 7, table A.2. The key to this method is to establish a correct exposure for the total combined developing time needed to produce rich shadow values without graying highlights. Watch the print carefully as it develops. As soon as the dark gray values are fully seen in the print, move it into a tray of high-energy developer (Beers B, or a standard developer diluted with half the recommended water).

---

**Table 11.6 Paper Contrast Controls**

**Fiber-based, Single Bath Development**

| *Increasing Contrast* | *Decreasing Contrast* |
|---|---|
| Increase potassium bromide | |
| Increase hydroquinone | Increase Elon |
| Increase carbonate | |
| Increase developing time | Decrease developing time |
| | Flash exposed print |

**Fiber-based, Two Bath Development**

| Increase time in low-energy developer | Increase time in high-energy developer |
|---|---|
| | water bath development |

**Fiber-based or RC, Either Development Plan**

| Increase contrast grade | Decrease contrast grade |
|---|---|
| Increase filter number | Decrease filter number |
| Selenium intensification | |

**Table 11.7  A Beers Fiber-Base Paper Contrast Control Developer Formula**

| Solution A | | Solution B | | Contrast Control Mixtures | | | | | | | |
|---|---|---|---|---|---|---|---|---|---|---|---|
| Water at 125°F | 750 ml (24 ounces) | Water at 125°F | 750 ml (24 ounces) | | Low | 2 | 3 | Med | 5 | 6 | High |
| Elon | 8 grams (2 1/4 teaspoons) | | | A | 500 | 435 | 372 | 310 | 250 | 190 | 128 ml |
| Sodium sulfite | 23 grams (1 tablespoon) | Sodium sulfite | 23 grams (1 tablespoon) | B | 0 | 65 | 128 | 190 | 250 | 310 | 872 ml |
| | | Hydroquinone | 8 grams (1 tablespoon) | Water | 500 | 500 | 500 | 500 | 500 | 500 | 0 ml |
| Sodium carbonate | 23 grams (1 tablespoon + 3/4 teaspoon) | Sodium carbonate | 32 grams (1 tablespoon + 2 teaspoons) | | | | | | | | |
| Potassium bromide | 1.5 grams (1/4 teaspoon) | Potassium bromide | 2 grams (3/8 teaspoon) | | | | | | | | |
| Cold water to make | 1 liter (1 quart) | Cold water to make | 1 liter (1 quart) | | | | | | | | |

Chemical quantities are listed in metric and common measures.

Other variations of two-tray processing are practical. One convenient method is to use any other concentrated, packaged liquid developer concentrate to modify Selectol Soft (in normal dilution). Minimum contrast (about half a paper grade less) is obtained by developing in Selectol-Soft alone. Contrast can be increased up to the normal for that paper grade by adding developer concentrate in 5–10ml increments. A variant is to begin with a liter of low-energy developer (Beers A or Kodak Selectol Soft) and add 20ml increments of liquid premixed developer concentrate as needed.

Sometimes it is convenient to make a "witch's brew," and modify a working tray of developer to produce changes in one or two prints. This is best done after the limits of standard solutions have been achieved. For more contrast, stir in 2 tablespoons of extra hydroquinone and 2 tablespoons of sodium carbonate to a tray for each liter of developing solution. Use a stirring paddle to move the chemicals around until they are dissolved. This produces a high-energy, although short-lived, developer.

Contrast can also be increased by adding 1/8 teaspoon of potassium bromide to a tray containing 1–2 liters of working developer. The bromide will cause a slight shift of color (toward a warm tone)—if you are making a portfolio of prints this may be important.

Contrast increase without color change can be had by using Edwal Liquid Orthazite instead of potassium bromide. Print exposure and developing time must both be increased slightly to allow for the effect of the bromide inhibitor.

Very contrasty negatives can sometimes be successfully printed (keeping both highlight and shadow detail) on fiber-based papers by using a basic-solution/water-bath development. Start by developing the print in a standard print developer until the middle gray values are just seen (about thirty seconds). Remove the print from the developer and (without allowing drain time) slide it in a tray containing *only* a 10% solution of sodium carbonate. Allow the print to stand in the second solution *without agitation* for one to two minutes.

The two-bath print developer described works because developer retained in the paper is accelerated by the strong basic solution and quickly exhausts itself in the heavily exposed areas of the print, but it continues working in the print highlights (where there is little image silver) until all available reduction is accomplished, and has a chance of producing a print with adequate highlights and open shadows. The developer/water-bath cycle may be repeated once. Subsequent repititions will produce a comparatively normal print. The print color may be affected (because the color of

the developed silver image changes slightly with the changed developer chemistry) and a warmer print may result. The warmer color may be corrected by toning.

## Contrast Control by Intensifying and Reducing

After development, the negative or the print may be chemically modified, increasing or decreasing the density or density range. Chemically changing the silver image almost always changes image color; this is not usually important for the negative, but always is for the print.

Modifications include adding metal to the silver image to increase contrast or removing silver to produce either less density or contrast. Intensification adds metal and increases density: more light is absorbed. Reduction removes silver and less light is absorbed.

When the negative lacks contrast, intensification may help. When a negative or a print is overexposed, reduction may help. Either intensification or reduction can be used to increase contrast in a print.

No intensification process can increase density where an original silver image does not exist. If the negative is underexposed, accept the fact it is underexposed, and acknowledge that *intensification cannot and will not create shadow detail.*

Chemical intensification should be regarded as a last resort because of the risks of damaging and staining the negative. If intensification must be done, be sure that all equipment is chemically clean, and the negative has been fully fixed. It is best to refix in plain sodium thiosulfate solution before beginning intensification.

Chromium was the metal used in the intensifier of choice from about 1860 until the late 1980s, when the oncological risks of chromic acid were fully acknowledged. Other metals were also used, including uranium and mercury. All of these involved health risks. Selenium is the only premixed metal intensifier commercially available for intensification of the negative or the print. Uranium and mercury as well as chromium can be used to intensify negatives, and the chemicals are available through the specialty sources listed in Appendix 5.

## Selenium Toning Negatives

Negatives that are well-exposed, underdeveloped, and lack contrast are suitable for selenium intensification (table 11.8). Selenium bonds easily to the silver image, absorbing more light and increasing the density. Where there is little silver, there is little or no increase in density; more silver produces more density after intensification. Selenium toner increases intensity negatives with little apparent change of grain. The maximum density change equals approximately a paper grade increase in contrast. Figure 11.7A is a straight print made before intensifying the negative. Figure 11.7B is a print on the same contrast grade of paper after intensification.

Intensification needs are usually discovered after film has been cut into strips and proof printed. Tank and trays must be clean; examine trays for rough places that might scratch the film. When processing negatives in a tray, a Patterson film clip or a Kodak No. 6 film hanger are good handles for the film.

a.

Figure 11.7

Demonstration of selenium intensification of the negative. a. Print from double-exposed negative made on contrast grade 3 paper. (Double exposure usually results in a low-contrast composite image.)

b. After intensification in Kodak Rapid Selenium Toner (1:8) for ten minutes, the print was made on contrast grade 3 paper. Intensification effects are noticeable in middle and upper gray values (e.g., the wood planks, face and neck).

### Health Hazard

Selenium is a known carcinogen; therefore, skin contact should be avoided. The selenium seems to be inert in the toning solutions commercially available, but there may be risk. (Note that even cosmetic products containing selenium are on restricted sale in Canada and the United Kingdom.) Work in well-ventilated spaces, as selenium toner can release hydrogen sulfide, hydrogen selenide, and sulfur dioxide gases. Wear rubber gloves or use print tongs. Potassium ferricyanide can release cyanide if heated or mixed with an acid. Dispose of exhausted ferrocyanide bleach solution carefully. If your school has an approved chemical disposal system, use that. If not, flush the trap of your sink with running water before pouring away the ferricyanide mixture, and flush the trap again afterward.

Table 11.8    Selenium Intensifier Solution for Negatives

| Pre-fix | Intensifier |
| --- | --- |
| 1 cup sodium thiosulfate crystals dissolved in 1 quart of water at 100°F; hypo is *endothermic* (i.e., absorbs heat as it dissolves and will chill the water). | 16 ounces of freshly mixed print-washing aid and 2 ounces Kodak Rapid Selenium Toner. Use both solutions at 68–70°F. |

b.

## Reducing Density with Farmer's Reducer

Farmer's Reducer (table 11.9) consists of separate **potassium ferricyanide** and sodium thiosulfate stock solutions. These are combined just before use. Once combined, they interact destructively and have a working life of only a few minutes.

Farmer's Reducer always removes some of the silver it contacts on either negative or print. Potassium *ferri*cyanide in the solution changes metallic image silver in the emulsion into silver *ferro*cyanide, which is *not soluble* in plain water but *will dissolve* in a sodium thiosulfate solution.

The solutions can be mixed or used sequentially. The combined solution is called a **cutting reducer.** It reduces overall density and slightly increases contrast because there is more reduction of lightly exposed areas than densely exposed highlights.

Work may be done in ordinary room light. Avoid touching the wet emulsion. It may be safer to process short pieces in reels and tanks than trying to handle them in trays. Maintain all solutions at 68–70°F.

1. Dissolve sodium thiosulfate crystals in warm water.

2. Prepare water, pre-fix, and intensifier solution.

3. Presoak the film one to three minutes in water.

4. Agitate film in thiosulfate solution for two minutes.

5. Drain, and place film in the selenium intensifier.

6. Agitate continuously for three to ten minutes (for maximum change).

7. Agitate in fresh print-washing aid solution for one minute.

8. Wash for two minutes (or fill and dump tank ten times).

9. Wet with wetting agent, and dry the film.

### Table 11.9  Farmer's Reducer Solutions

**Farmer's Reducer (Kodak R–4a) for overexposed negatives**

| Stock Solution A | Stock Solution B | Directions |
|---|---|---|
| Potassium ferricyanide, 37.5 grams, 2 T + 1 t and water to make 500 ml | Sodium thiosulfate (hypo), 480 grams, 1 1/2 cups and hot water to make 2 liters | Use solutions at 70°F. Have clean trays and a good working light. Prewet negative for at least 1 minute in water. Add 30 ml of A to 120 ml of B and add water to make 1 liter. Immerse the negative *immediately* after mixing. Agitate constantly. Watch the change in density, and remove the negative well before the desired reduction is achieved. Rinse negatives thoroughly in running water. Re-fix in hardening film fixer, use hypo-clearing agent, and dry normally. |

**Farmer's Reducer (Kodak R–4b) for overdeveloped negatives**

| Stock Solution A | Stock Solution B | Directions |
|---|---|---|
| Potassium ferricyanide, 12.5 grams, 1/2 T water to make 1 liter | Sodium thiosulfate (hypo), 200 grams, 1/2 cup hot water to make 1 liter | Presoak the negative at least one minute. Immerse negative in stock solution A for one to four minutes (depending on the amount of reduction desired), using constant agitation. Drain, and immerse in stock solution B for five minutes. Repeat if more reduction is needed. Fix, clear, and wash before drying. |

Both metric and common measures are listed: t = teaspoon; T = tablespoon.
Note: These solutions are stable when kept apart but interact immediately and have a short working life after being combined. Store stock solution A in a dark bottle. Avoid working in intense daylight.

Sequential treatment in two baths produces **proportional reduction**. The emulsion is wetted with the thiosulfate solution first, then either placed in or painted with the ferricyanide solution. Ferricyanide interacts with all the silver, causing a loss of density proportional to the original silver content.

## Reducing Negatives and Prints

Reduction should not be done to contrasty negatives with thin shadows. Negatives that are overexposed can be treated in variations of Farmer's Reducer to lower density. Negatives that are both overexposed and overdeveloped can be treated to reduce contrast as well as reducing overall density.

Farmer's Reducer is often used on prints to clean up highlights or to lighten it overall. Use Kodak R–4a Farmer's Reducer on a dry print that has been slightly overdeveloped—with good maximum black values and slightly veiled highlights. It can produce a *slight* intensification because the reducer etches away silver in the lightly exposed areas before it visibly removes density and lightens dark areas. The reduction brightens the highlights without weakening the shadows. Follow these steps:

1. Immerse the dry print in fresh reducing solution.

2. Agitate vigorously for ten to twenty seconds.

3. Remove print and flood with running water.

4. Re-fix print, use a hypo-clearing bath, and dry the print.

A prewetted print immersed in the same solution will be lightened evenly overall. The silver is removed proportionally from both highlights and shadows. Unlike starting with a dry print, this will not produce an intensification effect but can be used to correct a slight overall excess exposure.

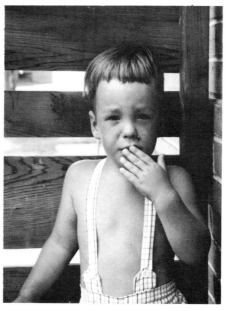

Figure 11.8
Demonstration of using ferricyanide bleach for local density control. **a.** Straight print without dodging or burning. Note darkening of the child's raised hand and face.

## Local Reduction

Large dark areas in a print are easily lightened by using Kodak R–4b Farmer's Reducer. The print is first soaked in thiosulfate solution and then treated with the ferricyanide solution. See the comparison figures 11.8*A* and 11.8*B,* in which the following procedure has been used:

1. Soak the print in the sodium thiosulfate (solution B).

2. Drain the print.

3. Place it face up on smooth work surface.

4. Squeegee the surface damp dry.

5. Paint the area to be reduced with solution A.

6. When reduction is achieved, rinse with running water.

7. Re-fix, use fixer remover, wash, and dry.

The ferricyanide solution may be painted on with a brush or applied with a cotton swab or a small sponge. Just

**b.** Local reduction of the raised arm and face by soaking the print in fresh nonhardening hypo and then painting those areas with a cotton swab saturated with a very dilute ferricyanide solution.

*before* the desired density has been achieved, the print is flooded with water. Because the loss of silver continues for a time, a weaker solution A is often used. Dilute it 1:5 or more (as in fig. 11.8). It may be used full strength, but only when vigorous reduction is desired.

It is a common practice to prepare only a ferricyanide solution, dilute it for daily use, and keep it in a small graduate near the fixer tray, and use the working fixer as part of the reducer. A disadvantage of this is that print fixer with hardener often produces a yellowish stain.

When local reduction is desired, the print is taken from the fixer, squeegeed dry, and painted with this diluted solution. It is very important to rinse the print thoroughly with running water before returning it to the fixer tray to avoid cyanide contamination of the fixer.

Ferricyanide bleaching can be used for small "pinhole" spots on the print, but they are more easily removed by using **Spotoff,** a commercial pre-

## Table 11.10 Selenium Intensification for Prints

| Pre-fix (This also can be the last fixer bath for any print) | | Intensification | Clearing | Final Wash |
|---|---|---|---|---|
| Water (125°F) | 80 ounces | Kodak Rapid Selenium Toner diluted 1:10 to 1:20 in Perma-Wash working solution or Kodak Hypo-Clearing Agent. Interleave prints constantly. Prints may tone adequately for intensification (increase of density only in the black and near-black tones) in as little as one minute, or they may take as long as ten minutes. Warm tone papers contain more silver chloride and will tone quickly; cold tone papers use silver bromide and tone slowly. Toning beyond intensification will change color toward the red. | Drain the prints and interleave three minutes in a working strength print-washing aid. | From five minutes to one hour, depending on print washer used and degree of permanency desired. |
| Sodium thiosulfate | 32 ounces | | | |
| Sodium sulfite | 4 ounces | | | |
| Cold water to make | 1 gallon | | | |
| Fix for three minutes at 68°F. Agitate prints constantly (by interleaving). Drain, and transfer directly to selenium bath. | | | | |

mixed solution which bleaches the silver. The resulting white spot can then be painted in with spotting dyes.

### Selenium on Prints

Selenium toner may be used in a weak solution to intensify a print, producing a slight change of color and adding density only to the dark shadows. The change is seen as an increase in blackness and a cool color shift but the effect is not strong enough to be represented in a printed reproduction; therefore, no comparison illustration is offered.

Prints are treated in a series of solutions (table 11.10). The prints are refixed (preferably in a plain sodium thiosulfate solution), drained, and then placed in a combination of selenium toner and a print-washing aid, which acts as a buffer and prevents the toner from staining the print.

### Selenium Toning for Print Color Change

Selenium toner in a concentrated solution will cause significant color change overall and will also reduce the print's contrast. Silver prints will tone to a dark red-brown color with selenium.

The change from a black to a red-brown image will darken highlights somewhat and apparently weaken shadow densities: the heavily toned print appears somewhat flat when compared to an untoned print from the same negative. The same sequence suggested for intensification is used for changing the print color, but the toning solution now consists of 1:3 toner to hypo-clearing agent. Toning should be done under a strong white light, in order to watch for the color desired: the longer you tone, the more red-brown the final print color.

An experimental validation of selenium toning can be made by bleaching a toned print in Farmer's Reducer. The resultant image consists only of selenium, showing just where and how much selenium has been deposited. This may also be seen as an experimental way to make a different kind of print. Tone an existing print with selenium until there is a significant change in color. Using one of the Farmer's Reducer mixtures specified in table 11.8, remove all the silver you wish, then refix, clear, wash, and dry the print. What is left is a balance of selenium and the silver that has not been removed by the ferricyanide and thiosulfate solutions.

### Sepia Toning

A sepia print is brownish yellow in color. Black silver is transformed into a silver salt by using a solution of potassium ferricyanide and potassium bromide. The iron and cyanide are displaced, leaving silver bromide alone in the emulsion (which is just what one started with!). The silver bromide is fogged and redeveloped as silver sulfide, a compound that looks yellow-brown (rather than the neutral gray-black of silver).

Kodak **Sepia Toner** is a packaged version of a bleach-redevelopment color change chemistry that has been popular for more than a century. Kodak's **Brown Toner** and **Polytoner** are also sulfide-based toners.

As noted above, ferricyanide interacts with silver and produces a compound that is not soluble in water but is soluble in hypo solution. Some of the image may be lost if the print to be toned has any residual thiosulfate (hypo). Photo books written before print-washing aids were common cautioned the photographer to make prints that were slightly darker than the desired final print to compensate for this loss of density.

## Summary

Silver print and negative developers are similar in composition but differ in pH; paper developers have more alkali. Water should be clean and of appropriate hardness. Elon (Metol) and hydroquinone are the two most popular reducing agents. Phenidone often replaces Elon and is less allergenic. Photo chemicals decay quickly in heat and light and should be stored in the dark at moderate temperatures. Developers can be mixed by the photographer and weights can be estimated using common measures. The effects of developer components are demonstrated in a two-tray experiment. Many RC papers respond differently than fiber-based papers to development controls. Modifying developer chemistry will often change the color of a print.

Contrast in negatives and prints can be increased by chemical manipulation. There is always physical risk to the film when intensifying or reducing negatives because the film is being rewetted. Negative density and contrast can be reduced by using Farmer's Reducer to remove silver. Lightening print highlights is easily accomplished.

Selenium intensification of the negative can produce about a paper grade increase in contrast, and the intensifier has little effect on apparent grain. Some intensification of the print is possible with selenium toning. Large changes in print color (with loss of contrast) are achieved by heavy selenium toning or by sepia toning.

## Discussion and Assignments

All silver process developers are similar, yet even small differences in pH, different concentrations of developing agents, percentage of restrainers, or the type of restraining agent used will create changes in the formation of the silver image and the way the print looks, its color and value scale.

### Assignment 1

Prepare a tray of your regular paper developer. First, mark #1 on the back of a piece of photographic paper, expose it correctly, and develop it for exactly two minutes. Process and set the wet print aside. Continue using the developer for at least fifteen prints for each liter of liquid in the developer tray. Second, expose a second print from the test negative identical to the first, mark it #2 on the back with a pencil and develop it for exactly two minutes. Third, add 1 tablespoon of sodium carbonate and 1 teaspoon of hydroquinone to the tray; stir with a stirring paddle until the chemicals are dissolved. Fourth, expose a new print (#3) and develop it for exactly two minutes. Finally, complete the processing and dry all prints. In a good light, examine the three test prints and see what differences can be observed. Especially examine the shadows. What conclusions can you draw?

### Assignment 2

Mix the two Farmer's Reducer (R–4a) stock solutions. Locate (or make) a print with good, solid shadow values but veiled highlights. Cut the print in half and be sure the cut passes through the important highlight areas. Wet the print, drain it, and squeegee it dry. Swab the highlight areas with B stock (using a small sponge), and sponge damp-dry. Dilute the A stock 1:8, and (using a small sponge, or a cotton swab) lightly and quickly paint the highlights. After thirty seconds, rinse the print in running water, re-fix, wash, and dry. Place the print halves edge to edge (holding them down with a sheet of plastic or glass) and see how much change has been effected by the density reduction.

### Assignment 3

Take a small bottle of rubber cement and thin it until it will paint smoothly onto a print. Paint out an interesting area and let the cement dry. Tone the print for color change in selenium toner. When the print is dry, use a small block of gum rubber to lift the film of rubber cement from the print without damaging the gelatin surface. Study the way the color change of the masked area within the picture affects its aesthetic impact.

### Assignment 4

Using contrast grade 2 paper, expose a normal contrasty negative and develop a print for two minutes, using constant agitation. The exposure and development should produce correct highlights, but the shadows may be somewhat lighter than you want, and will lack substance. This now becomes the reference print. Expose a second sheet about 10% less and develop it for five minutes in total darkness, agitating for the first minute, then with no agitation the rest of the time. Expose a third print (also a little less than the reference print). Before you develop it, add 2 tablespoons of sodium carbonate, 1 tablespoon of hydroquinone, and 1/4 teaspoon of potassium bromide to the tray of developer. Develop this print for three minutes, with constant agitation. When the prints have been processed and dried, examine them in a good light. Compare shadow values, print color, and overall contrast.

# 12 Other Aspects of Photography

Figure 12.1
**Untitled, 1956. Aaron Siskind.** Rock forms on Martha's Vineyard, Maine, were used by Siskind to make "abstract" photographic art. Siskind established a reputation with documentary street pictures in Spanish Harlem ("the most crowded block in the world") in the late 1930s. He was a teacher with Moholy-Nagy at the Chicago Institute of Design (ID) and the Rhode Island School of Design and was a founding member of the Society for Photographic Education.
Courtesy of the photographer.

## Restrictions

A photographer is free to photograph and display those photographs as he or she wishes, by and large, but there are limits on what can be photographed and what can be published. Some limits are established by law and local community standards and some by good taste. Government restrictions exist, privacy rights exist, and community standards limit what may be exhibited or displayed. For example, under the United States Code, it was formerly considered counterfeiting to photograph American currency. Now, in certain circumstances, for certain uses, it is permitted.

## Privacy

You can make pictures of almost anybody in a public place, unless that person is protected by the law and the public place is not one in which photographs are prohibited or in which a permit is required. Some seemingly public spaces in fact require you to obtain permission to take photographs, including the New York subway and many museums. But the right to make a picture does not always give you the right to use it.

We each own our faces, and therefore retain the right to privacy. An amateur photographer is under fewer constraints than a professional, but either amateur or professional needs to have permission from the person photographed or the owner of property to use photographs for sale, profit, and most public exhibitions.

The following have been legally established as violations of privacy:

- Publishing a photograph of a person's face or likeness or a photograph of his or her property for advertising or trade, without that person's permission
- Disclosing embarrassing private facts to the public
- Using a picture to suggest a falsehood
- Trespassing to take a photograph

Permission to reproduce a photograph must be obtained by the photographer, and anyone can release his or her right to privacy; permission to reproduce photographs is easily obtained by having subjects sign a **model release**. A sample model release is shown in figure 12.2. Another release form, which can be photocopied and carried for use when needed, can be found in the back of this book.

Professional photographers have favorite stories about advertisers using photographs of buildings that were privately owned and not in the public domain, and the sizable financial settlements made to property owners. The nuisance of obtaining a release is small when compared to the expense of protecting yourself in even one legal suit for invasion of privacy.

Not all publishing requires a release. No release is needed if the event is newsworthy. In general practice, a release is often not sought when the picture is used in an editorial, rather than advertising or trade, context. But this is a legal gray area. Many art and commercial photographers do use or exhibit pictures of people and private buildings without a release. At the least, they do so unethically, and they do so at their own financial risk. Recent expansions of *art* to include *appropriation* and reuse of photographs in new contexts have created an unclear legal environment surrounding fair use.

## Intrusion and Trespass

The photographer is prohibited from being intrusive in the act of making a picture. Intrusion is legally similar to trespass: you *need not* step foot on another's property to be intrusive. *Intrusion* can be defined as making your presence evident even when you are not physically on another person's property. Intrusion is often more difficult to prove legally than trespassing, but it is in any case unethical behavior, at the least. Photographers have been arrested for going to unreasonable lengths to produce photographs; for example, by hiring boats and using telephoto lenses to photograph a famous person seen on a private beach.

## Publicity and Libel

A right of publicity is retained by many people who have created a celebrity value in their name or features. Commercial use of photographs of such a person is considered subject to license contracts. This is different from being a newsworthy figure, and celebrity status has been considered as a capital asset by the courts. Taking pictures of such a person without permission or using the picture without a release is considered using their assets without a legal right.

*Libel* is defined as damaging a person's reputation by communicating a false statement. For many years, a newsworthy photograph of a public figure was not suitable for libel unless it was shown to be made with reckless disregard for the truth, or was deliberately false to the reality of the situation. Obviously, a photograph can give a false impression when it is changed by cropping, but powerful distortions of the physical reality of the situation can be created by choice of lens and point of view. Obviously, the immense sophistication of seamless manipulation (a recent example was placing the head of a famous TV woman personality on the body of another actress) and distortion possible by using digitized imagery and computerized rebuilding of the image complicate this legal situation. Libel law is now being reconsidered in the courts, and definitions of who is subject to libel may change.

## Copyright

Protection for photographs as well as writing is now provided by the U.S. Copyright Law as revised in 1978. Your unpublished photograph is automatically protected in this country under the copyright act if it is original work. Defining *uniqueness of the image* is difficult, and with digitized imagery and computerized assembly there will be complications. To protect it when it is exhibited or published, the print must bear the copyright symbol (©), your name, and the year, or the phrase "Copyright (year) by (name)," where it can be seen easily.

MODEL RELEASE

DATE: _____ DESCRIPTION OF PHOTOGRAPH(S):

For consideration received, I give _____ permission to reproduce the photograph(s) described, and I agree that said photographer and all licensees and assignees are entitled to use the photograph(s) described above in any manner or form whatsoever, either wholly or in part, in any medium, and in conjunction with any wording or other photos or drawings, worldwide. I understand that I do not own the copyright of the photograph(s).

[    ] I am over the age of majority *(or)*
[    ] I am the parent/guardian of _____ and I consent to these conditions.

Date: _____ Model's Name (printed):
Signature:
Address:

Date: _____ Witness signature:

Figure 12.2
Model permission form. Copy and carry in camera case or wallet. (Also see back of book.)

Figure 12.3
**Ringling Brothers Museum, Sarasota, Florida. Timo Pajunen.** Photograph made on an NEA Fellowship project using an 8″ × 20″ "banquet" camera. The format was invented to photograph large public dinners, popular at the end of the nineteenth century.
Courtesy of the photographer.

Under **copyright** law, you have five exclusive rights, four of which are of concern to photographers:

- The right to reproduce the picture
- The right to prepare derivative works
- The right to distribute the work to the public
- The right to exhibit in public

Definitions of most of these rights are evident, but the second also means that others (painters, photographers, anyone) *cannot reuse your photograph in modified form without permission.*

Photographs can be registered with the copyright office of the Library of Congress (Washington D.C., 20559), but whether registered or not, copyright protection for your original photographs extends for the duration of your life, plus fifty years. When photographs are made for hire, the law is a little different: the copyright protection is for seventy-five years from publication, or 100 years from creation (whichever is shorter). While the copyright registration does not have to be done until the work is published, if publication is considered, copyright should be completed, if only to avoid possible litigation.

## Who Owns the Picture

When you make a photograph to order for a client, it used to be that the client owned the pictures you made, including the negatives and all rights, *unless* a specific contract defining ownership had been prepared. Recent interpretations of the law indicate that there has to be a specific written agreement transferring ownership of the copyright to the client. This is obviously an improvement over the earlier tradition of the photographer being a photographic carpenter who merely manufactured and warehoused photographs.

When the photographer works on speculation or assumes the expenses and produces the pictures for his or her own profit, ownership is generally considered specific to the photographer. But it is most safe to draw up a written contract, in which ownership is specified and which may be retained by the photographer, or revert to the model who was photographed or to the client.

It is wise to have a licensing agreement before beginning any work. The contract helps assure the photographer that only the usage of the pictures has been purchased, not the original photographic materials themselves.

## Obscenity and Pornography

Our society is very confused about sex and art and photography. Between 1974 and 1989, an art gallery could safely show explicit nakedness and sexual statements that might be cause for arrest if displayed elsewhere. Recent lawsuits regarding the work of Robert Maplethorpe, or the example of the U.S. Customs sequestering a nude self-portrait-with-child by Walter Chappell, describe an ominous shift in political opinion about what may be photographed and displayed or distributed.

Community standards vary widely when defining art and pornography. The physical site where the photograph is exhibited affects a definition, as much as does the subject matter. The legal definitions of obscenity and pornography have been unclear since 1974, when the U.S. Supreme Court refused to establish a national criteria for defining lewd or obscene objects or publications. Unfortunately, it must be recognized that aesthetic quality has little or nothing to do with this judgement and that religious, feminist, and old-fashioned politics do play a significant part. Ultimately, should the ques-

tion be raised to show that the work, taken as a whole, has serious artistic value, both the proof of appropriateness and any legal risk falls on the photographer.

## Professional Possibilities

The opportunities for well-paid professional photographic work have increased steadily during the last four decades. The range of markets for photographs includes making photographs to order for other people to using photography as a means of intense, personal expression. You can use your knowledge of photographic processes, aesthetics, and history to provide professional services to the art community or commercial photographic markets. Photographers also find many different ways of supporting themselves, other than manufacturing photographs for publication or for gallery sales. Photographers work as photographic technicians as well as provide supporting services for gallerys, museums, and publishing, and some teach photography, or investigate the effects of photography on all the arts and teach photographic art history.

Although photographs are made and sold as art objects, very few photographers have ever been able to make a living by producing only art photographs, and, if truth were known, most famous art photographers have had alternative incomes. Some of the better known names who supported their art photography with outside income or through professional photographic work include Alfred Steiglitz, who inherited a photogravure company; Paul Strand, who was able to make films and produce photo books only through help from a trust fund; Paul Outerbridge, a successful fashion illustrator who kept independent through inherited money; Ansel Adams, who was for many years a commercial photographer in San Francisco; Wynn Bullock, who throughout his professional life owned and operated a photofinishing service in San Franciso; Syl LaBrot, who worked for years as a free-lance calendar and color stock-photo producer (and who

was also independently wealthy). Many, if not most, well-known and widely published contemporary art photographers are supported through teaching positions and an academic system in which they are encouraged to make photographic art as an adjunct to their school duties.

Within professional photography, there are many specialities: photocommunication, editorial, catalogue, fashion, architecture and interiors, portrait, advertising, biomedical, and corporate and industrial are a few of these specializations. The amount of special education needed for each of these varies. A photographer snapping babies with automated equipment in the supermarket can be trained to produce competent pictures within a company format in a few weeks, but an editorial illustrator photographing famous musicians, athletes, or writers for full-page ads in consumer magazines usually has years of training and experience.

New needs for photographers arise as technology changes: many companies now commission expensive slide shows, videos, and laser-disk productions to illustrate their products at corporate conventions, or for use in employee training. Even with the digital photographic manipulation now becoming common, the need for the new original image continues. Special needs arise and disappear often in the professional photography market. Although many schools "teach" photography, most teach it in a narrow, repetitive manner, in which the young photographer is trained to emulate very safe, traditional models. Very few schools really urge their students to explore a suitable style for the subject that cannot be taught: the expressive heart.

Future marketplace responses inevitably will create more training facilities to meet special technical and stylistic needs. One example is the corporate annual report, which appeared doomed when the Securities and Exchange Commission stopped demanding companies produce them. Many corporations have found these expensive, richly illustrated bulletins to be useful advertising, and they con-

Figure 12.4
Grain Elevator with Tar Patches,
Minneapolis, Minnesota, September 1939.
John Vachon. A Farm Security

Administration documentary photograph
that reveals the photographer's concern
with abstract form.

Library of Congress, FSA Collection.

tinue to hire expensive specialist photographers to illustrate the reports.

The independent photographer
can flourish in the American economy,
but only if he or she is a capable small-
business manager. As well as having
photographic skills, you must be prepared to cope not only with selling and
advertising your own efforts, but with
tax, insurance, capital amortization,
rent or lease agreements, medical, retirement considerations, workman's
compensation, and other business demands that being self-employed en-
tails. When the economy is good,
corporations tend to expand in-house
photographic staffs; when there is a

market drop, corporate accountants
make note of rising retirement and
medical benefit demands and the
number of in-house photographic staff
positions declines, and more jobs go to
independent, small-business free-lance
photographers.

## Media Labor Markets

The popular magazines now have few
or no full-time staff photographers:
everything is done by contract photographers. Not long ago, a typical photographer's dream was to work for *Life*
or *Look*. In the early 1960s, just before
suspending regular weekly publication,

*Life* had more than 200 photography
staff and contract positions, which are
now reduced to a handful. This trend
reflects a long-standing European practice. *National Geographic,* a bastion of
quality photographic reproduction, has
steadily reduced its ranks of staff photographers to about twenty, but it hires
more than fifty contract and free-lance
photographers each year. The reasons
are economic: an independent photographer does not represent a long-term
obligation.

The demand for photographs is
high, but the number of fixed-salary
jobs in magazine publishing is low. The

Figure 12.5
**Untitled. Mel Curtis.** A Widelux camera photograph. The lens rotates to make a 180° panoramic 2-inch long 35mm negative with a single exposure. The photographer combines the camera's extremely wide field of view and subtle use of infrared film to transform the subject.
Courtesy of the photographer.

economic implications of this change in publishing are complex. Many make a good living through photography, but the emphasis is on self-determination. Many more magazines exist now than did twenty or thirty years ago; almost 20,000 periodic publications use freelance photographs.

Though the number of newspapers has declined, the surviving papers have invested heavily in photographic communication. The number of photographers has held constant, and what is of importance is that there has been a notable editorial and graphic design shift toward making the photograph a more effective part of the newspaper page, which has created staff positions in photo editing, research, and graphics. More newspapers now publish extensive photo essays versus repetitive photojournalism. Even papers with limited circulations are producing 16–page special sections reporting on regional or national problems.

## Alternative Markets

The photographer may choose to sell services directly and make pictures for a client or a company, or to make pictures speculatively, which are sold through **stock agencies.** These are companies that store, catalog, and merchandize photographs. There are more than eighty stock agencies in the United States. Some are specialized (e.g., handle only aerial photographs or regional pictures), but most deal with a wide range of subject matter. For some time, stock houses wanted only color slides, but recently there has been renewed interest in excellent black-and-white photographs.

Many photographers make good livings from stock sales, but the income is unpredictable; you never know when someone will buy your pictures. You place your transparencies or prints with a stock house and it will be months or sometimes years before they find a home. A contract relation-

ship with a stock house is entered initially by presenting a minimum number (from 300 to 1,500) photographs of publishable quality; many houses require a guaranteed additional production of 500 to 1,000 images a year to maintain that contract.

The reproduction fee for using photographs varies widely, depending on the use and on whether model releases are available (essential for advertising; often ignored on editorial copy). The individual photographer *can* sell work directly, but an effective stock agency actively brings suitable images to many clients the photographer could never find, and also negotiates and collects a price reflecting the American Society of Magazine Photographers (ASMP) recommended prices for reproduction rights. After the client uses the picture, the agency regains physical possession and stores it until a new use arises; these services cost you approximately half the total fee paid.

## Photo Services

There is a service market need for people who know good photographs, know the history of photography and how it illustrates our culture, and know how to do cross-disciplinary research using libraries, film archives, galleries, museums, and uncatalogued collections. Even as simple a search as looking for recent photographs in the National Archives requires one to know not only what photographer's work is desired, but the entire panoply of federal agencies whose support might have been involved 40 to 100 years ago. As archives and museums fill with pictures, the difficulty of accessing the right picture to use for a TV show, textbook illustration, history book, or magazine feature article increases proportionately. Time-Life, Inc. charged (in 1990) $100 an hour to research pictures within their own collection.

A professional photographer may expose many dozen frames for each picture that is printed, and photographs in general are produced in far greater numbers than they were a generation ago. The need for specialists has increased, finding those with discerning vision who can examine a negative strip, find the dominant images, determine the important relationships that highlight a story, predict the interactions between pictures printed side-by-side on a newspaper page, and in fact determine a whole visual design where photographs are involved. This work, like most supporting roles in the photographic community, requires talent and extensive education. The graphics editor must be able to understand the full cultural implications in the picture as well as evaluate it for photographic quality.

## Entering the Field

A generation ago, the photographer was hardly ever more than a blue-collar hourly worker with a Speed Graphic or a darkroom technician. Now, the photographer may be a person skilled in reading, interpreting, and utilizing various imaging techniques. A contemporary professional photographer usually holds a college degree and is compe-

tent over a range of job classifications, from the traditional technician to managing a small business, or may be an artist, an arts administrator, a newspaper editor, or faculty in a university.

In a broad sense, the old definition of a photographer as "the person with a camera" has been supplanted by a skilled visual problem solver, a person who is skilled in creating, interpreting, and managing images as key communication elements. The silver photographic process continues to be important, but electronic camera photography, video, and graphics management of digitized images are replacing traditional production of the silver picture.

Portrait, illustration, newspaper, and other photographic specialities were traditionally learned by apprenticeships, and sometimes these began in high school, with summer jobs washing and drying prints, and mixing chemicals. Practically all of these now require college degrees. Unfortunately, training in these jobs rarely exposes you to larger ethical or philosophical photographic concerns. There is always a risk that the job may also be a poor example and encourage you to make only safe, mediocre pictures, and although the practical experiences may be fascinating, there is a risk they will narrow your interests.

Entry into any professional photographic discipline is probably best done by internship after completing most of a college degree. For example, some colleges teaching photojournalism encourage or arrange paid internships lasting a school term. Internships vary in the length and the intention of the relationship. There are wide variations in the demands made upon the beginner, but often the interns work as hard as the regular staff photographers and are given equally demanding assignments. Your own, the faculty, and the school's reputations are at risk when internships are negotiated, and these assignments are not taken lightly.

Internships are often arranged in the principal cities for illustration, fashion, and product specialities as well (what used to be apprenticeships are now subsumed in the role of photo-

graphic assistant). An assistantship will probably last from three to five years, and usually is mutually terminated when the assistant learns what can be learned. Three years is a normal healthy relationship. During the first year, much of the work is repetitive and often menial. The master provides mostly information. In the second and third year, the responsible assistant assumes more and more aesthetic and practical decisions. Mutual rewards—of assured, quality production by the apprentice and increased self-esteem on the part of the apprentice—justify both the initial low pay and the extra mental and physical labor (not to speak of botched work that has to be redone) by the master.

Beginning assistants are paid, though not very much. At first glance, it may look as though the pay may be equal to a minimum wage, but in fact, assistants rarely work a 40-hour week, and a 50 to 70 hour workweek for a fixed wage is standard. The assistant is expected to work long hours and to know how to improvise. One learns to find or create economical solutions to immediate, practical photographic, design, and structural set problems within minutes, all to produce pictures of professional caliber in an intensely competitive, demanding market. It is here that school experiences become useful. Three-dimensional design skills learned in school become essential when you are given a verbal sketch of a fashion concept in words and told to translate that into a studio assembly to be photographed.

## Education and Training

American primary and secondary education does little or nothing to support visual training, therefore a committed and intense self-education is basic to success in photography. To accomplish this, it is important to purchase and study photo and art books, then to view them critically and analytically. By and large, our training in visual literacy is extracurricular.

Academic education aside, the successful photographer must continually explore the production of new images and remain open to changing definitions of what is photography and what is currently important in the photographic scene. If you wish to be an exceptional person in photography, one needs to work constantly to acquire your own primary and secondary visual education.

The production, coordination, and manipulation of traditional photography or new image forms requires advanced aesthetic discipline, cultural awareness, as well as computer software managing skills. A humanities education, training in the visual arts, training in photographic skills, and practical experience are all needed to excel as a photographer. If you wish to be an editorial or journalistic photographer, you need to have a balance between creative seeing and journalistic excellence. In journalism, the event is foremost but the interpretation of that event is the result of visual training and cultural awareness.

Most well-paid photographic jobs now require an undergraduate college degree. Almost all newspaper jobs require a baccalaureate. The degree is only a minimum guarantee that you, the photographer, have a working knowledge of the society being photographed; but you also need higher education because of the complex business demands inherent in being a photographer today. Computer skills are also essential in the photographic marketplace, both for the increased digital manipulations of photographs that are being accomplished on a routine, daily basis and because more and more processes are being controlled by specialized computer circuits, not to mention the software management required to maintain adequate fiscal controls.

The popular short-term workshop system of photographic education is a very cost-effective way of acquiring knowledge and obtaining exposure to alternative aesthetics. Short workshops are intense experiences that economically bring significant figures from art and applied photography into contact with students. A college-level art or visual communication program is also an excellent way to acquire the basic knowledge that is needed to compete in the marketplace.

## Photography in College

Photography training of variable quality is available in many technical schools and traditional four-year colleges. Evaluating this education is more difficult than finding classes. College should provide a humanities as well as a visual education. In addition, in college one can easily acquire the broad business knowledge needed in today's market.

The "photo-techie" is a person who is competent with the camera but one who lacks visual understanding (culturally, aesthetically and visually illiterate). Full-time art schools and technical schools undoubtedly teach and demand more polished technical accomplishment than does a liberal-arts photo program, but there one also runs a risk of becoming a photographer in love with equipment, and not a photographer in love with the medium.

Photographic education is inevitably expensive because skill is acquired only through extensive use of costly equipment and materials. Most photo programs and even trade schools cannot afford to supply small camera equipment, though many have a tradition of owning and maintaining view cameras for student use. Photographic print and film materials have steadily increased in price faster than inflation, in part because they are tied to the precious metals commodity market price. In order to acquire an adequate level of knowledge for entry into a professional internship or graduate school, the cost of materials for a preprofessional undergraduate photography education can be expected to equal or exceed cost-of-living expenses, especially during the second and third year of major study.

A graduate program in photography should be considered as an intensive supplement to a traditional liberal-arts undergraduate humanities major. Graduate study in photography should be considered if one is dedicated to the medium. The baccalaureate years should be mostly time spent with the humanities, followed by a one- or two-year intensive study of photo-arts or photo-communication. School experience should be problem-solving times, where one is confronted with the limits of your own knowledge and helped to develop individual resources, a time to learn research techniques, photographic skills, alternate aesthetic solutions, understanding of ethical problems in visual communication, an explorations of what the photograph might mean other than what is obvious at first glance. When college experience is right, the rewards are visual acuity, technical excellence and an understanding of ethics in photographic practice and use. These experiences build the armature for a successful professional career.

## Networking

Networking is of immense importance in the professional community. Job stability is usually linked with supervisory roles or self-employment. Obtaining enough on-job experience to survive the first years is always painful, and the people you meet become conduits of information that lead to survival. The general experience is that most professional photographers make three to seven career moves in the first fifteen years of their professional life. The exceptions to this are those photographers who accept industrial and corporate positions.

An aspiring professional photographer should join one or more of these professional organizations:

- ASMP (American Society of Magazine Photographers)
- APA (Advertising Photographers of America)
- PPA (Professional Photographers of America)
- NPPA (National Press Photographers Association)
- State divisions of the NPPA
- SND (Society of Newspaper Designers)

All of these provide networking and information for the professional, as well as informative trade magazines. A few hours of conversation with experienced professionals, editors, and possible future employers will more than pay for the modest student membership dues now offered by all these organizations. Professional organizations sponsor conferences and training days. These give you the chance to meet other professionals, potential employers, and teachers when they are away from their usual work—and are therefore more relaxed and willing to chat and share their experience.

## Presenting Yourself

Your portfolio shows your ability to generate a photographic concept, to create images of quality, and to demonstrate your control of the tools and processes. Your personal style should remain personal; do not try to just borrow what is fashionable. It is inevitable that you will frequently see the same people over time within a given marketplace as you learn to sell your skills, which is another way of saying *sell yourself*. The rules are the same for any presentation: do the best work you can, be yourself (because ultimately that is what you are selling) and keep your portfolio current.

Figure 12.6
**Homesteader's Shake Cabin, 1910. Darius Kinsey.** Large-format documentation of the American West 8″ × 10″ view-camera. Color-blind film produced a white sky. The depth of field demanded a small aperture and long exposure: note the static poses and the blurred smoke.
Library of Congress.

The sequence and variety of images in your portfolio reveal the range of your imagination, your sensitivity, and your understanding of how photographs interact. The physical portfolio itself should be neat and presentable. If it is disorganized, that implies you are disorganized. When someone considers hiring you, they are commiting you and themselves to spending most of the day together, month after month, and often the decision is heavily influenced by subtle and unverbalized assessments. Details of presentation of your work are important as these reveal whether your visual awareness will carry over into other aspects of working with you.

Visually literate people have excellent visual memories, and there will be a presumption that you haven't made anything new if you show an editor pictures you have shown before. It is all right to be soft-spoken and laid-back, but that should not stop you for asking for feedback on your portfolio from every qualified professional you meet.

In professional photography, the technical quality of your work is the first thing observed by most people; after this knee-jerk response, what distinguishes one portfolio from another is the quality of visual concepts. No matter how interesting the aesthetic concept, prints must be well-crafted and copy slides be well made. For example, black-and-white originals are best copied on black-and-white reversal film rather than on color reversal, and color copies must be colorbalanced for the copy lights used. If you present color that is improperly filtered or exposed, you have far less chance of being hired because the assumption is you do not know the difference. An employer looks at all these things (and often does this so automatically, without being conscious of it) and then judges you. Bluntly stated, in a tight market, to give an excuse to not hire you means you won't be hired.

## Photographic Arts

The history of photography as art in the marketplace is comparatively thin. There are photographers who make a living directly through sales of photo-

Figure 12.7
**Patricia Grean as Charles Chaplin. Elise Mitchell Sanford.** A psychological reenactment, one of a series assisted by a Midwest Arts Fellowship. The photographer and her models work cooperatively and discover possible personalities which publicly exist only for a moment, for the camera alone.

graphic art, though the odds are about the same as making a living as a ballet dancer or as a professional musician. Making photographic art prints may best be compared to making music at the piano: it is a healthy discipline that nourishes the soul.

Art galleries that sell photography do not sell much contemporary work, and all commercial galleries depend heavily on the sale of historical photography—nineteenth and early twentieth century prints—where the supply is limited and prices are well established.

A recent listing for New York and the surrounding metropolitan area indicated that approximately 5% of all the galleries and museums exhibit photographs. But about 20% of these are museums whose exhibits include photographic art concentrated on established (i.e., deceased) masters.

Selling art photographs is more difficult than exhibiting them. An exhibit of your photographs can easily be obtained if you have a valid aesthetic concept, a body of photographs made in a particular style, and are willing to assume principal exhibition costs (opening and publicity expenses). The photograph, as any other piece of art, must be considered as a decorative object as well as an aesthetically moving experience, or as a collectable commodity (which one hopes will increase in value).

The decorative photograph is usually, though not always, sold in reproduction (e.g., as a poster, used to decorate a dorm room). A framed and matted photographic print is rarely purchased to be displayed permanently unless it is a "master print" by Ansel Adams, Edward Weston, or other photographers whose images have become icons in the art world.

---

The photographic print market received an enormous boost with the death, in 1959, of Edward Weston. Until a few months before his death, original prints could be purchased for less than $100; within months after his death, the price rose into the thousands. The market in print continued to rise for two decades, but reflected the idea that limited editions made the best investments. For example, Alfred Stieglitz produced an 11" × 14" photogravure edition of an indeterminate number in 1919–1920 of *The Steerage,* a photograph of the massed immigrants refused admission at Ellis Island, sullenly returning to Europe. A copy of this print was available at a New York bookstore for less than $20 until 1967, when the last copy was sold. By 1975, the auction price rose to more than $4,000.

The monetary value of the print depends on whether the photographer

is alive and who made the print, the photographer or another. Photography was initially popular in part because it seemed that any number of identical prints could be produced. It quickly became clear that even with rigid technical controls, there were variations between one print and the next, and the idea of a "master print" that revealed the exact vision of the photographer grew in importance.

With the rise in price in the 1950s of lithographs (which became marketplace models for other prints), there was greater value assigned to the nearly unique photographic print produced by the master rather than an assistant or heir. More and more photographers and collecters have come to believe that a print made by the photographer has a value not found in a print made by another.

Most photographers subscribe to the idea that any number of similar prints can be made from a negative, but a few believe that only prints made by their own hand deserve to survive. The most dramatic example of this is found in the self-destruction of Brett Weston's negatives on December 16, 1991. "Nobody can print it the way I do. It wouldn't be my work," is how he justified this act to a *San Francisco Chronicle* reporter as he burned a sixty-year-old collection of negatives on his eightieth birthday. This act is unique in the history of photographic arts.

After Edward Weston's death, his sons Brett and Neal continued to print the elder Weston's negatives for sale, and though these prints are valuable, they are much less expensive (and of notably different visual quality) than the prints made by the father. The controversial issue of *imprimatur,* (i.e., who authorizes a print to be published) and its effect on both price and aesthetic meaning continues.

In the 1970s, a number of photographers produced portfolios of prints (in editions of ten to one-hundred sets) for sale to the new market created by the new interest in photographic arts, and many of these portfolios were produced by commercial labs or even by students working under the direction of the photographer. The price of these works is immensely variable. An example is the *Jupiter* portfolio of photographs by Minor White, printed

and processed by workshop students under Professor White's direction. The first few copies sold for less than $1,000, and the last copy was sold several years after the photographer died for more than $70,000.

---

Collectors purchase photographic prints that fulfill their collector's criteria, which relates to artistic concept, uniqueness of subject, use of materials, and rarity. A dead nineteenth-century photographer is more collectable than a fashionable young twentieth-century artist who is going to continue producing pictures and who likely will fall out of fashion before the final value of the work is realized. Collectors are often not individuals but institutions that are building sets of prints and tend to purchase portfolios of prints, rather than single prints. For either type of collection, the decision to buy is often controlled by factors that at a glance have little to do with the aesthetic quality of the pictures.

Some financial assistance for the art photographer is available from state and federal granting agencies. None of the granting agencies provide assistance to students pursuing a degree. The National Endowment for the Arts (NEA) has biennial grants for photographic artists, but the rationale for the presentation of these awards is shrouded in controversy. The Simon P. Guggenheim foundation also offers annual grants to photographers, and their criteria is opaque. The "Guggie" grants provide roughly a year's living expenses to the artist.

Funding agencies require applications be supported both by slide copies of prints, written artist's statements, and/or references from professionally qualified figures in the arts; it is wise to attend the public application reviews and learn how the language of these presentations relates to the photographs presented. It is informative to realize that any photographer's *total body of work supporting the grant* is usually seen by the reviewing committee for less than thirty seconds.

In recent years, state arts councils have offered grants in a range of values from a few hundred to several thousand dollars, and these agencies have a much better track record for providing grants to candidates who are needy as opposed to fashionable. The process of applying for any of these grants is unique to each agency, and your local arts council should be contacted for details.

Most photographic artists who wish to make images to meet their own criteria rather than the criteria of others support themselves by doing other work—sometimes in areas allied to the arts. There continues to be openings for persons skilled in photographic conservation and art history, as a number of new regional and local museums add photographic collections. Unfortunately, few colleges simultaneously offer training in photography, photographic print conservation, and art history; most of the necessary education is at the graduate level and much training is by internship and apprenticeship.

Written criticism and historical research and writing is another allied field offering support. These jobs may be associated with professional journals or with organizations like Friends of Photography in San Francisco, or the Center for Creative Photography in Tucson. The competition is fierce; there are many eager hands at work. Significant writing skills and a rigorous graduate education are required.

Finally, many photographic artists continue to support themselves through teaching photographic arts in college. The minimum requirements for this usually are a terminal graduate degree and experience as a teaching assistant. Here, as elsewhere in the arts, the competition is brisk and there are no assured jobs.

## Summary

A photographer may photograph freely in most places, but is limited by rights of privacy and definitions of trespass and intrusion. Sometimes these are hard to prove legally, and the photographer's own ethical standard prevails. Obscenity is determined by community standards and pornography definitions are constantly being revised. A release is required for the photograph of a person or place to be used for profit. All unpublished original photographs are protected by copyright.

The photographer's social and professional position reflects a spectrum of possibilities, from blue-collar to middle-management. Most photography-related employment requires at least a liberal arts undergraduate degree and many positions demand a graduate degree in visual communication, photographic arts, or art history. Making a living through photographic art is risky but not impossible. Photographs made for personal and commercial reasons are both marketable. Researching and writing skills acquired through learning photographic disciplines are also marketable.

Portfolio presentations reveal individual concepts, production quality, and technical control, and are central to professional evaluations. There are many specialized photo markets, and most require the photographer to be a business person with some education beyond high school; many require an advanced degree. Photographers are now involved in sales, research, and education as well as technical production. Photographic training involves education in the humanities as well as internships, and a balance between these needs to be maintained. Most specializations may best be entered through internships and apprenticeships. Professional organizations provide a rich source of network information for a young photographer.

## Discussion and Assignments

Make a trial decision to work as a professional in photography.

### Assignment 1

If you are interested in the arts, contact your state arts council and prepare a complete grant application (including an artist's statement and slide documentation of your work).

### Assignment 2

Attend the public review of the local or state arts council applications. Note how the slides are reviewed, how the supporting documentation is presented, and what concepts of photographic art are being supported/minimized by the committee.

### Assignment 3

Make appointments with two potential employers and ask what their criteria are for employment. Learn how many photographers are employed, what are their responsibilities, and whether they are considered hourly or salaried employees.

# Appendixes

## 1 Photographic Education and Workshops

Nearly sixty colleges and universities offer graduate degrees in applied photography, photographic arts, and history of photography. Kodak publishes *A Survey of College Instruction in Photography: Motion Picture, Still Photography and Graphic Arts* (Kodak Publication T–17).

These regular educational programs are often supplemented by workshops (usually in the summer) that bring together professionals and students from all skill levels for short, intensive periods. They advertise largely through college and university photography and art school faculty mailing lists, and since they are seasonal, the brochures and bulletins are usually disseminated between March and May.

Workshop classes last from three days to six weeks. Most often they are not graded—the reward is the experience rather than an addition to one's academic record. Some workshops have lasted for years; others fail to catch on and quickly fade away. Two workshops have proven themselves: The Maine workshop faculty is largely drawn from the ranks of professional photojournalists and editorial illustrators, while the California workshop inherits the photographic art tradition of Ansel Adams.

Maine Photographic Workshop, Rockport, ME 04856.
Friends of Photography, 101 The Embarcadero, San Francisco, CA 94105.

## 2 Information

Knowing where to find information is a great help, especially when you are not quite sure what you want to ask for in the first place.
For more information on chemical hazards:

McCann, Michael. *Health Hazards Manual for Artists* (New York: Nick Lyons Books, 1985).
*Safe Handling of Photographic Chemicals,* (Eastman Kodak Co., Rochester, NY 14650).

Photographic education questions can be directed to the Society for Photographic Education, P.O. Box BBB, Albuquerque, NM 87196.

Equipment catalogs themselves are excellent sources of information that often lead one to ask questions that lead in unexpected directions.

Trade photo magazines are excellent sources of information about machinery and processes. The best of these is *Photomethods,* 50 South Ninth Street, Minneapolis, MN 55804. This monthly magazine offers specific craft information for professionals and also prepares an annual "source directory," a special issue dedicated to equipment location.

Books specializing in photographic problems include:

*Professional Photo Source* (110 West 17th Street, New York, NY 10011; 1987).

*Photographer's Market* (Writer's Digest Books, 9933 Alliance Road, Cincinnati, OH 45242; 1987).

Information on galleries, exhibits, and competition deadlines:

*Afterimage,* Visual Studies Workshop, 31 Prince Street, Rochester, NY 14607.
*Artweek,* 1628 Telegraph Ave., Oakland, CA 94612.
*FYI,* Center for Arts Information, 625 Broadway, New York, NY 10012.
*Lens on Campus,* 645 Stewart Ave., Garden City, NY 11530.
*New Art Examiner,* 230 E. Ohio, Rm. 207, Chicago, IL 60611.
*Photographers Forum,* 614 Santa Barbara St., Santa Barbara, CA 93101.
*Re-Views,* Friends of Photography, 101 The Embarcadero, San Francisco, CA 94105.

Each state has its own granting agencies for the arts, and these should be contacted directly to obtain schedules for grant application deadlines.
Legal information on photographic arts:

Caplin, Lee Evan, ed.*The Business of Art* (New York: American Council for the Arts, 1982).
Crawford, Tad. *Legal Guide for the Visual Artist,* revised edition (New York: Madison Square Press, Inc., 1985).
Mellon, Susan and Tad Crawford. *The Artist-Gallery Partnership* (New York: American Council for the Arts, 1981).

# 3 Books

In excess of 80,000 books are published each year in the United States, and of that number at least 1,000 deal with photography, or use photographs as important illustrations. The following dealers offer an important editorial service in bringing new photographic books to your attention and providing distribution services (often at a discount from the regular bookstore price).

A Photographer's Place, P.O. Box 274, Prince Street Sta., New York, NY 10012.

Amphoto, American Photographic Book Publishing Company, Garden City, NY 11530.

Aperture Inc., 20 East 23 Street, New York, NY 10010 (212-505-5555).

Eastman Kodak Company, Department 454, 343 State Street, Rochester, NY 14650.

Focal Press, 80 Montvale Avenue, Stoneham, MA 02180 (617-438-8464).

Light Impressions, 439 Monroe Avenue, Rochester, NY 14603-0940 (800-828-6216 or 800-828-9629 in New York).

Maine Photographic Resource, 2 Central Street, Rockport, ME 04856 (800-227-1541).

Morgan and Morgan, Inc., 145 Palisade Street, Dobbs Ferry, NY 10522.

Photo-Eye Books, P.O. Box 2686, Austin, TX 78768 (512-480-8409).

Printed Matter, 7 Lispenard St., New York, NY 10013.

# 4 Cameras and Other Equipment

Talk to local dealers first. This offers you a chance to have hands-on experience of the equipment (and often things feel different than you expected them to, causing you to reassess equipment needs). Both new and used equipment can be purchased by mail. It is important that you know exactly what you want, how much you are willing to pay for it, how much you should pay for it, and what kind of guarantee you have of getting what you ordered. Even when the local price is higher, it is often worthwhile to pay more, considering the goodwill involved, access to service, and (with certain foreign merchandise) a valid American service guarantee. A significant percentage of the more expensive cameras in this country are "gray-market" (i.e., are imported without full warranty contracts).

Aristo Grid Lamp Products, Inc., P. O. Box 769, Port Washington, NY 11050.

Arkay, 228 South First Street, Milwaukee, WI 53201 (800-862-7529).

Calumet Photographic Inc., 890 Supreme Drive, Bensenville, IL 60106 (800-225-8638 or 312-860-7447 in Illinois).

Garden Camera, 345 7th Avenue, New York, NY 10001-4076 (800-223-5830).

Hartco Products Company, Inc., P.O. Box 46, West Jefferson, OH 43162-1496 (614-879-8315).

Helix, 310 South Racine Avenue, Chicago, IL 60607 (800-621-6471 or 312-421-6000 in Illinois).

Hoos Photo, 1745 Sherman Avenue, Evanston, IL 60201.

Porter's Camera Store, Inc., P. O. Box 628, Cedar Falls, IA 50613.

Zone VI Studios, Inc., Putney, VT 05346.

For preservation and storage materials, as well as specialized equipment, contact:

Archivart Process Material Corp., 301 Veterans Blvd., Rutherford, NJ 07070.

Hollinger Corporation, P. O. Box 6037, Arlington, VA 22206.

Light Impressions, 439 Monroe Avenue, Rochester, NY 14603-0940 (800-828-6216 or 800-828-9629 in New York).

Maine Photographic Resource, 2 Central Street, Rockport, ME 04856 (800-227-1541).

Portfoliobox, Inc., 166 Valley St., Bd. 3-402, Providence, RI 02909.

Spink and Gabor, Inc., 32 W. 18th St., New York, NY 10011.

University Products, Inc., P.O. Box 101, South Canal St., Holyoke, MA 01041.

Used photographic equipment can usually be located by examining the ads in *Shutterbug,* a monthly magazine and catalog. The address is P.O. Box F, Titusville, FL 32781.

Finally, for experimental lenses, small tools, inexpensive polarizing filters, ventilating fans, and many other useful objects, contact Edmund Scientific Company, Department 2099, Industrial Catalog #8741-2099, 101 East Gloucester Pike, Barrington, NJ 08007.

# 5 Chemicals

Photo chemicals can usually be purchased at a camera store. Kodak packages and sells photo chemicals in convenient quantities. The major chemical supply houses often do not sell to individuals, and when they do, there is usually a sizable minimum order required (by weight or dollar amount). If you are associated with a school, orders can often be placed through the purchasing office to one of the following:

Curtis Matheson Scientific Company
Fisher Scientific Company
Sargent-Welch Scientific Company
VWR Scientific
Canadian Laboratories Supplies, Ltd.

These major distributors have branches throughout the United States and Canada.

Small quantities of any photographic chemical, and complete processing kits for hundreds of different formulae can be purchased from a unique source: Photographers' Formulary, P.O. Box 5105, Missoula, MT 59806 (406-543-4534).

If your local dealer does not carry a photographic solution you wish to try, contact the manufacturer and ask for the name of the nearest distributor.

Acufine, Inc., 439 East Illinois Street, Chicago, IL 60611.

Edwal Scientific Products Inc., 12120 South Peoria Street, Chicago, IL 60643.

Ethol Chemicals, Inc., 1808 North Damen Avenue, Chicago, IL 60647.

Fuji Photo Film USA, Inc., 350 Fifth Avenue, New York, NY 10001.

Heico, Inc., Delaware Water Gap, PA 18327.

Ilford, Inc., P.O. Box 288, Paramus, NJ 07652.

Sprint Systems of Photography, 100 Dexter Street, Pawtucket, RI 02860.

Unicolor Division Photo Systems Inc., PO Box 306, Detroit, MI 48130.

# 6 Metol-free Developers

Many people eventually become Metol (or Elon) sensitive and may develop a skin rash, which can be avoided by using developers that do not contain it (table A.1).

# 7 Packaged and Homemade Chemicals

There are few occasions now for the contemporary photographer to mix solutions from raw chemicals. The premixed, powdered, or liquid developers, fixers, and toners provide dependable and easy processing for almost any need. You may wish to experiment with the formulas listed in table A.2, or to experiment with basic developer components in order to understand more thoroughly the silver process.

# 8 Chemical Notes

Most of the chemicals listed in tables A.2 and A.3 are packaged in convenient sizes (if not the most economical) and sold through retail photo stores. Formulas that are not frequently used often disappear from sight. You are urged to examine older editions (dating back to the 1930s) of the *Photo-Lab Index* and other reference books for formulas that are often still useful and adapt well to modern films and paper.

# 9 Parametric Densitometer Controls

## Equipment Needed

A transmission densitometer measures the absorption of light passing through a film emulsion, and is needed to prepare parametric analysis of film and developer relationships. These instruments range in price upwards from about $300.

Data is acquired by using the densitometer to measure both test and working exposures. The densities are plotted as parametric curves. All the parametric curve illustrations presented in this appendix have been prepared on a Macintosh computer, using MacDraw II® software, but a number of other drawing programs would work. If you do not have a computer available or if you wish to produce the charts by

## Table A.1  Metol-free Developers

| Manufacturer | Product | Description |
|---|---|---|
| Acufine, Inc. | Acufine | High-energy film developer |
| | Diafine | Contrast control, two-bath film developer |
| | Posifine | Paper developer |
| Agfa-Gevaert | Rodinal | High-acutance film developer |
| Edwal | FG–7 | Fine-grain film developer |
| | Platinum | Paper developer |
| Eastman Kodak | HC–110 | High-acutance film developer |
| | Ektaflo | Warm-tone paper developer |
| Ethol | LPD | Paper developer |
| Ilford, Inc. | Microphen | Fine-grain film developer |
| | Bromophen | Paper developer |
| | Ilfospeed | Paper developer |
| | Multigrade | Paper developer |
| Sprint System | Quicksilver | Paper and film developers |

## Table A.2  Film Developers

All units of measure are metric (i.e., gram or ml units). The chemicals are listed in the order in which they are mixed (unless noted). All formulas are for a final solution of 1 liter. Start with 750ml of water (distilled is preferred) at about 125°F. Avoid chemical dusts, and mix thoroughly with a stirring paddle. When chemicals are dissolved, add cold water to make 1 liter.

| Chemical | D–23 | D–25 | D–76 | POTA[2] | Beutler[1] A | Beutler[1] B | D–8[3] |
|---|---|---|---|---|---|---|---|
| Elon | 7.5 | 7.5 | 2.0 | — | 10 | — | — |
| Sodium sulfite[4] | 100 | 100 | 100 | 30 | 50 | — | 90 |
| Phenidone–A | — | — | — | 1.5 | — | — | — |
| Hydroquinone | — | — | 5 | — | — | — | 45 |
| Sodium bisulfite | — | 15 | — | — | — | — | — |
| Sodium hydroxide[5] | — | — | — | — | — | — | 37.5 |
| Sodium carbonate | — | — | — | — | — | 50 | — |
| Borax | — | — | 2 | — | — | — | — |
| Potassium bromide | — | — | — | — | — | — | 30 |

[1]The Beutler developer is mixed as separate stock solutions that are combined just before use. See chapter 11 for details.

[2]The POTA developer is an alternative to Kodak Technidol developer for Kodak Technical Pan film, a high-contrast emulsion that can be developed for lower contrast. This formula is also useful for other emulsions where very low contrast is desired. Agitation with Technical Pan film should be reduced to two slow inversions of the tank each minute; develop between ten and fourteen minutes.

[3]D–8 is a high-contrast developer originally used for photoetching plates. It is worth experimenting with when high contrast is desired. Normal developing time is about two minutes.

[4]Use dessicated sodium sulfite. Stir thoroughly to assure that the sulfite is completely dissolved to avoid pinholes.

[5]Sodium hydroxide is a dangerous chemical that generates heat when mixed with water and *must* be stirred in slowly. The chemical can cause serious burns to skin and eyes. Always wear protective gear when working with concentrated solutions.

All units of measure are metric (i.e., gram or liter units). The chemicals are listed in the order in which they are mixed (unless noted). Print developer is rarely used in small quantities, and all formulae are for a final solution of 4 liters. Start with three liters of water (distilled is preferred) at about 125°F. Pour chemicals in smoothly, avoiding chemical dusts, and mix thoroughly with a stirring paddle. When chemicals are dissolved, add cold water to make 4 liters.

| Formula Names | Kodak | Ansco[1] | | | DuPont | |
|---|---|---|---|---|---|---|
| *Chemical* | D–72[2] | 120[3] | 130[4] | 135[5] | 54–D[6] | 59–D[7] |
| Elon | 12 | 49 | 9 | 6.4 | 10.8 | 12 |
| Sodium sulfite[8] | 180 | 144 | 200 | 96 | 160 | 144 |
| Hydroquinone | 48 | — | 44 | 26.4 | 42.4 | — |
| Sodium carbonate[9] | 320 | 144 | 312 | 96 | 352 | 84 |
| Potassium bromide | 8 | 7.2 | 22 | 11.2 | 3.2 | 16 |
| Glycin | — | — | 44 | — | — | — |

[1]Ansco was an American film and chemical company that became Agfa-Ansco in the 1930s and became GAF Corporation in the 1950s.

[2]D–72 is very similar to Kodak Dektol developer.

[3]Ansco 120 is a low-contrast developer; Adams suggests it as an alternative to Kodak Selectol-Soft, used from full strength to a 1:2 dilution for 1 1/2 to 3 minutes developing time.

[4]Ansco 130 is the only developer suggested here that uses developing agents other than Elon or hydroquinone. This developer produces excellent separations of shadows and highlights. The developer darkens to a light brown color immediately after mixing, but this is *not* an indication of exhaustion.

[5]This is a *warm-tone* developer, and will produce a more brown-black image than the others. Dilute 1:1; to increase the warm-tone, increase bromide to twice the quantity noted.

[6]A *cold-tone,* vigorous developer, used diluted 1:2. A very good developer for two-tray development, used full strength or 1:1.

[7]An alternative to Ansco 120, this is a soft working developer that is an excellent replacement for Selectol-Soft, or for use in two-tray development.

[8]The dessicated form of sulfite is used.

[9]The monohydrated form of carbonate is used.

hand, these plots may be drawn on ordinary graph paper (engineering tablets with a light green pattern printed on the back of the sheet, with ten divisions to an inch, are the best to use). Straight lines may be used to connect the data points.

## Photographic Parameters

A parameter has been defined as a quantity to which one can assign arbitrary values, and this is of use when you wish to determine *what might happen* if you change one part of a relationship. In the basic photographic equation, there are three parameters: exposure, development, and film speed (or ISO).

Exposure is the product of two variables, the intensity of the light acting upon the emulsion and the time of exposure.

Development is affected by time and the amount of reducing agents in the developer, the developer pH, the developer temperature, the agitation style, and the vigor of the agitation of the developer.

Film speed has been traditionally considered invariable by physicists, and yet is considered variable by many (if not most)

photographers. Strictly speaking, film speed *is* fixed—determined by standardized sensitometric tests—and this speed is indicated by the ISO number (100, 400, 3200, etc.), which is determined by ANSI testing. Development affects the separation of densities produced by standardized exposures and the effectivity of these separations can be interpreted to result in different personal or working exposure indexes (EI) for a given film, depending on what is an acceptable picture for the photographer.

## Characteristic Curves

Characteristic curves (D log E, or H & D curves) are graphs of density against exposure (with development time held constant). These graphs are solutions of an equation. Normally, density is plotted on the ordinate, or vertical axis, and development time on the abscissa, or horizontal axis. The characteristic curve of *any* silver emulsion is determined by its inherent sensitivity to light, the exposure (the product of intensity *and* time), and the development (chemistry, time, temperature, and agitation).

The H & D curve is only one version of a parametric equation. Figure A.1 shows generalized D log E curves for two popular films. These parameters are held constant:

Emulsion sensitivity
Developer formula
Temperature
Agitation

and these parameters are variables:

Exposure
Density

A number of characteristic curves may be drawn on the same chart as shown in Figure A.1 to facilitate comparisons, and each curve describes how density changes as a function of exposure and development time.

The traditional H & D curve is most useful for describing overall contrast but is not revealing of how one development time compares to another when attempting to predict changes in shadow or highlight densities.

Comparing curves shows how silver emulsion responds to development. It is obvious that as the development time lengthens, overall density range (or contrast) increases (for a given range of exposure). What is less obvious are subtle relationships within a given curve or between graphs of different development times.

These changes are important, and it is exciting to discover what happens when one switches parameters and plots density against developing time, keeping *exposure constant*. This is an alternative to the traditional representation of the same data, and we give it a new name and call these curves *parameters*, or *parametric curves*. It is important to realize this is a new look at the same information.

## Parametric Family of Curves

Parametric presentations are most useful as a *family of curves* that are created when one of the parameters is changed over a useful range while the rest are held constant, and all the resulting data are plotted on a single chart. The family of curves has immediate practical applications.

With little film and time invested, the parametric curve family indicates precise *development times* for contrasty, normal, and flat scenes. All that is needed to produce this information are a few film tests, careful measures of the densities, and plots of density against developing time (with ex-

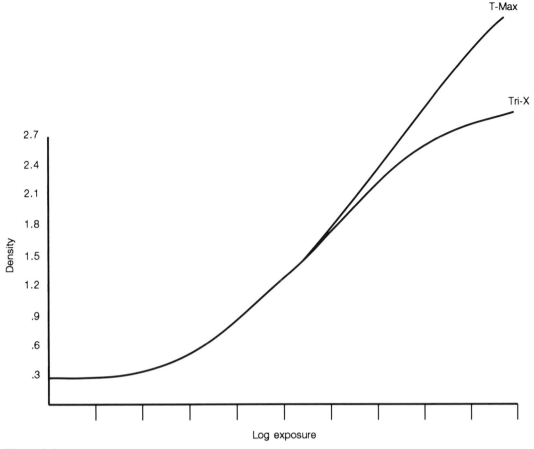

T-Max

Tri-X

Density

2.7
2.4
2.1
1.8
1.5
1.2
.9
.6
.3

Log exposure

Figure A.1
Generalized D log E curves for Tri–X and
T–Max films.

posure held constant). Patterns of curves within the family also suggest how changing exposure or metering (EI) will change density range. Parametric curves also often reveal film development, agitation problems, and mechanical irregularities in the camera's shutter or diaphragm mechanisms. Parametric curves become a validation of the entire photographic system, from meter to print.

First, understand that what you are photographing in these tests is a *field of light,* and you specifically *do not* wish to record detail. Focus your camera on ∞, stand close enough to the target that it completely fills the frame, and feel free to handhold even slow shutter-speed pictures: a little blur will actually help.

Make and develop three exposure tests. Hang a blank sheet of paper as a target so that it is evenly lighted in the light for which the film is being tested (daylight, fluorescent, tungsten). Many films have a different, and lower, EI under tungsten light. Use a reflected-light meter to measure the inten-

sity of light reflected from the target to calculate the exposure. The meter can be TTL or hand-held.

Expose the first frame of a new roll at the metered exposure (to provide a definite reference frame of density when the developed film is examined). The second frame is exposed 5 stops less than the indicated exposure, the third frame −4 stops, and for each subsequent frame the exposure is increased one stop until the last frame is exposed 5 stops *more* than the indicated exposure.

If a 36-exposure roll is used, then expose the mid-section of eight to ten frames on another subject (one which will provide useful information on how the image of typical shadows and highlights for your work typically look) and then *repeat the step exposure test exactly* with the last third of the film. Expose a second roll in exactly the same way. With these two rolls, you now have four sets of test film, separated on each roll by several frames. When you are ready to develop the tests, these

films may be cut in two equal lengths in the darkroom and each test strip will produce an 11-frame density test plus some other exposed frames.

Develop three of the half-roll test strips for a different time, using exactly the same developer temperature and agitation. Use fresh developer for each test strip. To ensure similar developing temperatures, keep the developing tank in a water bath. The fourth strip should be kept and used if a mistake is made in processing one of the first three.

Start by developing one test for about 50% of the manufacturer's recommended time, a second for the recommended time, and the third for twice the recommended time. In the example in figure A.2, T-Max film, rated at EI of 400 was developed in D–76 1:1 @ 68°F, with standard agitation.

When the three strips have been processed and dried, each frame is measured with a densitometer in three specific areas. (Areas A1, B, and C1 are appropriate densitometer metering targets for test film.)

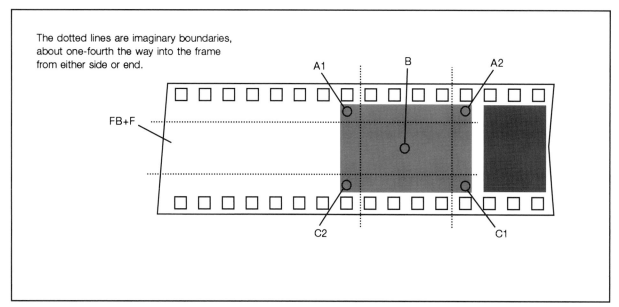

The dotted lines are imaginary boundaries, about one-fourth the way into the frame from either side or end.

Figure A.2
Locations of roll film critical density measurement areas.

## Preliminary Evaluations

Examine the film by eye first to see if densities obviously vary across the frame. Figure A.2 shows critical areas of the 35mm film frame that should be compared. Look for density streaks adjacent to the sprocket holes, then for a band of greater density parallel to the sprocket holes (areas A1–A2 or C1–C2).

Streaks reaching from the sprocket holes toward the center of the film are caused by excessive agitation and indicate that the developer is being "pumped" through the sprocket holes. This is usually the result of the tank being flung back and forth instead of being inverted about its own center. A band of excess density parallel to the edge and extending about 1/4th the way into the frame is most often caused by too little agitation (and is a common fault with plastic tank developing reels).

Use the densitometer to measure areas A1, B, and C1 in each of the ten test frames. There will be three density readings for each frame, and these should be added together and divided by three to produce an average density for each test exposure frame. There will inevitably be some differences of density, but they should be within a range of 0.02. When the differences exceed this range (are greater than 0.02 from center to corner, or corner to corner), look for some possible causes in table A.4.

Table A.4 Density Variations in 35mm Test Frames

| Location | Comment |
| --- | --- |
| A1 = A2 = B = C1 = C2 | Ideal. Differences should ≤ .02. |
| A1 > C1 | Target may be unevenly lighted. If cloth shutter, and C2 > C1, then curtains are out of adjustment. |
| A1 < B | And C1 > B, then lens may not cover field adequately and evenly. And C1 > B, then see if C2 and A2 are also greater than B; if so, increase agitation. |

## Graph Presentation of Densities

The averaged densities should be plotted to reveal the useful relationships they contain. If a paper graph is produced, the following scales have been found to be successful in presenting the data in a way that reveals significances and yet does not promise more accuracy than is actually available from this simple test:

*Development times:* 1 inch equals 1 minute (for development times of 10 minutes or less), or 1/2 inch equals 1 minute (for times of 20 minutes or less ), and total time ranges from 0 to 10 minutes or 0 to 20.

*Density:* 1 inch equals 0.6, and density ranges from 0 to 2.5 or 3. This scale produces a 6 × 10 inch graph, which is a convenient size and comfortable proportion to work with.

An alternative method of charting the results is to plot the information with a computer, using standard graphics software. There are advantages to using the computer, the most obvious being that data can be saved to disk, and revised easily. Although any computer with a graphic program can be used, the illustrations for this appendix have been prepared with a Macintosh computer using MacDraw II.

All text illustrations shown here were prepared on the Macintosh, though pencil-and-paper produces similar results. Figure M.1 through M.4 (at the end of this appendix) outline preparation of Macintosh MacDraw II software to chart parametrics.

Figure A.3 shows a blank format that can be prepared and called to the screen when needed. The ordinate is scaled from 0 to a density of 2.7; the abscissa from 0 to 20 minutes developing time. Although T–Max will produce densities above 2.7, usable small camera densities rarely rise above 2.4, and contemporary developing times almost never exceed 20 minutes.

In this example, using the data from table A.5, figure A.4 shows development time lines established at 5, 10, and 20 minutes. If you are using paper and pencil, then the next step would be to locate the

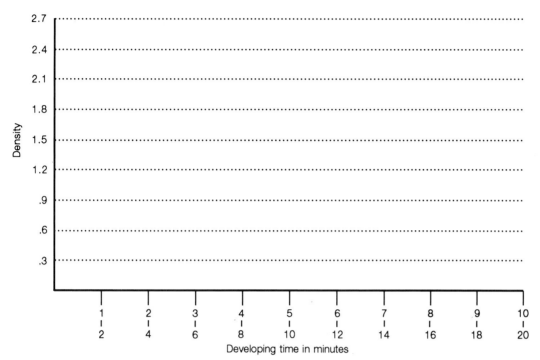

Figure A.3
Blank chart for plotting density as a
function of developing time.

densities for each frame on the vertical time lines as shown in figure A.5. The densities presented in Table 2 have been Xed in on the development time lines. When using a computer and a graphics program, this is not necessary because each time-density coordinate can be located directly—a line can be drawn directly from one data point to the next using the mouse and/or arrow keys, depending on the software.

Figure A.6 shows densities for each frame and all developing times connected point-to-point with straight lines. When drawing the lines, evaluate them immediately in a common-sense way. The pattern of the lines should be regular and the spaces between lines fairly even. A density line will *never* decrease as developing time increases (and if your drawing says it is so, stop and look for the error). Density lines can never cross.

Large irregularities in the pattern probably indicate errors in metering, translating exposures from meter to camera, changing camera exposures from one frame to the next, mechanical mistakes in using the densitometer, recording the data, averaging the data, or transcribing the readings. Since this data is the result of a single test, there are small irregularities that would average out and disappear were you to make a number of tests and average the results.

Table A.5    T–Max 400 at EI = 400: D–76 1:1 Test Densities

| Exposures | 5 | 10' | 20' | Comments |
| --- | --- | --- | --- | --- |
| FB + F | .28 | .30 | .30 | Unexposed film |
| 1/30 @ f–32[1] | .58 | .92 | 1.23 | Metered exposure |
| 1/1000[2] | .30 | .31 | .32 | −5 stops |
| 1/500 | .31 | .34 | .35 | |
| 1/250 | .33 | .42 | .45 | |
| 1/125 | .38 | .54 | .65 | |
| 1/60 | .48 | .72 | .94 | Important shadow |
| 1/30[1] | .58 | .92 | 1.23 | Metered exposure |
| 1/15 | .68 | 1.11 | 1.48 | |
| 1/8 | .79 | 1.24 | 1.70 | |
| 1/4 | .89 | 1.40 | 1.92 | Typical highlight |
| 1/2 | 1.04 | 1.59 | 2.12 | |
| 1 | 1.10 | .98 | 2.27 | |

[1]This density and the mid-roll target density may differ as much as .03.
[2]This value should be > FB + F by .01 to .03. If it equals FB + F, the test should be repeated using a 50% lower EI. If greater than .03, repeat with a doubled EI.

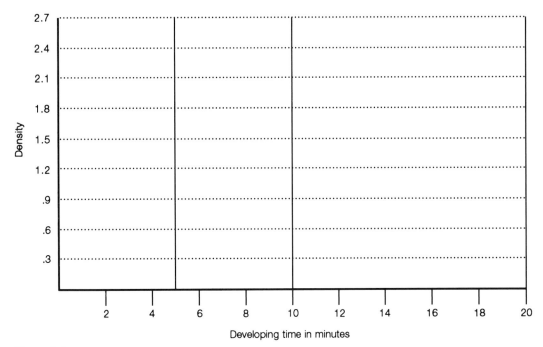

Figure A.4
Time lines drawn at 5, 10, and 20 minutes.

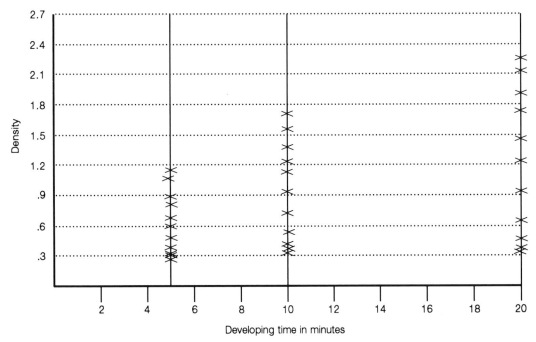

Figure A.5
Densities for exposures from −5 to +5
stops posted for 5, 10, and 20 minutes
developing times.

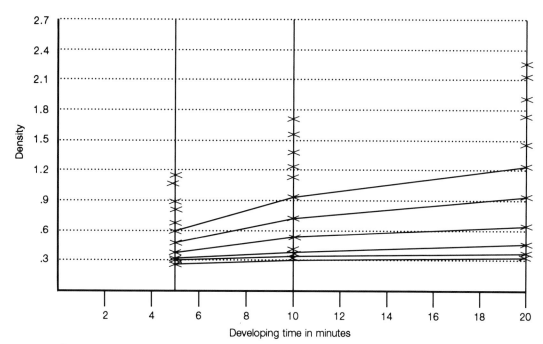

Figure A.6
Draw connecting lines between equal
exposures.

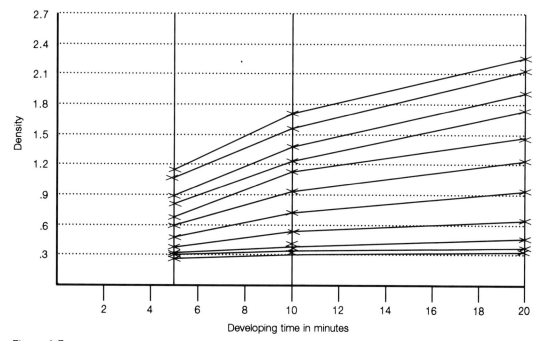

Figure A.7
Complete set of density lines from −5 to
+5 stops of metered exposure.

The complete array of data lines is shown in figure A.7. When the data is posted on the computer, it is easy to delete the vertical time lines.

Remember, if you are using a computer to draw the family of curves, the X's need not be drawn, and if you are using paper and pencil you may now wish to carefully erase the time lines and the data-locating marks so that the pattern of the family of curves representing changes in density is more clearly seen.

It is actually better to draw the lines as broken curves because rounding the lines to a smooth curve produces a misleading sense of precision. When using the Macintosh, do not use the curve-smoothing option available: the software algorithm eliminates the knee in the curve and usually drops the line down slightly, creating a density error that will result in an indicated increase of development time.

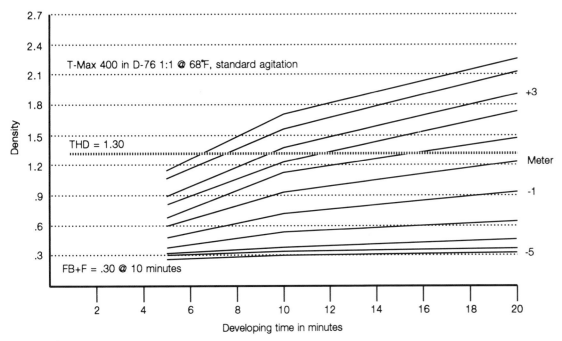

Figure A.8
Typical highlight density (THD) line and other identifying information.

## Densitometer Metering Targets and THD

The densitometer light-sensing probe has a field of view controlled by a fixed aperture. Accurate (repeatable) measurement of densities requires the target area on the negative be at least as large as the aperture. Most densitometers have an aperture of 13mm, or about 1/16 to 1/8th of an inch in diameter. This large an area of even density may be difficult to find in 35mm negatives of everyday scenes. Often only sky areas are large enough in the negative to be accurately metered, and it is necessary to find test scenes with large, simple tonal areas that illustrate the lighting and are also compatible with the mechanical needs of the densitometer. Experiment with your densitometer to discover how large an area of even density you must have for repeatable measurements.

Once you have determined the minimum-sized accurate metering target, locate several negatives of your own that have meterable highlight details (THD).

Typically, these areas are found in pictures of a person wearing a white shirt, or where there is a large area of detailed snow or billowing cloud. A correct meterable THD has a sizeable off-white subject that reveals good detail in a well-made print. Assuming correct exposure, these negatives also print on normal grade paper (contrast grade or filter 3 when using 35mm film), with good shadow detail and separation of the lower values in the picture, and do not require burning in the highlights or dodging, holding back the shadow areas.

Make density readings of several THD areas from these negatives. You will probably find that the negatives you pick do not have *identical* THD densities, partly because of the variations in brightness range of the original scenes and standardized development. However, if your negative exposures and development have been well-controlled, the THD readings will cluster around a density of about 1.20. Photojournalists tend to make and use a negative with a THD of about 1.30 to 1.40 (or even higher). This is unnecessarily high; such de-

velopment produces vigorous tonal separation but it also produces excess grain. A more fine-grain negative will have a THD of about 1.20.

## Normal Development Time

For the time being, accept the THD you discover in your negatives. You may wish to change to a lighter or darker THD later, but accept the fact that you have a working system, even though the densities may not be ideal.

Figure A.8 shows a line drawn clear across the parametric graph at the THD. It will intersect several of the exposure/density curves. Find the intersection of the +3 line, which is the record of exposing film for 3 stops more than the indicated meter exposure (as shown in figure A.9). Carefully draw a vertical line from that intersection straight down. The time indicated on the horizontal axis by this vertical is the *normal* developing time. It indicates that developing a normal contrast scene exposed on this type of film for that time will produce a negative that will print easily on normal contrast grade paper.

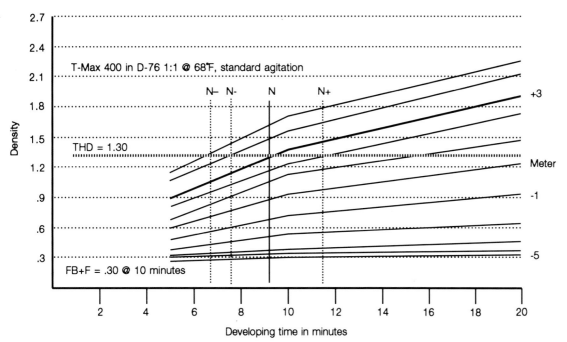

Figure A.9
Trial development times for scenes of
varying contrast predicted from the
intersection of THD for very contrasty,
contrasty, normal, and flat scenes.

## Exposure and EI Prediction

The parametric curves suggest corrections
of minimum exposure and the system EI.
Look at the −5 stop density line and compare it to the FB + F at or near the normal
developing time suggested in figure A.8.
Table A.6 indicates the −5 stop density
should be slightly greater than FB + B.
The metering system is providing a safe
minimum density exposure when the −5
stop density line is a little greater than FB
+ B. If the density were the same as FB +
F, it would be impossible to say if the exposure were absolutely correct or not.

When the −5 stop exposure density is
greater than FB + F by more than .03 (but
less than .06), then the EI should be *doubled* for future exposures. This increase of
EI will decrease the exposure and lower the
−5 stop density toward FB + B.

When the −5 density is more than .06
above FB + F, then either the metering
method is in error (somehow one was measuring a lighter subject as well as the selected target), the meter battery is weak, or
a mechanical problem may exist in the
meter. A meter battery nearing exhaustion
will consistently indicate an overexposure.

### Table A.6   Parametric Exposure Correction Logic

| Condition | Suggested Correction |
|---|---|
| −5 = FB + F and −4 is not more than .03 above FB + F | Decrease EI 2 stops |
| −5 = FB + F and −4 is at least .03 but not more than .06 above FB + F | Decrease EI by 1 stop |
| −5 > FB + B but not more than .03 | Accept EI |
| −5 > FB + B + .03 but less than .06 | Decrease EI by 1 stop |
| −5 > FB + F + .06 but less than .09 | Decrease EI by 2 stops |

If the differences exceed the values in this table,
redo all testing. Monitor the procedure carefully
for metering errors and equipment problems.

Errors of underexposure can be estimated by examining the lower curves of
the parametrics. When the −5 stop line
equals FB + F, examine the −4 stop line.
The separation between it and FB + B can
be used with the help of Table A.6 to calculate a corrected EI.

When an indicated adjustment requires
an EI correction of 2 stops or more in either
direction, the test data should be set aside
and the testing redone. When the indicated
error is overexposure, first replace the TTL
meter battery in the camera. For indicated
underexposure, review the metering
method.

## Development Effects on EI

Figure A.10 is an enlargement of the intersection of the normal development time
and the −1 stop density line. The −1 line
equates with the exposure required to produce richly detailed, important shadow
values (Zone IV). Look at this line and you
will see there is a change in density with
changing development time, although the
change is much less than those in the
higher stops. As development is decreased, density will be lost; the parametric
family of curves permits you to estimate an
appropriate increase in exposure (decrease
in EI) necessary to produce a *correct and
safe minimum density*. When development
is increased, some extra shadow density is

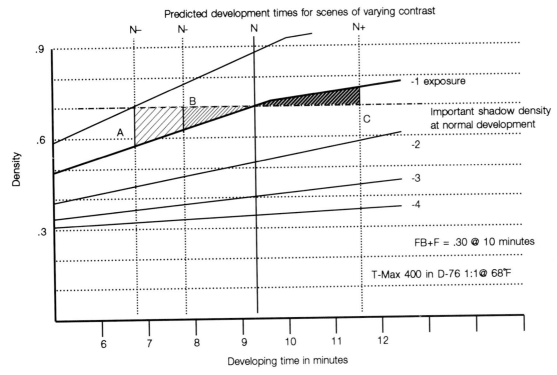

Predicted development times for scenes of varying contrast

Figure A.10
Enlarged detail of important shadow
density, showing the loss or gain in EI as
development time is increased or
decreased.

produced, meaning that in critical work, the
exposure can be reduced slightly (i.e., EI
can be increased).

In general, contrasty scenes require
both reduced development and increased
exposure. The parametric curves permit accurate prediction of the desired amount of
exposure and development correction.
Using figure A.10, reducing film developing
time to decrease the density range for contrasty scenes lowers the important shadow
density about 1/2 the distance between the
metered exposure and −1 density lines (as
indicated by the shaded area beside B).
This loss of important shadow area density
can be avoided by increasing exposures by
1/2 stop. In this example, contrasty scenes
require shortened development times and
an exposure increase of 1/2 stop.

Very contrasty scenes require less development time and increased exposure, in
this example an increase of a full stop.
Look to the left of the normal development
time line in figure A.10 and see the change
of density produced by the shorter development time suggested for a very contrasty

scene. As indicated by the shaded area
beside A, the loss of density is almost a full
stop.

Finally, look to the right of the normal
time line and see how important shadow
area densities increase with increased development time. In this example, about a
half-stop of density is gained. With large-
format films, this could be ignored, but with
35mm, where any increase in density
means a corresponding increase in grain
size, the EI for flat scenes that are going to
be developed for longer than normal times
could be increased by 1.5 times.

The parametric graphs you make are the
results of very economical testing; they
should be validated and modified through
testing with typical subjects. Assume the EI
for this T-Max film parametric presentation
was 400, then the suggested EI for flat
scenes would be 600 and you would validate this assumption by making test exposures before using this combination of
controls on important scenes. For contrasty
scenes, it would be 300, and very contrasty
scenes 200. These are suggested values
that would be validated through testing.

## Other Information

The overall pattern of the parametrics reveals the effects of a film-developer combination. Effects of developer dilution or
formula strength, which most often change
the high value separations, are immediately
made clear in the parametrics. Film speed,
on the other hand, is most clearly apparent
in the lower densities. In general, high-
speed films (EIs of 400 or more) tend to
crush shadow details. This squashing together appears clearly in the bottom lines
of the parametric, which lie closer together
than they do for the first lines of a medium-
to-low speed film (one with a sharper
"toe").

Because their characteristic curve has a
toe that bends up more sharply on a traditional H & D curve than does a highspeed
film, a medium or slow film produces better
separation of shadow densities. The H & D
curve indicates this separation, but the parametric family of curves transforms the toe
into a clearly readable pattern. This array of

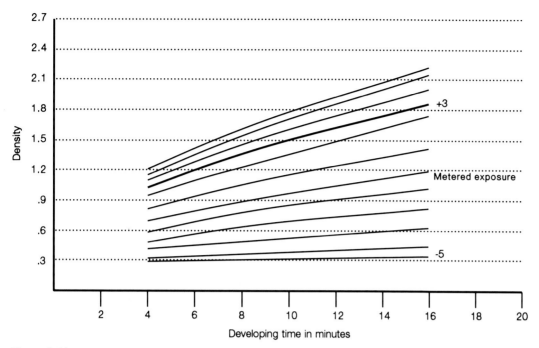

Figure A.11
Idealized parametric data sheet for film
developed in a compensating developer.
Note the more even separation of shadow
values and the diminished separation of
highlight densities, a useful combination for
very contrasty scenes.

well-separated lower density lines is shown
in figure A.11, a parametric presentation of
an idealized low-speed film developed in a
*compensating developer* (i.e., one that provides normal shadow and midrange development and limits highlight separation). An
example of this might well be Tri–X film developed in HC–110 at dilutions of 1:64 or
higher, or T–Max in T–Max developer diluted two to four times more than the
normal dilution suggested by Kodak.

Parametric data presentation truly
comes into its own when unusual combinations of film and developer are desired. For
example, Kodak recommends using T–Max
film developer in a dilution of 1:4. Experimental evidence indicates that there is no
observable difference in the finished print
when this developer is used at 1:7 or 1:11
dilutions (for correspondingly longer developing times), yielding both a significant
savings in cost and greater control of the
highlight densities of T–Max films, which
are notorious for producing unprintable
highlight densities with even moderate
errors of development.

New combinations of film and developers are quickly and easily investigated.
Kodak HC–110 developer when used with
T–Max emulsions can be diluted with more
water than indicated in the popular Dilution
B; the more dilute solutions produce linear
separation of the lower (shadow) values
and avoid excessively dense highlight
values. Many other film-developer combinations are both possible and useful. The parametric test and presentation permits
accurate predictions of development time/
temperature/agitation relationships.

## Using MacDraw II

Figures A.12 through A.15 illustrate set-up
procedures for using MacDraw II software
on the Macintosh to draw parametrics.

Having established ordinates, use the
**Pen-Line** menu to create dashed lines and
draw them in at 0.30 density intervals.
(Draw the first one and then duplicate it
using Command–D—i.e., press both keys
at once. Place the duplicated line carefully
at 0.60. Type Command–D again and a
third line will be produced at 0.90, or repeat
the initial interval you established. Continue
duplicating until the grid is drawn.)

Use the irregular polygon command
from the shape menu to draw each parametric density line. Note that as you move
the cross-hair cursor on the grid, a dotted
line moves across and up the rulers on
screen at top and left, permitting you to accurately place the beginning and end of
each line segment. Place the cursor at the
minimum time and minimum density; click
the mouse; draw the cursor to the middle
time and the correct density for that frame;
click the mouse again; draw the cursor to
the third time and its correct density; click
the mouse twice. The parametric line can
be marked and moved, deleted, or re-
shaped (using Command–R) if needed.

Additional information can be derived
from these curves, relating to change of EI
when shorter or longer developing times
are used, and approximate developing
times to use when flat or contrasty subjects
are being photographed.

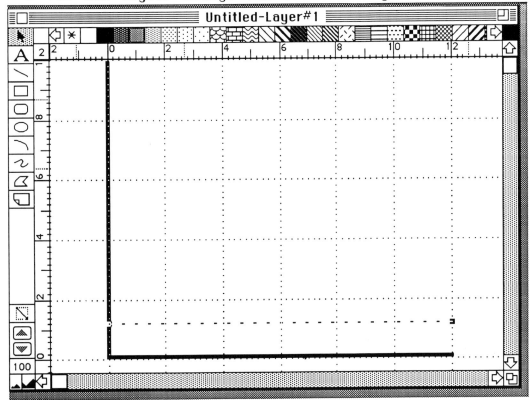

Figure A.12
The Macintosh screen using MacDraw II to
present parametric data. Establish
ordinates (here using a metric Ruler option)
and then create density reference lines at a
density interval of 0.30.

© 1991 Claris Corporation. All Rights Reserved.
MacDraw is a registered trademark of Claris
Corporation.

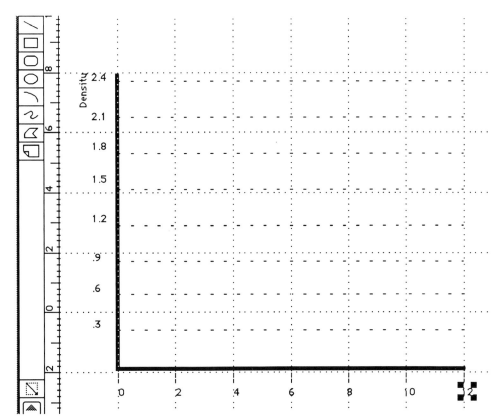

Figure A.13
The basic grid for presenting parametric
data. The developing time scale should be
appropriate to your testing.

© 1991 Claris Corporation. All Rights Reserved.
MacDraw is a registered trademark of Claris
Corporation.

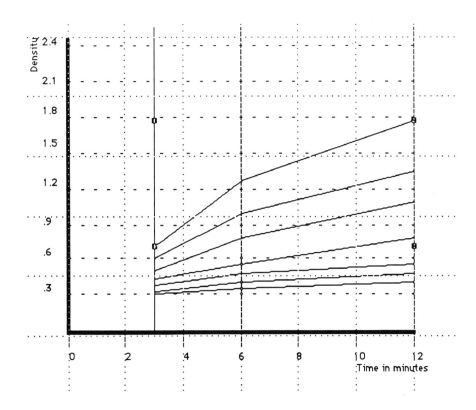

Figure A.14
Establish vertical development time lines.
Use the cursor to draw the connecting lines
between development times.

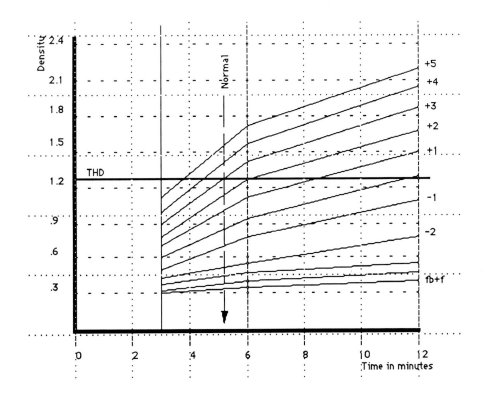

Figure A.15
Identify the density lines. Establish an
appropriate THD (typical highlight density)
valve. Mark the intersection of THD and the
+3 density line as ''normal'' developing
time.

# Glossary

**absorption**  Transforming light into another energy form.

**accelerator**  Creates strong alkaline pH in developer.

**additive primary**  Red, green, or blue light.

**albumen print**  Nineteenth-century silver print: paper was coated with egg albumen that supported the silver halides used to make the image.

**antihalation**  Dye absorbs light passing through emulsion, which otherwise causes secondary image (halation).

**artificial light**  Supplementary light source that modifies ambient light.

**Autochrome**  First commercial color transparency made using three-color separation. First manufactured in 1919 by Dufay, a French firm.

**Automatic Tray Siphon**  Print-washing aid for small numbers of prints.

**backlight**  Light that is directed toward the lens of the camera and that separates a portrait subject from the background.

**baseboard**  Support for enlarger, on which a printing paper easel is placed.

**bleach**  Transforming dark silver metallic image into white silver salt.

**bounce light**  Light directed at ceiling or other reflector rather than directly at subject.

**bracketing**  Exposing more and less than the calculated exposure.

**Brown Toner**  Kodak commercial version of a sepia redevelopment toner.

**burning-in**  Giving extra exposure to an area of a print to darken it.

**Calotype**  (Greek, meaning "beautiful print") William Henry Fox Talbot's invention; a positive print made from a paper negative.

**camera obscura**  Darkened room with a lens in one wall.

**candela**  Term for measure of light intensity that has replaced *candle*.

**carte-de-visite**  A small photograph (about the size of contemporary school photographs) that became popular in the 1860s. Made by a camera with eight lenses.

**changing bag**  Lighttight bag with armholes.

**characteristic curve**  Graph of film or print density change created by increasing exposure and a fixed development.

**Chem-Wipes**  Lint-free sheets used to wipe final rinse water from negatives.

**clearing**  Removal of unused silver salts from film or papers.

**cliche-verre**  Hand-made negative.

**color temperature**  Color of light in degrees Kelvin (K°), a measure of temperature above absolute zero.

**complementary colors**  Opposing light and pigment colors: red-cyan, green-magenta, blue-yellow.

**compression**  Shortened development time, which reduces contrast.

**contrasty**  Common speech term describing a scene that has both very dimly lit and very brightly lit areas.

**copyright**  Protection by law for creative work.

**covering power**  Negative area from which an acceptable sharp image can be made.

**cross light**  Light striking the photographic subject at right angles to the lens, illuminating surface detail and producing high contrast.

**cutting reducer**  Diminishes image density and contrast.

**daguerreotype**  Unique silver process photograph from the 1840s: a mercury-silver image on a polished copper plate.

**densitometer**  Machine for precise measurement of light absorption by negatives or prints.

**developer**  Solution that makes visible a latent image.

**developing agent**  Active ingredient in developer that changes white silver salt to dark metal image.

**developing out**  Darkening of latent image in a developing solution.

**diffraction**  Spreading of light rays.

**diffuse density**  Density measured using uncollimated (scattered) light passing through a negative.

**dodging**  Holding back light from an area of a print.

**dry-mount tissue**  Heat-sensitive adhesive sheet used to bond photograph to mounting board.

**drying down**  Loss of contrast and brilliance in a print as it dries after processing.

**Dust Off**  Compressed gas used for blowing dust from negatives.

**DX**  Acronym for directed exposure, referring to machine coding of film speed electronically accessed from conductive stripes on the film cannister.

**edge sharpness** Subjective perception of crisp detail in photographic image created by best compromise of lighting, exposure, and development of the negative.

**EI** Abbreviation of Exposure Index, the number used to indicate film speed for contemporary photographic metering systems.

**enlarging lens** Wide-field lens designed for printing negatives.

**expansion** Lengthened development time that increases contrast beyond normal.

**exposure** Sum of light intensity and time, creating latent image on film or paper.

**fiber base** Printing paper with emulsion coated on paper support.

**figure** Principal area in a two-dimensional composition.

**figure / ground** Relationship between the nominal subject of an image and the area framing it.

**fill light** Secondary light source used to limit contrast.

**film base** The plastic support for the emulsion and the dyes, which are incorporated into it for contrast control.

**filter factor** Linear multiplier of prefilter metered exposure.

**fisheye lens** Extreme wide-angle lens producing a picture with distortions of parallel lines.

**flash bulbs** Magnesium ribbon or wire sealed in a glass bulb and electrically ignited. Used from about 1930 through 1970 as a portable light source for interior and night photography.

**flash meter** Incident meter that calculates exposure by integrating ambient and flash light.

**flash powder** Powdered magnesium metal (ignited by gun powder). Used from about 1880 through the 1930s to photograph inside and at night.

**flat** Descriptive term describing light on the subject parallel to the lens and from the back of the camera; also a print that has little apparent density range from dark to light areas.

**focal length** Distance from optical center of a lens to focal plane.

**focal plane** Plane in which parallel lines of light are brought by a lens to a point.

**fog** Non-image silver emulsion density.

**glacial acetic acid** Concentrated acid that freezes at about 50°F.

**GN** Guide Number: estimating factor for predicting flash exposures.

**graded contrast** Printing paper with a singular characteristic curve.

**ground** Surround area in a two-dimensional composition.

**guide number** Predicts flash f−number as dividend of light-to-subject distance.

**hardening fixer** Thiosulfate solution with chrome alum to tan gelatin.

**hardness** Amount of calcium in water.

**highlights** Highly reflective surfaces in the subject that have texture or detail.

**hot shoe** Synchronization connection through mounting clip on camera body.

**HTH** Highest Textured Highlight; brightest subject area that shows detail.

**hydroquinone** Low-energy, high-contrast developing agent; synergetic with Metol.

**Hypo Chek** Edwal product to estimate activity of fixer.

**incident light meter** Meter that integrates light directly toward the subject.

**indicator stop bath** Acetic acid with pH-indicating dye.

**inhibitors** Chemicals in the developing solution that tend to prevent silver reduction.

**intensification** Adding density to negative or print image to increase contrast.

**intensity** Measure of light energy impacting on film or paper.

**intention** Planned subject of the photograph.

**inverse square law** Intensity is inversely proportional to square of distance from light.

**IR** Infrared (radiation below threshold of visible light).

**ISA** Important Shadow Area; large shadowed area of subject with significant detail.

**ISO** International Standards Organization; arithmetic number indicating film or paper sensitivity to light.

**key light** Primary light source that determines overall direction of shadows.

**kicker card** Small white card (often 3″ × 5″ file card) used at the electronic flash in bounce-light position to reflect light onto nearby subject.

**Kodachrome** Three-color transparency process invented in the 1930s.

**latent** Invisible but real image in a silver emulsion, produced by exposure and made visible by development.

**latitude** Ability of emulsion to produce a usable picture with varying exposure.

**Leica** First 35mm camera, invented to use standard movie film.

**LFN** Edwal brand low-foaming wetting agent.

**Liquid Orthazite** Edwal compound restrainer that causes less color change than potassium bromide to prints.

**luminance** Amount of light, measured in candelas.

**M** Flash synchronizaton timing connector found on older cameras, used to ignite magnesium ribbon flashbulbs.

**mat cutter** Holds blade at angle to permit cutting window mats.

**Metol** Low-contrast, high-energy developing agent (same as Elon).

**model release** Contract defining permissible use of photographs.

**modeling light** Low-intensity, steady-state light on electronic flash.

**momentary light** Light source with short duration.

**monopod** Camera support with only one leg.

**nanometer** Measure of wavelength of light.

**negative** Image with values reversed from original subject.

**negative-positive** System where a printing master with reversed values is created by the camera and then used to produce any number of prints with dark and light areas suggestive of the original scene.

**neutral density** Filter that affects all colors of light equally.

**normal** Field of view seen by a lens that approximates the "sharp" area of human vision (about 38°).

**normal** Metered brightness range between important shadowed areas and highest textured highlights is four stops.

**normal contrast** Describes subject reflective range.

**orthochromatic** Sensitive to all colors except red.

**panchromatic** Sensitive to all visible light.

**PC connector** Coaxial connector for electronic flash synchronization.

**peak action** Photograph that describes most intense moment of play in sports event.

**Perma-Wash** Solution that transforms thiosulfates into soluble compounds.

**Phenidone** Hypo-allergenic, high-energy, low-contrast developing agent; replaces Elon.

**Photo CD** Kodak alternative to color print. Digital transcription of customer's negative onto compact disk for viewing on TV screen.

**Photo Flo** Wetting agent used for films.

**Photo Mount** Scotch Brand (3M) aerosol cement.

**Photo-Wipes** Lint-free sheets used to wipe final rinse water from negatives.

**pictorialism** Where printmaking is more important than the photographic subject.

**point source** Sun or other light source that generates parallel rays of light.

**polarized**   Light vibrating in only one plane.

**Polaroid**   Originally Polaroid-Land print process. Silver-diffusion print process that produces a finished picture in the camera.

**Polytoner**   Kodak commercial variation of sepia-redevelopment toner that produces a range of brown-to-red print tints.

**Positionable Mounting Adhesive**   3M contact sheet adhesive.

**positive**   Image with values that parallel those of subject.

**potassium bromide**   Commonly used restrainer in developer.

**potassium ferricyanide**   Combines with silver to form soluble silver salt in thiosulfate solution.

**pre-fix**   Treatment in thiosulfate solution prior to toning or intensification.

**preservative**   Chemical that protects developing agent from oxygen in solution.

**prewet**   Water treatment of film to minimize uneven development.

**primary**   Color of light: red, green, or blue.

**printing out**   Darkening of silver emulsions by the action of light alone.

**projection**   Personal perception imposed on the photograph.

**proportional reducer**   Diminishes image density without affecting contrast.

**push development**   Developing film longer than the manufacturer recommends, producing overall greater contrast to enhance image legibility.

**range finder**   Optical-mechanical system for focusing lenses.

**rapid fix**   Ammonium thiosulfate fixer.

**Rapid Selenium Toner**   Kodak selenium toning solution.

**reciprocity**   Exposure = time × intensity.

**reciprocity effect**   Loss of expected density produced by failure of reciprocity law in low light or with very short exposures.

**redevelop**   Developing chemically altered silver during intensification.

**reducing agent**   Active ingredient in developing solution.

**reflected light meter**   Meter that measures light reflected by the subject.

**reflection**   Reversal of light direction on impact with polished surface.

**refraction**   Change of light direction on entering another medium.

**release**   Contract permitting use of photographs.

**replenish**   Adding stock or concentrate to working solution to restore original state.

**resin-coated**   Polyethylene-coated paper isolating print emulsion from paper support.

**resolve**   Smallest detail in original subject which can be seen in the negative or print.

**restrainer**   Provides bromine ions, which inhibit developing of latent image.

**safelight**   Light of low intensity and color that has minimal effect on photosensitive emulsions.

**secondary primaries**   Subtractive primaries: cyan, magenta, yellow.

**shadows**   Dark subject areas that are perceived to have significant detail.

**Sepia Toner**   Bleach-redevelopment process used to change print color from black to yellow-brown.

**single-shot**   Solution that is used once and then discarded.

**skylight filter**   Eliminates ultraviolet; filter factor = 1.

**SLR**   Abbreviation of single lens reflex, describing a camera that uses one lens and an internal mirror system to frame, focus, and expose the picture.

**snapshot**   Photograph made in the instant, without planning.

**specular density**   Density measured using collimated light passing through a negative.

**split-image**   Internal optical-mechanical system for focusing the lens; the target image is sliced in two but merges when the lens is focused.

**sodium carbonate**   Moderately strong alkali used as accelerator (activator) in developer.

**sodium hyposulfite**   First name given to thiosulfate compound used to fix negative; also called *hypo.*

**sodium sulfite**   Weak alkali used as preservative in developer.

**sodium thiosulfate**   Used to remove unused silver from negatives and prints; ''fixer'' or ''hypo.''

**spot meters**   Reflected light meters with supplemental optical telescope, which permit measuring small target areas at a distance.

**Spotoff**   Commercial silver image bleach.

**Spotone**   Transparent dye for retouching prints.

**standard Gray Card**   Cardboard with a surface that reflects 18% of the incident light, a value seen subjectively by the eye as ''middle gray.''

**steady-state light**   Light with constant intensity over time.

**stock**   Concentrated solution that is diluted for use.

**stock agency**   Sales center for photographs made on speculation.

**stop**   2:1 change of exposure; also f–stop.

**stop bath**   Acetic acid solution that stops print or film development.

**straight**   An unmanipulated photograph.

**strobe light**   Repeating light used to analyze rotary motion; misnomer for flash.

**subtractive primary**   Perceived primary color of pigments: cyan, magenta, yellow.

**synchronized**   Electrical connections permit flash exposures to occur only when the shutter is open.

**taxonomy**   Classification of objects.

**Technicolor**   Three-color sequential dye-matrix print made from master separation negatives (exposed simultaneously in a special camera).

**threshold**   Minimum exposure required to create developable latent image.

**TTL**   Through-the-lens metering; standard on most 35mm cameras.

**variable contrast**   Paper with color sensitive emulsions, one high-contrast and one low-contrast.

**virtual image**   Image that exists in optical space (rather than projected onto ground glass).

**water bath**   Tray of water in which developing tanks or trays rest. (Alternate: plain water solution used for development of film or paper to limit contrast.)

**wet-plate**   A nineteenth century photographic process.

**wide-angle**   Lens with field-of-view significantly greater than 40°.

**X**   Electronic synchronization indication for electronic flash exposure timing.

**Xacto knife**   A commercial knife with a small, interchangeable blade.

**zero-balanced**   Adjusting a scale so that zero mass is indicated despite the presence of a chemical tray.

**Zone System**   Method of metering the subject, calculating exposure, and predicting development to produce a predictable negative.

**zoom lens**   Lens with internal movable optics that mimic lenses with a wide range of focal lengths.

# Index

## MODEL RELEASE

DATE: _____ DESCRIPTION OF PHOTOGRAPH(S):


For consideration received, I give _____ permission to reproduce the phototograph(s) described, and I agree that said photographer and all licensees and assignees are entitled to use the photograph(s) described above in any manner or form whatsoever, either wholly or in part, in any medium, and in conjunction with any wording or other photos or drawings, worldwide. I understand that I do not own the copyright of the photograph(s).

[      ] I am over the age of majority (or)
[      ] I am the parent/guardian of _____ and I consent to these conditions.

Date: _____ Model's Name (printed):
                              Signature:
                              Address:

Date: _____ Witness signature:

---

## MODEL RELEASE

DATE: _____ DESCRIPTION OF PHOTOGRAPH(S):


For consideration received, I give _____ permission to reproduce the phototograph(s) described, and I agree that said photographer and all licensees and assignees are entitled to use the photograph(s) described above in any manner or form whatsoever, either wholly or in part, in any medium, and in conjunction with any wording or other photos or drawings, worldwide. I understand that I do not own the copyright of the photograph(s).

[      ] I am over the age of majority (or)
[      ] I am the parent/guardian of _____ and I consent to these conditions.

Date: _____ Model's Name (printed):
                              Signature:
                              Address:

Date: _____ Witness signature:

---

## MODEL RELEASE

DATE: _____ DESCRIPTION OF PHOTOGRAPH(S):


For consideration received, I give _____ permission to reproduce the phototograph(s) described, and I agree that said photographer and all licensees and assignees are entitled to use the photograph(s) described above in any manner or form whatsoever, either wholly or in part, in any medium, and in conjunction with any wording or other photos or drawings, worldwide. I understand that I do not own the copyright of the photograph(s).

[      ] I am over the age of majority (or)
[      ] I am the parent/guardian of _____ and I consent to these conditions.

Date: _____ Model's Name (printed):
                              Signature:
                              Address:

Date: _____ Witness signature:

This 18% gray card approximates a Zone V value.